THE
NEW
RESIDENTIAL
COLLEGES
AT
YALE

THE NEW RESIDENTIAL COLLEGES AT YALE

A CONVERSATION ACROSS TIME

Robert A.M. Stern
with
Gideon Fink Shapiro

Foreword by
Paul Goldberger

Edited by
Melissa DelVecchio
Arianne Kouri
Graham S. Wyatt

THE MONACELLI PRESS

Library of Congress
Control Number
2017949272
ISBN 9781580935043

Frontispiece: Benjamin Franklin
College, view south along Prospect
Street toward the Schwarzman Center.

Design: Pentagram
Printed in The United States

Portfolio Photography by
Peter Aaron/Otto

The Monacelli Press
6 West 18th Street
New York, New York 10011

From James Gamble Rogers to Robert A.M. Stern: Yale and the Arc of Historicism

It is a splendid historical coincidence that the completion of Pauli Murray and Benjamin Franklin Colleges comes precisely one hundred years after James Gamble Rogers received the commission to design Yale's Memorial Quadrangle, the extraordinary set of buildings (later converted into Branford and Saybrook Colleges) that was in every way the inspiration for Robert A.M. Stern's design of today. In the century between 1917 and 2017, the arc that spans the years from Rogers to Stern, we have seen the historicist sensibility hold sway over American architecture, fall from grace, and assert itself again; as Rogers was one of its more accomplished, not to say nimble, practitioners in the early twentieth century, Stern is one of its most agile in the twenty-first.

It is no exaggeration to say that the opening of these new colleges—Yale's first since Eero Saarinen's Ezra Stiles and Morse Colleges were completed fifty-five years ago—is more than a notable event in the history of Yale University and in the oeuvre of Robert A.M. Stern Architects. It has far broader implications. This pair of residential colleges is among the most ambitious and serious attempts to design new architecture in a traditional mode in our time, and it marks an equally intentional break from more recent history. Yale commissioned some of the greatest historicist buildings of the twentieth century from Rogers, John Russell Pope and others, then changed course abruptly after World War II and became an equally enlightened client of modern architecture as it added to its campus important works by Louis Kahn, Paul Rudolph, and Philip Johnson, as well as Saarinen. Stern is well aware that the return to historicism that the new colleges represent would be surprising, and controversial; he devotes much of the opening portion of the text of this book to a defense of the decision to reject the modernism of postwar Yale in favor of a quest to express a sense of physical continuity with the Yale that existed before he was born.

Stern has unquestionably sought to evoke the Yale of James Gamble Rogers, even more directly than Rogers himself recalled the colleges of Oxford and Cambridge. But whether the inspiration is Gothic architecture itself or previous American evocations of Gothic architecture, the basic question of the choice of historicism in 2017 inevitably hovers over the new colleges—even as they seek to make, at least implicitly, the argument that the debate over historicism versus modernism should not matter as much as we tend to presume it does.

The premise is that a good building is a good building, and what makes it good isn't whether its style is of the moment, but whether it is well-planned, well-detailed, and well-built. By that measure Pauli Murray and Benjamin Franklin Colleges are a triumph. Stern and his partners, Melissa DelVecchio and Graham Wyatt, have channeled James Gamble Rogers with a mix of erudition, design skill, and wit. They have handled difficult urban design challenges masterfully, recognizing that this was one of Rogers's strengths. (And their site is more difficult than any of Rogers's.) They have used the most advanced construction technologies, as Rogers did, since they, like him, always favor picturesque effect over ideological purity. Stern's own instincts, like Rogers's, are both romantic and pragmatic, and he, too, conjures out of his romantic pragmatism buildings that have a compelling visual allure. The colleges seek to be like cultivated, easygoing companions: with their excellent manners, they never assault you, although they do not fail to remind you in myriad ways that they know their way around the world. Thus, the Bass Tower, the colleges' tall anchor on the cityscape, is a loose architectural quotation from Nicholas Hawksmoor, and the dining hall facade of Pauli Murray College alludes to Palladio; thus, the walls

are carved with literary quotations from *Ulysses* on the one hand and Cole Porter on the other.

Stern is counting on the idea that context is largely a physical thing: the urban surround, the physical fabric, that his buildings respect and so skillfully seek to extend. But there is also the intellectual and cultural context into which these buildings have been set, and that is a more complex matter. The Yale of 2017 is not the Yale of 1917. Rogers's buildings were designed for an institution whose members represented a narrow stratum of society: men of the upper class, or men who aspired to join it. To Yale in 1917, diversity was, if not meretricious, at least irrelevant. The world is different today. Stern, I suspect, would not deny these differences, but he would suggest that they are irrelevant to the design decisions that he, and Yale, have made here, and he would ask why the admirable fact that Yale is a more democratic institution in the twenty-first century than it was at the beginning of the twentieth should mean that a different kind of architecture is called for. The Memorial Quadrangle, after all, houses the inclusive Yale of today as graciously as it housed the exclusive Yale of its own time; why shouldn't this process work in reverse, and these new buildings, conceived in a more democratic era, be considered equally unburdened with irrevocable associations?

All of these buildings, Rogers's and Stern's alike, force us to ponder the question of how architectural associations work. How much does our experience in these buildings come from what the architect has done with space, composition, light, proportions, and materials, and how much comes from our views of the world in which they were made and of the values they were intended to express? In other words, is architectural experience shaped by what is inherent in form, or by the associations, positive or negative, that we have with it?

Now, nearly a century after the completion of the Memorial Quadrangle, it is hard to look at it or at any of the other colleges Rogers designed and not wonder if the real message they carry about their time is not about its social and intellectual milieu but about its innocence. There is no irony to Rogers's architecture. There is not much irony to Stern's either, even though we live in an age of irony. For all the architectural sophistication that Rogers's buildings represent, they possess a certain ingenuousness; I think that Rogers's greatest gift, in the end, was in his ability to combine brilliant and knowing architectural composition with a relatively simple, utterly unselfconscious, air. The result was an architecture of earnestness, constructed in the belief that all of these associations with Oxford and Cambridge were sure to uplift, certain to inspire a love of education, because that is how the world works. Whatever else can be said about our time, it is surely less inclined to believe that the world works in such un-mysterious ways.

The subtitle of *The New Residential Colleges at Yale* is "A Conversation Across Time," an intentional reference to Vincent Scully's observation that urban architecture is "a continuing dialogue between the generations which creates an environment developing across time." Pauli Murray and Benjamin Franklin Colleges make it clear that Robert A.M. Stern has listened intently to the earlier parts of this conversation, learned from it, and responded with respect, dignity, and even verve. It will be for the users and observers of these new buildings to determine how much they add to the ongoing discourse, and what their architecture has to say as it joins the conversation and extends it into the next generation.

PAUL GOLDBERGER

Introduction

History is essential for architecture, because the architect, who must now deal with everything urban, will therefore always be dealing with historical problems — with the past and, a function of the past, with the future. So the architect should be regarded as a kind of physical historian, because he constructs relationships across time: civilization in fact. And since civilization is based largely upon the capacity of human beings to remember, the architect builds visible history.

VINCENT SCULLY
American Architecture and Urbanism, 1969

Unlike many of its peers, since 1717 Yale has been an urban university, embedded within the grid of city streets. As the campus has grown over time, the character of its architecture has played an increasingly important role, helping to distinguish it from the commercial and civic life of its host environment. Yale has, from its earliest days, taken its architecture seriously. Decisions regarding which elements of architectural heritage are to be discarded or burnished and what new buildings and landscapes are to be added to the mix reflect the university's ever-evolving assessment of its mission, which has at its core the education of undergraduates at Yale College.

Much of the university's architectural and institutional history can be understood through the lens of undergraduate housing, which, from the Colonial-era "Old Brick Row" to the modern residential colleges, has aimed at once to provide suitable living spaces and cohesive educational communities. The Memorial Quadrangle (1917–21), designed by James Gamble Rogers (who would ultimately design eight of the ten original residential colleges), adopted many aspects of the demolished Brick Row, especially the entryway system of separate stair halls leading to student suites, but for a much-enlarged student body. Just as importantly, the Memorial Quadrangle deliberately appealed to the emotions: as President Arthur Twining Hadley said upon breaking ground in 1917, a great building "gives a visible and permanent object around which life and loyalty can grow and to which tradition and sentiment can attach."

Buoyed by the social and architectural success of the Memorial Quadrangle, Yale established ten undergraduate residential colleges in the 1930s and built two more in the 1960s. Quadrangles were also constructed for student housing and academic functions of the Law School and the Graduate School. Whether Gothic or Georgian in style, each of these was deliberately connected to historical Yale but never at the expense of new modes of living and new technologies of construction.

In 2008, as part of an anticipated 15 percent expansion of the undergraduate student body to 6,200 students, our firm was asked to undertake the design of two new residential colleges, each accommodating more than 450 undergraduates and a plethora of social and academic functions. These became the thirteenth and fourteenth residential colleges at Yale, named in 2016 in honor of statesman and scientist Benjamin Franklin (Hon. MA 1753) and Pauli Murray (JSD 1965), the civil rights activist and legal theorist who was the first African-American to earn a doctor of juridical science degree. Our design work was guided by extensive research of Yale's existing architecture and by clear guidelines set forth in a 2008 report by a study group composed of Yale faculty, administrators, and students appointed by President Richard C. Levin, tasked with advising him and the Yale Corporation on "what would be needed to preserve the special nature of the Yale College experience."

The two new colleges are among the most interesting and important commissions I and my colleagues have ever been privileged to undertake. I first came to appreciate the special character and value of the architecture of the Yale campus as a graduate student at the School of Architecture. My admiration deepened later, when, as its dean from 1998 to 2016, I became an advocate for the preservation of numerous significant buildings, including that embattled masterpiece of hyper-expressive Modernism, Rudolph Hall, home to the School of Architecture since 1963. During these years, I also became better acquainted with the work of Rogers while serving with Cesar Pelli and Thomas H. Beeby on a three-member architectural advisory panel to the president where our responsibilities included the review of aspects of the comprehensive program to rehabilitate the twelve extant residential colleges.

Our design for Benjamin Franklin and Pauli Murray Colleges reflects our ambition to perpetuate the undergraduate experience to the fullest by providing additional accommodation that captures in physical form the essential spirit of residential life at Yale. As we designed the new colleges, we allowed Rogers to show us the way, not only with his resourceful interpretation of the Gothic but also with his ability to reconcile complicated patterns of everyday use and urbanism, equally attentive to both the part and the whole. In effect, we attempted to climb on Rogers's shoulders as we set out to meet twenty-first-century standards of collegiate living and environmental responsibility.

Evidently we have not heeded the warning that Rogers offered as part of his comments on the Memorial Quadrangle in *The American Architect/The Architectural Review* of November 9, 1921: "The chances are that the architect will receive more harm than good from writing, because in his eagerness and enthusiasm—which most architects have—he will in all probability propound principles, creeds and dogmas that will later adversely affect his freedom of design." At the risk of being held forever accountable for our dedication to context and continuity, we have ventured, with this book, to try to tell the story of the conception, design, and realization of Benjamin Franklin and Pauli Murray Colleges in relation to their surroundings and inner functional requirements.

This book, part historical analysis and part architectural monograph, builds upon valuable studies such as *Yale in New Haven: Architecture & Urbanism* (2004), edited by Lesley K. Baier, with essays by Vincent Scully, Erik Vogt, Catherine Lynn, and Paul Goldberger; Patrick Pinnell's *Yale University: An Architectural Tour* (1999; 2013); Elizabeth Mills Brown's *New Haven: A Guide to Architecture and Urban Design* (1976); monographic studies of architects who made significant contributions to the Yale campus, especially Aaron Betsky's *James Gamble Rogers and the Architecture of Pragmatism* (1994); and general histories and memoirs of Yale. Primary resources consulted include the James Gamble Rogers Papers, conserved in the Manuscripts and Archives of Yale University Library, and architectural drawings by Rogers and other architects held in the Yale Plan Room. Thanks are due to the archivists and librarians at Yale and elsewhere who facilitated research during the design process and again during the preparation of this book.

I want to thank Yale University for entrusting me with shaping so much of its future. I thank in particular President Levin, who deemed these two new colleges necessary to achieving the larger ambition of increasing and further diversifying Yale's undergraduate population, and I wish to thank his successor, President Peter Salovey, who has enthusiastically embraced that vision. I want to also thank the incomparable Linda Koch Lorimer, former Vice President for Global and Strategic Initiatives, who so gracefully kept me in line during the long process of design; the Yale Corporation, especially G. Leonard Baker, Edward P. Bass, and Roland W. Betts, who have been great friends to me and to this project, as have other officers who supported our efforts, particularly Vice President Bruce D. Alexander, Associate Vice President for Facilities John Bollier, University Planner Laura A. Cruickshank, and Project Planner Alice J. Raucher, who offered continuing support over these many years. I would also like to thank all the New Haven city officials who, even prior to my involvement, worked closely with Yale for many years to prepare the way for the new colleges and various neighborhood improvements.

The design of a building is not a singular act. It is a collaboration among many. At the end of this book are the names of the project team members, including those in our office as well as other key collaborators and consultants, who helped bring the new colleges from idea to built reality. I do wish to call special attention to the invaluable contributions of my partners Melissa DelVecchio, who co-led the design process with me, and Graham S. Wyatt, who served in a management and oversight capacity; Associate Partner Jennifer Stone, who served as project manager; Associate Partner Kurt Glauber, who, joined by Senior Associate Sungchan Park, led our technical effort; and Associate Ken Frank, who was instrumental throughout design and construction.

I extend my gratitude to Gianfranco Monacelli and Elizabeth White who, as with so many of our editorial efforts in the past, have made this book possible; to Michael Bierut, Laitsz Ho, Tess McCann, and their team at Pentagram, whose inspired sense of graphic design has given life to the pages of this book; to Paul Goldberger for contributing a wonderful foreword; to our photographers, Peter Aaron and his colleague Francis Dzikowski, whose ongoing documentation of our firm's work, and especially the portfolio that is crucial to this book, captures the essence of our intentions; and to Arianne Kouri and M. Leopoldo Villardi who tirelessly researched archives for illustrations and historical data. Finally, I want to celebrate the collaborative effort of Gideon Fink Shapiro, a talented scholar and one who can write beautifully.

ROBERT A.M. STERN

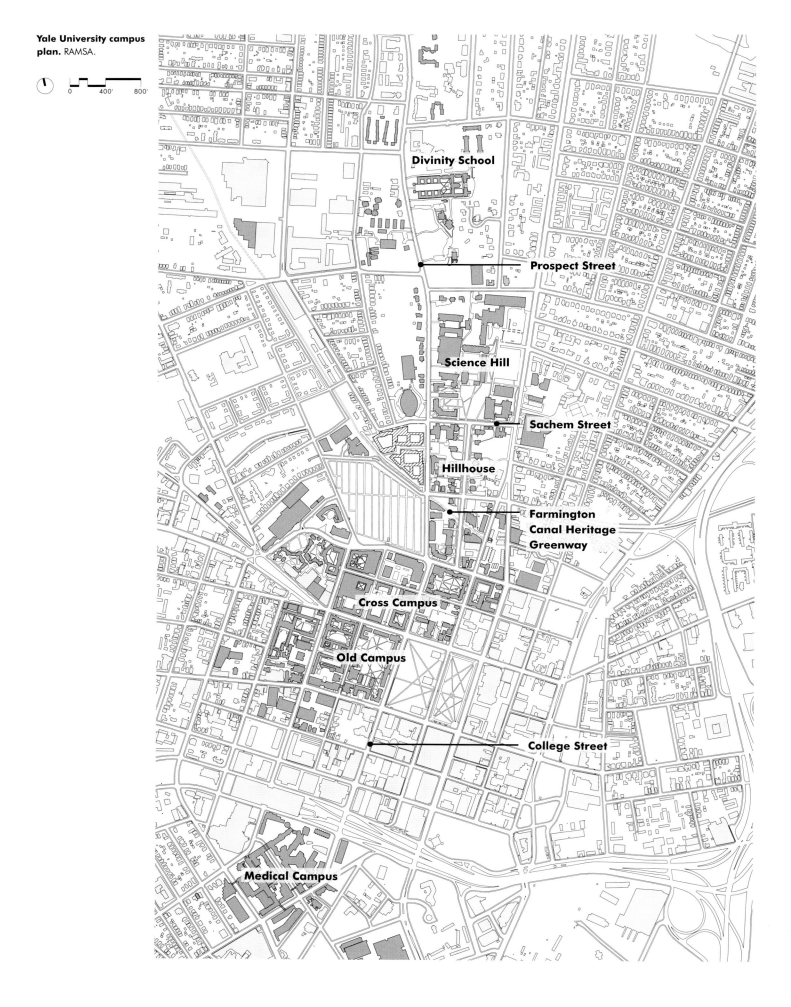

Yale University campus plan. RAMSA.

0   400'   800'

Divinity School

Prospect Street

Science Hill

Sachem Street

Hillhouse

Farmington
Canal Heritage
Greenway

Cross Campus

Old Campus

College Street

Medical Campus

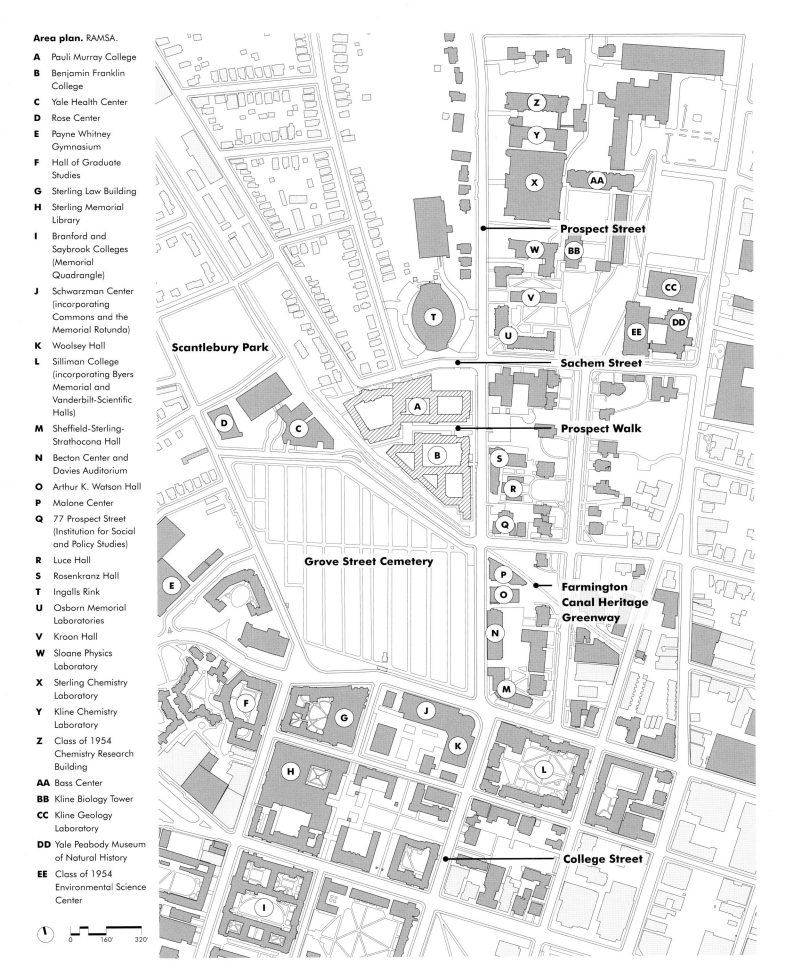

Area plan. RAMSA.

A   Pauli Murray College

B   Benjamin Franklin College

C   Yale Health Center

D   Rose Center

E   Payne Whitney Gymnasium

F   Hall of Graduate Studies

G   Sterling Law Building

H   Sterling Memorial Library

I   Branford and Saybrook Colleges (Memorial Quadrangle)

J   Schwarzman Center (incorporating Commons and the Memorial Rotunda)

K   Woolsey Hall

L   Silliman College (incorporating Byers Memorial and Vanderbilt-Scientific Halls)

M   Sheffield-Sterling-Strathocona Hall

N   Becton Center and Davies Auditorium

O   Arthur K. Watson Hall

P   Malone Center

Q   77 Prospect Street (Institution for Social and Policy Studies)

R   Luce Hall

S   Rosenkranz Hall

T   Ingalls Rink

U   Osborn Memorial Laboratories

V   Kroon Hall

W   Sloane Physics Laboratory

X   Sterling Chemistry Laboratory

Y   Kline Chemistry Laboratory

Z   Class of 1954 Chemistry Research Building

AA   Bass Center

BB   Kline Biology Tower

CC   Kline Geology Laboratory

DD   Yale Peabody Museum of Natural History

EE   Class of 1954 Environmental Science Center

Prospect Street

Scantlebury Park

Sachem Street

Prospect Walk

Grove Street Cemetery

Farmington Canal Heritage Greenway

College Street

0   160'   320'

Gothic Yale: Scholastic Ideal and Urban Type

In matters of grave importance, style…
is the vital thing.

OSCAR WILDE
The Importance of Being Earnest, 1895

Benjamin Franklin College and Pauli Murray College have been designed in the Gothic style, a choice that may startle those who expect a timely Modernist mode of expression. Skeptics today may have similar concerns to those in 1921, who, beholding the architecture of the newly completed Harkness Tower and Memorial Quadrangle at Yale, would "decry any use of the Gothic in these days when we have apparently travelled so far from Gothic traditions," as noted by the editors of the monthly *Architecture*, raising the inevitable question: "Why Gothic? Why not something distinctively modern and American?" But the editors defended the quadrangle's design by James Gamble Rogers (1867–1947; BA 1889), contending that its architectural language signified "the spiritual and intellectual aspirations of the world," and likened it to "the venerable buildings of Oxford and Cambridge . . . where the surrounding architecture seems to be the silent and fitting expression of the scholarly environment," yet placed in a busy urban quarter "in such a way as to harmonize it with its surroundings." Our answer to the question "Why Gothic?" regarding the design of Benjamin Franklin and Pauli Murray Colleges is not so different. If anything, the logic has grown stronger in light of an additional century's worth of architecture at Yale.

Style is not all that counts on the Yale campus, important as it may be. Beneath dramatic variations in architectural design, many Yale buildings can be seen as reiterations of relatively stable organizational typologies such as quadrangles, courtyards, and in the case of residential buildings, entryways, common rooms, and dining halls, characteristically planned around durable patterns of use and the university's location in the heart of a city. The notion of "Gothic Yale" includes these typological aspects as well.

Yale's architectural history effectively begins with the move of the Collegiate School, founded in 1701 in Old Saybrook, Connecticut, to New Haven in 1717. Renamed the following year in honor of Welsh merchant Elihu Yale, who donated funds and 417 books, the college, for the first time, had a permanent base in the Yale College House, a hurriedly completed wood structure that was a triple-wide version of an ordinary colonial house. Located at the corner of College and Chapel Streets, it pressed up against the street line across from the New Haven Green, a vast public open space, suggesting a collegiate "household" on equal footing with other members of the New Haven community. Its presence fulfilled a long-deferred dream by New Haven cofounder John Davenport (1597–1670), who had attended Merton and Magdalen Colleges at Oxford University, that the new city have a college to prepare young men for careers in both church and state.

Yale assumed an ambivalent stance relative to the life of the city with the construction of Connecticut Hall (1750–53), a dormitory, and the adjacent College Chapel (1761–63), which were both set back markedly from the street, signifying the college's wish to "reserve its right to withdraw for the sake of constructing its own community," as the historian Patrick Pinnell (BA 1971, MArch 1974) observes. The dormitory and the chapel had virtually identical brick facades, windows, and rooflines, establishing the architectural flavor of the campus for the next century. Yale did not yet own the entire block known today as the Old Campus, bounded by College, Chapel, High, and Elm Streets; it only owned the southern frontage along College Street, with decidedly unsavory boarding houses, taverns, and a prison with an open yard occupying the northern part of the block.

The young college struggled through the War of Independence and the recession that followed, but when the ramshackle College House was torn

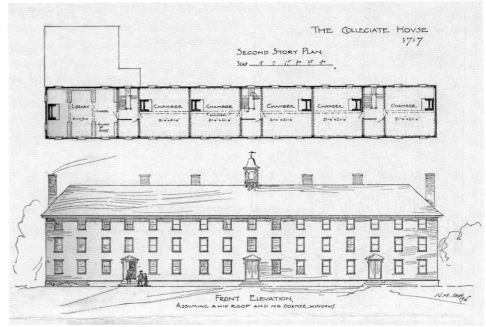

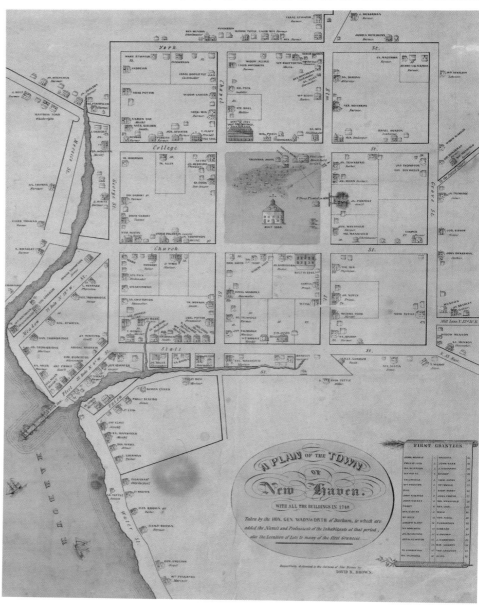

Gothic Yale: Scholastic Ideal and Urban Type

1.3. **"A Front View of Yale College and the College Chapel in New Haven" (June 26, 1786). Printed by Daniel Bowen from a woodcut.** Yale University Library, Manuscripts and Archives. Image no. 43272.

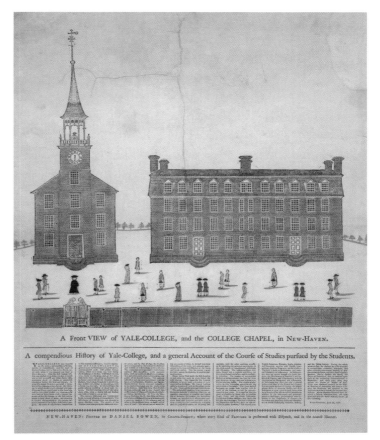

1.4. **Plan and elevation for the development of Yale College (John Trumbull, 1792).** Yale University Library, Manuscripts and Archives. RU 1/Drawer 1/Folder 3.

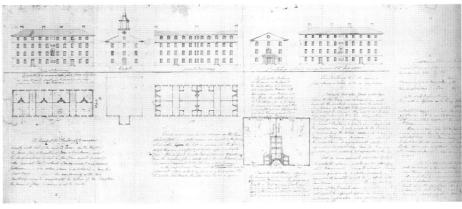

1.5. **Landscape plan for the development of Yale College (John Trumbull, 1792) showing deep setback of the Old Brick Row from College Street.** Yale University Library, Manuscripts and Archives. RU 1/Drawer 1/Folder 3.

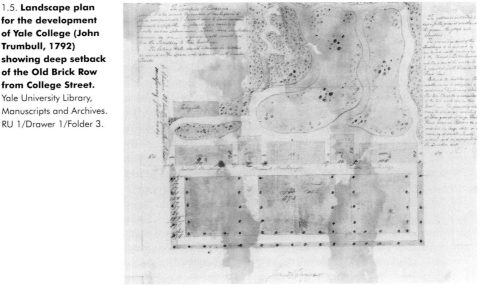

down in 1782, partly at the hands of riotous students, a new dormitory was urgently required. After exploring several expansion plans—the first one having been rejected by the citizens of New Haven, according to historian Erik Vogt—President (1778–95) Ezra Stiles and the Yale Corporation approved what amounted to the first college campus plan in the United States. Submitted in 1792 by the artist John Trumbull (1756–1843) together with James Hillhouse (1754–1832), a New Haven businessman and statesman, the scheme established a reciprocal spatial relationship between the college yard and the town common. To realize the expansion plan, Yale purchased the remainder of the College Street front facing the Green between 1796 and 1800, aided by debt relief from the State of Connecticut, which was the college's on-and-off sponsor.

The Trumbull Plan provided the framework for open-ended growth through the repetition of two building types, resulting in the Brick Row, an alternating series of Georgian-style dormitories and assembly halls that by 1836 came to include eight buildings along College Street and, behind them, a college yard ringed on three sides by "The Fence," an unpainted wood enclosure remembered as a favorite student gathering place. The almost bucolic nature of Yale at this time was chronicled by Charles Dickens, whose *American Notes* of 1842 describe the college buildings nested "in a kind of park or common in the middle of the town, where they are dimly visible among the shadowing trees. The effect is very like that of an old cathedral yard in England."

As New Haven grew increasingly industrial and socially and ethnically diverse, the buildings of the Brick Row seemed too much like the utilitarian mill and factory buildings proliferating in the town and throughout New England. Starting in the middle decades of the nineteenth century, as Yale sought to leave behind its provincial origins and emphasize its growing academic and social distinction, it began to purge its Colonial-era buildings, instead signaling the seriousness of its intellectual aspirations by association with the architecture of the English Scholastic tradition. For an academic community moving gradually toward secular humanism, putting aside the Puritan ideal of a theology-based curriculum, the embrace of Gothic architecture may seem odd, but it was seen as ennobling the quest for secular knowledge with a sense of spiritual striving amid an increasingly materialistic culture.

The first Gothic-style structure at Yale was also the college's first purpose-built library, designed by Henry Austin (1804–1891) in 1842 and completed in 1846. Representing a significant financial investment and an imaginative leap for Yale, the library resembled a scaled-down version of King's College Chapel at Cambridge, England (1446–1515), a building already loosely reprised in Harvard University's Gore Hall (Richard Bond, 1838–41; demolished 1913). Austin's library, which survives today as Dwight Hall and has been repurposed, fittingly, as a chapel, was a radical departure from the austere, boxy buildings of the Brick Row. Not only did its placement at the back of the college yard liberate it from the constraints of the row, providing stylistic and compositional license for a different kind of architecture, but, just as importantly, it reduced the library's exposure to the risk of fire from adjacent buildings, an all-too-real threat in an age of coal-burning hearths in every dormitory room tended individually by students.

Second in Yale's Gothic lineage, also reflecting Tudor influences, was Alumni Hall (Alexander Jackson Davis, 1851–53; demolished 1911), built at the corner of High and Elm Streets and remembered for its two octagonal turrets, which were carefully disassembled and, in 1918, resurrected within a

1.6. **Colored engraving of the Old Brick Row (A.B. Doolittle, 1807). Left to right: Union Hall, also known as South College (1793–94; demolished 1893), the Athenaeum, also known as First Chapel (1761–63; demolished 1893), Connecticut Hall, also known as South Middle College (1752), Connecticut Lyceum (Peter Banner, 1803–4; demolished 1895), Berkeley Hall, also known as North Middle College (Peter Banner, 1801–3; demolished 1895).** Yale University Library, Manuscripts and Archives. RU 703/Cabinet B/Drawer 21/Folder 70. Gift of James M. Hoppin, B.A. 1840.

1.7. **Yale students at the Fence. View looking north from Chapel Street. College Street and the New Haven Green on the right. Old Brick Row on the left and Farnam Hall (Russell Sturgis Jr., 1869–70) ahead. Photograph 1879.** Yale University Library, Manuscripts and Archives. Yale University buildings and grounds photographs, 1716–2004 (inclusive). Image no. 3177.

1.8. Yale College Library, now Dwight Hall (Henry Austin, 1842–46), flanked by Mineral Cabinet on the left and the Trumbull Gallery (John Trumbull, 1830) on the right, both demolished. Photograph n.d. Yale University Library, Manuscripts and Archives.

1.9. Gore Hall, Harvard University (Richard Bond, 1838–41; demolished 1913). Photograph 1905. Library of Congress Prints and Photographs Division.

1.10. **King's College Chapel, Cambridge (Reginald Ely, Simon Clerk, John Wastell, 1446–1515). Left to right: Clare Bridge, Clare College, King's College Chapel, Gibbs Building. View from King's College Bridge. Photograph c. 1926.** King's College, Cambridge, Archive Centre, JMK/RV/1.

few hundred feet of their original location behind the opaque stone "tomb," or headquarters of the Skull and Bones Society. An anonymous article in the *Yale Literary Magazine* from 1853 expressed concern that the newly completed building did not look old enough; its plastered interior walls lacking "that substantial, venerable air" befitting "an old and honored university."

The last building of Yale's original Gothic trio was Street Hall (Peter B. Wight, 1864–66), originally the home of the School of Fine Arts and today part of the Yale University Art Gallery. On the heels of his acclaimed Venetian Gothic–style National Academy of Design in New York (1863–65), inspired partly by the ideas of John Ruskin, Wight designed the art school with conical spires and finials to give a sense of lightness and upward thrust, but to his everlasting chagrin, these features were omitted. Taken together, these three buildings along High Street expressed what historian Paul Turner called the "new connotation" of Gothic Revival architecture, apart from any notion of religious piety, and focused on "the appearance of age and permanence."

It was only after the Civil War that Gothic architecture began to reshape Yale's College Street frontage with the gradual enclosure of what is now known as the Old Campus. Tensions between Yale students and city residents had spilled over in the 1850s into protests, clashes, and even the alleged murder of a fireman and a bartender at the hands of students, leading Yale to consider leaving its center-city location in favor of a more bucolic one to the west. Instead it opted to hunker down and defend itself by means of a nearly continuous wall of battlemented buildings hugging College Street, expressing President (1871–86) Noah Porter's belief that "the college community is emphatically an *isolated* community; more completely separated and farther removed than almost any other." Porter's proposed quadrangle began to take shape in 1869 as, one by one, the detached buildings of the Brick Row were replaced with medievalizing dormitories joined into a solid barrier against the city.

In these post–Civil War buildings, the use of Gothic and Romanesque elements conveyed not the spiritual striving of medieval religious architecture, but the defensive function of medieval citadels such as Carcassonne, France, famously restored by the French architect Eugène Emmanuel Viollet-le-Duc in the 1850s and 1860s, and apparently an inspiration for the blockading dormitories Farnam (1869–70), Durfee (1871), and Lawrance (1886) Halls designed by the New York Gothicist Russell Sturgis Jr. (1836–1909). According to the critic Montgomery Schuyler, writing in 1909 in *The Architectural Record*, the Sturgis buildings showed an advance upon the college's mid-century Gothic pioneers "both in the respect of scholastic accuracy and in the respect of artistic freedom."

In 1871 future Yale President (1886–99) Timothy Dwight the Younger, then a professor in the Divinity School and an editor of the literary journal *New Englander*, in the last of a series of five reform-minded articles called "Yale College: Some Thoughts Respecting Its Future," affirmed the view that "the old line of unsightly brick buildings might give way, not only to beautiful ones, but to those made of stone," and endorsed Porter's idea of enclosing the college square to form a quadrangle. However, Dwight differed from Porter in urging that all new buildings on Yale's Old Campus should be designed with a "double frontage" facing both inward and outward, on which account he criticized Farnam and Durfee Halls for standoffishly turning their backs to New Haven, "one of the most beautiful of our American cities." Dwight also implicitly championed the Gothic style by invoking "the grand old edifices of Oxford and

1.11. **Alumni Hall (Alexander Jackson Davis, 1851–53; demolished 1911). Durfee Hall (Russell Sturgis Jr., 1871) to the right. Photograph 1901.** Library of Congress Prints and Photographs Division, Detroit Publishing Company.

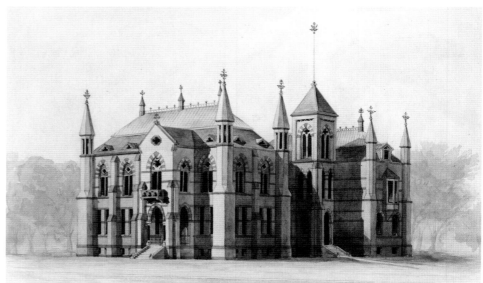

1.12. **Preliminary design for Street Hall (Peter B. Wight, 1864–66). Drawing 1864.** Yale University Library, Manuscripts and Archives. Image no. 2041.

1.13. **Street Hall, originally the Yale School of Fine Arts (Peter B. Wight, 1864–66). Photograph n.d.** Yale University Library, Manuscripts and Archives. Image no. 3168.

Gothic Yale: Scholastic Ideal and Urban Type

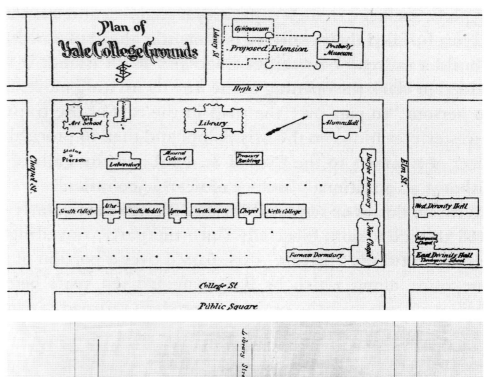

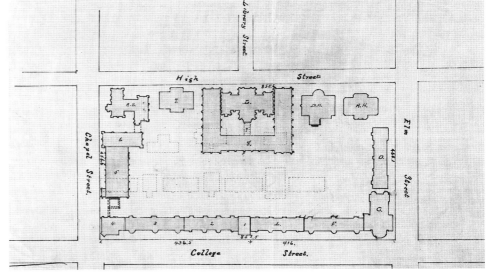

Cambridge," which lift "the minds and hearts" of those who dwell within them, promising that the Yale student of the future would similarly glean knowledge and inspiration from "the very buildings that have met his vision from day to day." As the last minister to be president of Yale, Dwight advocated the building of a chapel at the center of the new quadrangle, the better to ward off increasingly powerful secular interests that seemed to foretell "a serious conflict of opinion" on the nature of Yale as a Christian institution.

New buildings soon plugged the remaining holes along College Street and rounded the corner of Chapel Street, offering a modicum of permeability to the street. Embracing medievalism but relaxing the tendency toward fortification, the first building commissioned by Dwight once he became president was Osborn Hall (Bruce Price, 1888; demolished 1926), designed in the Romanesque style of Henry Hobson Richardson (1838–1886), then the most respected architect in America. Osborn Hall, before being replaced by the far more imposing and militaristic Bingham Hall (Walter B. Chambers, 1926–28), opened the campus to the city with wraparound stairs, five round-arched entrance portals, and a rotunda at the historic corner of College and Chapel Streets, where the first Yale

25

1.16. Farnam Hall (Russell Sturgis Jr., 1869–70). Looking southwest along College Street. Photograph 1888. Yale University Library, Manuscripts and Archives. Image no. 2249.

1.17. Carcassonne, France. Photograph 1994. Yale University, Visual Resources Collection.

1.18. Durfee Hall (Russell Sturgis Jr., 1871) and Battell Chapel (Russell Sturgis Jr., 1874–76). Looking northeast from inside the Old Campus quadrangle. Photograph 1900. Library of Congress Prints and Photographs Division, Detroit Publishing Company.

Gothic Yale: Scholastic Ideal and Urban Type

1.19. **Osborn Hall (Bruce Price, 1888; demolished 1926), corner of College and Chapel Streets. Flanked by Vanderbilt Hall to the left. Looking from southeast. Photograph 1901.** Library of Congress Prints and Photographs Division, Detroit Publishing Company.

1.20. **Phelps Hall (Charles C. Haight, 1896). Welch Hall (Bruce Price, 1891) to the left. Lawrance Hall (Russell Sturgis Jr., 1885–86) to the right. Photograph 1901.** Library of Congress Prints and Photographs Division, Detroit Publishing Company.

1.21. **Vanderbilt Hall (Charles C. Haight, 1894). View from Chapel Street. Street Hall (Peter B. Wight, 1864–66) to the left. Photograph c. 1900–15.** Library of Congress Prints and Photographs Division, Detroit Publishing Company.

College House had once unguardedly faced the Green. A casualty of the construction of Osborn Hall was the last stretch of the old Yale fence torn down despite the objections of the students and 2,100 alumni who petitioned against the destruction of this informal interface between campus and city, its upper rung "as comfortable as an easy chair," according to alumnus author John Seymour Wood.

Price was engaged once again to design a dormitory along College Street, Welch Hall (1891), distinct from the Sturgis buildings in that it was pierced by a vaulted archway to the street, since blocked. A larger gateway building, Phelps Hall (Charles C. Haight, 1896), containing classrooms and offices, filled the space between the Welch and Lawrance dormitories, evoking the alternating rhythm of buildings of the Brick Row, but without leaving any space between them. Its turreted, monumental Tudor-Gothic facade amplified the initial Gothic impulse of Austin's library and Davis's Alumni Hall from a half-century earlier, as if summoned from the relative sanctuary of High Street and presented at greater scale to the public theater of College Street, forming a minimally permeable buffer, at once physical and psychological, to Yale's urban milieu. It was Haight (1841–1917), too, who designed Vanderbilt Hall (1894), the dormitory which, positioned between the stylistically opposed Osborn Hall and Street Hall, stepped back from the street but addressed the city with a generous courtyard entrance facing Chapel Street.

During the last decades of the nineteenth century, Yale was also expanding beyond the Old Campus quadrangle with buildings in a heterogeneous mix of medievalizing and classicizing styles. Some, like the Berkeley Oval (J. Cleaveland Cady, 1893–1903; demolished 1930), a collection of brick dormitory, office, and classroom buildings, were soon regarded as too utilitarian and too much like the austere buildings of the early college. More significantly from our perspective, in 1858, a separate campus of sorts began to take root north of Grove Street, just beyond New Haven's foundational Nine Square Plan, along Prospect Street and Hillhouse Avenue, where the Sheffield Scientific School, founded in 1847, migrated from the original college area. The new school gained a foothold on Prospect Street by renovating and enlarging the former medical school at Prospect and Grove Streets, then expanded north along Prospect Street, facing the Grove Street Cemetery, and along Hillhouse Avenue one block to the east. Lacking either the means or the will (or both) to create a quadrangle comparable to the Old Campus of Yale College, the scientific school expanded in piecemeal fashion with three austere buildings designed by Cady (1837–1919): North Sheffield Hall (1872–73), Winchester Building (1892–93), and Sheffield Chemical Laboratory (1894–95), later called Arthur K. Watson Hall, were realized in red brick with rounded arches, suggesting medieval keeps but with open, loft-like interiors.

The scientific school struggled to gain equal footing with the college in the eyes of conservative administrators and members of the Yale Corporation, the governing body, who prioritized the college and the religious tradition from which it emerged. In 1886 President Timothy Dwight the Younger successfully prevailed upon the Corporation to adopt the name Yale University, and he subsequently implemented reforms to give equal status to the science, law, medicine, graduate, arts, music, and divinity schools alongside the liberal arts college. Nonetheless Yale did not cultivate the sciences as avidly as other leading universities of the day, and "Sheff" students and faculty were marginalized culturally as well as physically by their counterparts in the college.

1.22. Sheffield Scientific School buildings. Exterior and interior images of Winchester Hall (civil engineering), Hammond Metallurgical Laboratory (mining), Mason Laboratory (mechanical engineering), and Dunham Laboratory of Electrical Engineering. Print c. 1918. Yale University Library, Manuscripts and Archives. Image no. 4145.

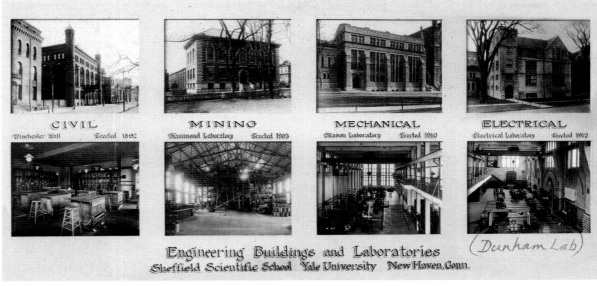

1.23. North Sheffield Hall (J. Cleaveland Cady, 1872–73; demolished 1967). View from southwest. Photograph 1875. Yale University Library, Manuscripts and Archives. Image no. 2277.

1.24. Map of the campus (1909) showing the growth of the Sheffield Scientific School to the north (right) and the new Bicentennial Buildings (Carrère and Hastings, 1901–2), as an intended hinge with the campus core. Yale University Library, Manuscripts and Archives. *Yale 1883*, the book of the class compiled after its quartercentenary reunion. Image no. 010539.

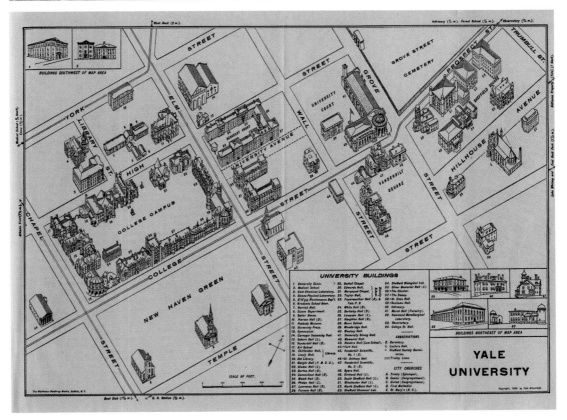

29

1.25. Bicentennial Buildings (Carrère and Hastings, 1901–2). View from northeast. Left to right: Woolsey Hall; Memorial Rotunda and Commons, now the Schwarzman Center. Photograph c. 1902. Yale University Library, Manuscripts and Archives. Image no. 2028.

1.26. Bicentennial Buildings (Carrère and Hastings, 1901–2). View from south. Left to right: Commons and Memorial Rotunda, now the Schwarzman Center; Woolsey Hall. Woodbridge Hall (Howells & Stokes, 1901), is on the far right. Photograph c. 1905. Library of Congress Prints and Photographs Division, Detroit Publishing Company.

1.27. Byers Memorial Hall (Hiss and Weekes, 1903) and Vanderbilt-Scientific Halls (Charles C. Haight, 1906), buildings of the Sheffield Scientific School were incorporated into Silliman College in 1940. College Street facades. Photograph c. 1910. Library of Congress Prints and Photographs Division, Detroit Publishing Company.

The university made a brief foray into Beaux-Arts Classicism to celebrate its bicentennial in 1901, realizing a grand ensemble of buildings—University Commons, Memorial Rotunda, and Woolsey Hall, known collectively as the Bicentennial Buildings (Carrère and Hastings, 1901–2)—with the Rotunda echoing the gesture of Osborn Hall and strategically situated between the older college campus and the nascent science campus.

Many agreed with the critic Montgomery Schuyler, who dryly remarked in 1909 that "the bicentennial buildings are as they are, and past praying for," but commended the "unpretentious, easy and delightful cloistrality" of the Sheffield School's newer Gothic-style dormitories and nearby tower, Vanderbilt-Scientific Hall (Charles C. Haight, 1903–6), which seemed destined to become "a complete and separate quadrangle" and perhaps even a "college" in the Oxford and Cambridge sense—an event realized three decades later when the Sheffield buildings were made part of Silliman College (Eggers & Higgins, 1940). "In spite of many more or less lamentable exceptions," Schuyler judged that Yale's architects over several generations "have upon the whole fixed as 'Gothic' the style of Yale."

Schuyler's pronouncement was reaffirmed when the scientific school commissioned a series of buildings in the "Collegiate Gothic" style—a term probably initiated by Schuyler in 1911 and used interchangeably with "English collegiate" and "collegiate"—as it made a decisive leap onto the knoll of Prospect Hill, thereafter Science Hill, turning first to Haight, who designed the Sloane Physics Laboratory (1912), with its corner towers and subtle features animating its relatively flat facade, and the Osborn Memorial Laboratories (1913–14), with castellated gateway towers recalling those that once guarded Alumni Hall and Haight's own Phelps Hall on the Old Campus. Two more Collegiate Gothic

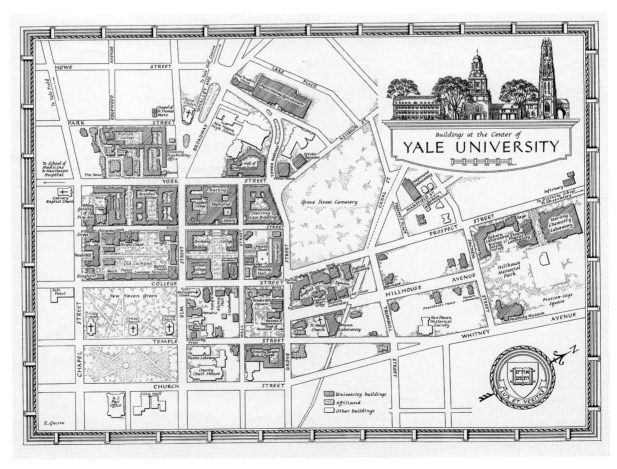

1.28. **Map of the campus (1938) showing new buildings on Science Hill: Sloane Physics Laboratory (Charles C. Haight, 1912), Osborn Memorial Laboratories (Charles C. Haight, 1913–14), Sterling Chemistry Laboratory (Delano & Aldrich, 1921–23), and Yale Peabody Museum of Natural History (Day & Klauder, 1923–24).** Yale University Library, Manuscripts and Archives. Yale University buildings and grounds photographs, 1716–2004 (inclusive).

1.29. **Sloane Physics Laboratory (Charles C. Haight, 1912) from the north side. Photograph 1912.** Yale University Library, Manuscripts and Archives. Image no. 6457.

1.30. **Osborn Memorial Laboratories (Charles C. Haight, 1913–14). View from southwest, at the corner of Prospect and Sachem Streets. Photograph c. 1914.** Yale University Library, Manuscripts and Archives. Image no. 6458.

1.31. **Sterling Chemistry Laboratory (Delano & Aldrich, 1921–23). View from Prospect Street. Photograph 1923.** "Sterling Chemistry Laboratory," *Architecture* v. 48, n. 5 (November 1923): 377–79.

1.32. Sterling Chemistry Laboratory (Delano & Aldrich, 1921–23). Typical laboratory with view of roof skylights to the right. Photograph 1923. "Sterling Chemistry Laboratory," *Architecture* v. 48, n. 5 (November 1923): 377–79.

1.33. Sterling Chemistry Laboratory (Delano & Aldrich, 1921–23). Roof skylights. Photograph 1923. "Sterling Chemistry Laboratory," *Architecture* v. 48, n. 5 (November 1923): 377–79.

1.34. **Preliminary plan for Sterling Chemistry Laboratory (Delano & Aldrich, 1921–23).** "Sterling Chemistry Laboratory," *Architecture* v. 48, n. 5 (November 1923): 377–79.

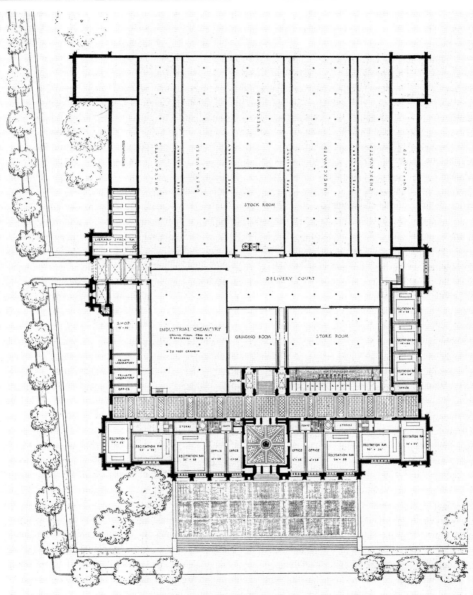

buildings, the Sterling Chemistry Laboratory (1921–23) and Sage Hall (1924), both designed by Delano & Aldrich in a notable departure from the firm's Georgian specialty, were subsequently added to Science Hill facing Prospect Street. Behind the arched entrance and buttressed stone facade of the sprawling chemistry building—praised as "not too damn Gothic" by none other than Bertram Goodhue (1869–1924), a renowned if inconsistent practitioner of the English Gothic style—lay open-plan laboratories and flexibly partitioned classroom spaces illuminated through a sawtooth roof.

This first generation of buildings on or near Science Hill, also including the Yale Peabody Museum of Natural History (Day & Klauder, 1923–24), accommodated the rapid expansion of the scientific disciplines while signaling their desire to be fully integrated with the rest of the university. Built for the most part on steel structural frames, they demonstrated that the Gothic idiom was compatible with modern construction technology and scientific research. Moreover, building by building, they began to form a science quadrangle commensurate in scale with the Old Campus. The most prominent of all the Sheffield buildings to adopt Gothic garb came much later: Sheffield-Sterling-Strathcona Hall (Zantzinger, Borie & Medary, 1932), the steel-framed, limestone-clad building whose 166-foot-tall tower rises catercorner from the Memorial Rotunda and represents a bold, if somewhat crudely realized, tectonic bid on the part of the scientific school to directly confront Yale College in full view of all.

Paralleling the scientific school's embrace of the Gothic style, Yale College moved in the same direction, all but officially adopting it at the behest of John Villiers Farwell of Chicago, newly appointed to the Yale Corporation and its Committee on the Architectural Plan. Farwell was convinced that there was

1.35. **Yale Peabody Museum of Natural History (Day & Klauder, 1923–24), from Whitney Avenue. Photograph c. 2005.** Yale Peabody Museum of Natural History.

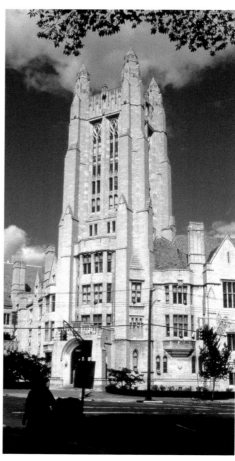

1.36. **Sheffield-Sterling-Strathcona Hall (Zantzinger, Borie & Medary, 1932), corner at Prospect and Grove Streets looking northeast. Photograph Robert A.M. Stern, 2000.** RAMSA.

"certainly something" about the Gothic "with its perpendicular lines . . . to point the mind upward," as demonstrated by new campus architecture designed by the firms of Cope & Stewardson and Day & Klauder at the University of Pennsylvania, Washington University in St. Louis, and Princeton University, among other American institutions. Farwell was related by marriage to James Gamble Rogers, a Yale College graduate of 1889, whom he approached in 1912 for advice on hiring a consulting architect to the university. Rogers declined the appointment, preferring instead to hold out for an architectural commission.

The Yale Corporation appointed the accomplished Gothicist Frank Miles Day (1861–1918) of Day & Klauder as consulting architect in 1913. Three years later, Day was asked to make a preliminary design for "a series of dormitories in the form of a quadrangle," housing more than six hundred men, funded by Yale alumnus Edward S. Harkness. Day died only months later, and Rogers assumed the job of designing what became the Harkness Tower and Memorial Quadrangle. He not only had an ally in Farwell, but also the all-powerful backing of Harkness himself, a fellow Yale College graduate (1897) who had previously commissioned Rogers to design at least four buildings, including his New York townhouse (1907–8). The motivation behind the quadrangle, which was dedicated to the memory of the recently deceased Charles W. Harkness, Edward's elder brother, was to provide communal accommodations for upper-classmen who, pushed off campus by growing enrollment, were forced to live in private boarding houses, and hence miss out on some of the informal social bonding that was supposed to underpin each graduating class.

As a graduate of the École des Beaux-Arts, Rogers had designed works in the Classical tradition, such as the monumental Roman US Post Office (1913) on Church Street facing the New Haven Green, as well as commercial buildings in Chicago. His only experience designing in the Gothic style was for the School of Education at the University of Chicago (1901–4), where his buildings fit within the context established in 1891 by Henry Ives Cobb (1859–1931), who favored the Gothic for "adaptability and variety within a controlled plan." The Midwest-born Rogers, who had never visited Oxford or Cambridge during his trips to Europe as either a baseball player or a graduate student, turned for inspiration to his collection of postcards of European architecture, many apparently from the Musée de la sculpture comparée in Paris, to initiate what historian Aaron Betsky described as a "collage-like form of design," employing a rich and flexible vocabulary of individual elements that could be deployed within a Classical architectural grammar. Rogers developed his own modern interpretation of the "English secular Gothic," according to an art historian of his own day, the noted museum curator William H. Goodyear (1846–1923), writing in *The American Architect/ The Architectural Review* in October 1921.

In addition to clipping Gothic and Renaissance details from his eclectic but carefully arranged postcard albums, Rogers familiarized himself with the new college buildings being realized in the United States in the Collegiate Gothic style. A recent benchmark for quadrangular planning could be found in Princeton University's Graduate College (Ralph Adams Cram, 1913), which nonetheless differed from the situation at Yale in that it was separated from the main college campus and unrelated to city streets. Moreover, Cram's quadrangle at Princeton had only two courts surrounded by buildings of generally equal height, similar to English precedents, but the Memorial Quadrangle was to be an orchestrated composition of six courts of various sizes, surrounded by buildings

Gothic Yale: Scholastic Ideal and Urban Type

1.38. **Princeton Graduate School (Ralph Adams Cram, 1913). View from the southeast. Photograph c. 1913.** Princeton University Library. Department of Rare Books and Special Collections. Seeley G. Mudd Manuscript Library. Box MP83, Item 3378.

of changing heights, in a more inventive take on *Oxbridge* tradition — a portmanteau referring to both Oxford and Cambridge. And while Cram's single tower at Princeton had an extruded form, Rogers's Harkness Tower, inspired by St. Botolph's Tower in Boston, England, was more dynamic and was supplemented by a second, smaller tower, Wrexham Tower, modeled loosely after the tower of St. Giles Court in Wrexham, Wales, where Elihu Yale is buried.

"In this one project," writes the critic Paul Goldberger in his 2004 essay in *Yale in New Haven: Architecture & Urbanism*, based in part on his 1972 honors thesis as a Yale undergraduate, "Rogers established a kind of soft, highly picturesque Gothic as Yale's primary style; he gave the university a physical symbol, Memorial Tower, that has never been supplanted; and he created the prototype for the completely enclosed quadrangle that was to become the university's main mode of building for the next generation." Disparaged as retrograde by Modernist critics, Rogers saw no contradiction between the functional demands of modern planning and the representational benefits of traditional design.

Three key associates assisted Rogers in the design of Harkness Tower and the Memorial Quadrangle: Beaux-Arts–trained Otto Faelten, who would serve as head designer in the office for several decades; E. Donald Robb, an architect who had worked for Cram, Goodhue & Ferguson and was known for his atmospheric perspective renderings; and George Nichols, who had helped Rogers complete the New Haven Post Office. The independent sculptor-artisans Lee O. Lawrie and René Paul Chambellan held major responsibilities for the sculpture and ornament. In an arrangement that would be highly irregular today, it was Harkness, not the Yale Corporation, who acted as the client in charge of the development of the Memorial Quadrangle.

In a larger sense, the Memorial Quadrangle responded to anxieties about a world order collapsing as a result of World War I, suggesting that Yale was

1.39. Memorial Quadrangle (James Gamble Rogers, 1917–21), Branford Court looking southeast toward Harkness Tower. Photograph 1921. Yale University Library, Manuscripts and Archives. Image no. 6691.

1.40. Memorial Quadrangle looking southeast along York Street. Photograph 1921. James Gamble Rogers, "The Memorial Quadrangle of Yale University and the Harkness Memorial Tower," *Architecture* v. 44, n. 4 (October 1921): Plate 153.

1.41. Memorial Quadrangle, Wrexham Tower from Branford Court. Photograph 1921. William H. Goodyear, "The Memorial Quadrangle and the Harkness Memorial Tower at Yale," *The American Architect/The Architectural Review* v. 120, n. 2379 (October 1921): 299–321.

1.42. Memorial Quadrangle, view from Killingworth Court. Photograph 1921. William H. Goodyear, "The Memorial Quadrangle and the Harkness Memorial Tower at Yale," *The American Architect/ The Architectural Review* v. 120, n. 2379 (October 1921): 299–321.

1.43. Memorial Quadrangle, corner in Linonia Court. Photograph 1921. William H. Goodyear, "The Memorial Quadrangle and the Harkness Memorial Tower at Yale," *The American Architect/ The Architectural Review* v. 120, n. 2379 (October 1921): 299–321.

1.44. **Memorial Quadrangle, Wrexham Tower from Silliman Entry. Photograph 1921.** William H. Goodyear, "The Memorial Quadrangle and the Harkness Memorial Tower at Yale," *The American Architect/The Architectural Review* v. 120, n. 2379 (October 1921): 299–321.

1.45. **Memorial Quadrangle, Mason Entry. Photograph 1921.** William H. Goodyear, "The Memorial Quadrangle and the Harkness Memorial Tower at Yale," *The American Architect/The Architectural Review* v. 120, n. 2379 (October 1921): 299–321.

1.46. **Memorial Quadrangle, Waite Entry. Photograph 1921.** William H. Goodyear, "The Memorial Quadrangle and the Harkness Memorial Tower at Yale," *The American Architect/The Architectural Review* v. 120, n. 2379 (October 1921): 299–321.

1.47. **Memorial Quadrangle, Pierpont Gateway from Linonia Court. Photograph 1921.** William H. Goodyear, "The Memorial Quadrangle and the Harkness Memorial Tower at Yale," *The American Architect/The Architectural Review* v. 120, n. 2379 (October 1921): 299–321.

1.48. **Memorial Quadrangle, Memorial Gateway viewed from High Street. Photograph 1921.** William H. Goodyear, "The Memorial Quadrangle and the Harkness Memorial Tower at Yale," *The American Architect/ The Architectural Review* v. 120, n. 2379 (October 1921): 299–321.

1.49. **Memorial Quadrangle, detail of facade on Library Street showing moat wall. Photograph 1921.** William H. Goodyear, "The Memorial Quadrangle and the Harkness Memorial Tower at Yale," *The American Architect/ The Architectural Review* v. 120, n. 2379 (October 1921): 299–321.

poised to pick up the pieces, at least in the arts. President (1899–1921) Arthur Twining Hadley gave voice to this idea in his remarks of October 1917, upon the laying of the Memorial Quadrangle's cornerstone, noting that "a university is something more than a school, or group of schools. It is a complex of traditions and influences; of sentiments inherited from the past, and aspirations reaching out to the future." The destruction caused by World War I could only be countered by building "new centers of beauty and affection," Hadley added, and the wartime pressure to seek "immediate efficiency rather than permanent utility; to seek tangible effects and disregard intangible ones" made it all the more necessary to "renew our supply of tradition and inspiration by buildings like this," instilling in students, who "breathe the spirit of the place," a "love of the beautiful."

In 1919, before the Memorial Quadrangle was completed, John Russell Pope (1874–1937) furthered the use of the Gothic style in his plan for Yale's future development, commissioned by Yale alumnus and benefactor Francis P. Garvan. The plan's most striking features included a series of proposed axial connections, as discussed in Chapter 2, but Pope's choice of the Gothic was in itself notable given his record as an accomplished Classicist who had studied at the American Academy in Rome and the École des Beaux-Arts after graduating from Columbia University. Pope, like Rogers, thus followed Cope & Stewardson and other firms in adapting Anglo-Gothic precedents to the American context, though they differed in their exercise of creative license.

Also in 1919, Everett Victor Meeks (1879–1954), who served at Yale as chairman of architecture, at that time a department within the School of Fine Arts, from 1918 to 1945, and dean of the School of Fine Arts from 1922 to 1947, lobbied for a second quadrangle to provide classroom, studio, and museum space as well as dormitories specifically for art and architecture students. Working with architecture student Hyman I. Feldman (1896–1981), then preparing his thesis, Meeks proposed an elevated courtyard bounded by Skull and Bones to the east, a new art gallery (Egerton Swartwout, 1926–28) to the south, dormitories for art students to the west, and Weir Hall (Meeks, 1924, after a 1912 design by Tracy and Swartwout) to the north. Opened in 1924, the Gothic dormitories, designed by Rogers, housed Yale College undergraduates, not just art students. They were incorporated into Jonathan Edwards College in 1932.

The dramatic growth of the university and especially the college, with enrollment increasing 43 percent from 1,190 undergraduates in 1900 to 1,697 undergraduates in 1929, gave rise to a widespread sense that a certain cadence of life at Yale had disappeared in the rush toward modernization. The success of the Memorial Quadrangle suggested that comparable arrangements could be offered to all undergraduates by building a series of residential quadrangles, at once solving the perennial housing shortage and eliminating the need for upperclassmen to live in scattered boarding houses. President (1921–37) James Rowland Angell proposed a residential college system in 1925, whereby Yale College could manage its growth and recover a sense of a shared life and purpose for its members. Beyond providing student dormitory space, each college would also include dining and recreational facilities and a limited number of faculty residences, as in the Oxbridge model.

As early as 1926, Harkness indicated that he was prepared to fund the massive construction effort required to create the new colleges, but he insisted

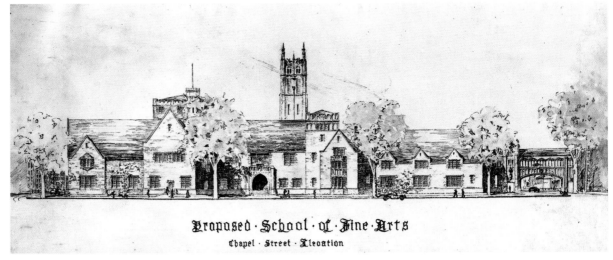

1.51. **Proposed School of Fine Arts (Hyman I. Feldman, 1919), forming a quadrangle with a raised garden court at the center. Second floor plan.** Yale University Library, Manuscripts and Archives.

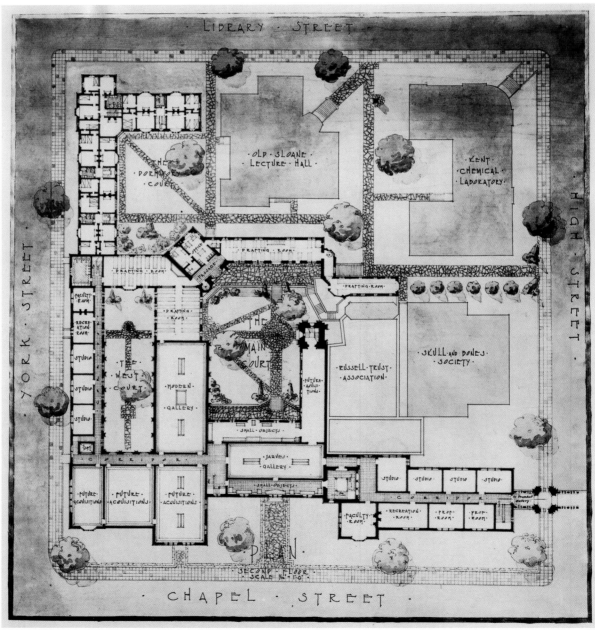

that his offer be kept secret until the university resolved of its own accord to move toward a residential college model. Harkness grew impatient as the faculty and the Yale Corporation, not knowing of his offer, dithered until December 8, 1928, when they finally took the first steps toward adopting the residential college or "house" system, followed by the Yale Corporation's approval on October 4, 1929, based on the findings of a committee that residential colleges would "provide definite social values which have disappeared from Yale . . . assuming that at Yale social elements play a significant role in education." Yale made amends with Harkness — who in the interim had promised a substantial gift to Harvard for the construction of the Georgian-style "River Houses" — and in 1930 he made a generous gift to his alma mater to establish the residential colleges.

Yale reaffirmed its preference for English architectural styles, both Gothic and Georgian, as the Memorial Quadrangle served as the architectural template for the ten residential colleges that would be constructed between the two World Wars, mostly with Harkness funds. Construction on five new quadrangles began in 1930, and in 1933 Yale opened seven residential colleges: Branford and Saybrook Colleges within the Memorial Quadrangle; Jonathan Edwards, incorporating and expanding upon the two existing Rogers-designed dormitories intended for art and architecture students; Trumbull, designed by Rogers, on the former site of the gym; Calhoun (now Grace Hopper), designed by John Russell Pope in a Rogers-friendly Gothic on the former site of the Divinity School; Davenport, designed by Rogers primarily in the Georgian style in deference to the residential neighborhood to the west, but with a Collegiate Gothic facade along York Street to complement the Memorial Quadrangle across the street and Rogers's scenographic vision for an all-Gothic corridor along High Street; and Pierson, Davenport's all-Georgian fraternal twin with its primary frontage on Park Street. The Sterling Memorial Library (1927–30), the Sterling Law Building (1929–31), and the Hall of Graduate Studies (1931–32), all designed by Rogers, gave Yale a new Gothic center.

Although the Rogers-era residential colleges and academic buildings varied in their particulars, all had modern structural underpinnings wrapped with Gothic or Georgian facades, drawing the ire of some undergraduates who argued for Modernist expression. The sight of medievalizing forms and materials cladding the welded steel tower of Sterling Memorial Library drove the future journalist William Harlan Hale, then a Yale senior, to passionately decry the hypocrisy of "Girder Gothic" in a widely circulated article first published in issue of the *Harkness Hoot* on November 15, 1930. Hale conceded that the Memorial Quadrangle was "a delightful place to live in" but deemed it morally outrageous that its architect had "put water tanks into church towers, and lavatories into oriels." In 1959, however, Hale acknowledged that Yale's architecture of the past had "become authentic in the sense that any canon of taste portrays the mores and feelings of its time."

Following World War II, Yale embarked upon further physical expansion, but in a very different spirit, with individual Modernist "trophy" buildings inserted here and there amid the continuous and characteristic fabric built by previous generations of architects. Among the most renowned of these symbols of a forward-looking university are the Beinecke Rare Book & Manuscript Library (Gordon Bunshaft; Skidmore, Owings & Merrill) and Paul Rudolph's School of Art and Architecture, both completed in 1963. More germane to this

1.52. **Yale University, aerial view from the southwest showing construction of the residential colleges west of York Street. Photograph 1931.**
Yale University Library, Manuscripts and Archives. RU 703/Series I/Box I/ Folder 10.

Branford College
James Gamble Rogers, 1917–21; 1933

Saybrook College
James Gamble Rogers, 1917–21; 1933

1.53. **Residential colleges, 1932–1940.** Yale University Library, Manuscripts and Archives.

Davenport College
James Gamble Rogers, 1932–33

Jonathan Edwards College
James Gamble Rogers, 1933

Grace Hopper College
John Russell Pope, 1933

Pierson College
James Gamble Rogers, 1933

Berkeley College
James Gamble Rogers, 1934

Trumbull College
James Gamble Rogers, 1929; 1933

Timothy Dwight College
James Gamble Rogers, 1935

Silliman College
Eggers & Higgins, 1940

1.54. **Reprint of Harkness Hoot (1930)** in **The American Architect** v. 139, n. 2591 (January 1931): 24–25.

project are the buildings completed by Eero Saarinen (1910–1961), including Ingalls Rink (1958), adjacent to the site of Pauli Murray College, and Morse and Stiles Colleges (1960–62), which were intended to help Yale accommodate a jump in enrollment after World War II—from 1,520 in 1940 to 2,533 in 1950—stimulated by the Servicemen's Readjustment Act, better known as the GI Bill, which made college affordable to returning soldiers.

Saarinen had been an architecture student at Yale in the early 1930s when the first wave of residential colleges was being built and, before coming to Yale, had grown up amid the medievalizing campus of Michigan's Cranbrook Academy of Art, designed by his father, Eliel Saarinen. His design of Morse and Stiles Colleges caused a stir in the architectural press with their combination of Modernism and Medievalism, evoking both the forms, spaces, and textures of Yale's Gothic residential colleges and those of the Italian hill town of San Gimignano. Saarinen, forced to contend with an irregularly configured site unlike those that his predecessors had to face, remained true to the sensibility of Rogers in designing Morse and Stiles not as stand-alone object-buildings, but as an irregular, picturesque grouping of courts, walls, and towers bisected by a winding pedestrian walk similar in spirit (if not in geometry) to Library Walk, a de-mapped street separating the Memorial Quadrangle from Jonathan Edwards College. The British critic Reyner Banham accused Saarinen of evoking "Gordon Craig–type scenic effects" (Craig was an innovative theater designer and director), an idea Saarinen's widow accepted, stating after his death that "he thought of college architecture, in its relation to students, as stage scenery."

Gothic Yale: Scholastic Ideal and Urban Type

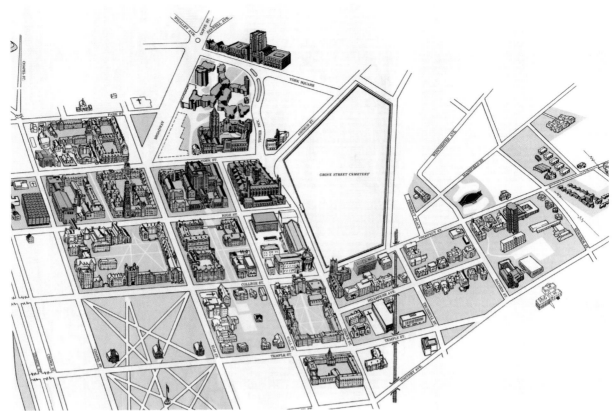

1.55. **Diagram of significant Modernist buildings completed between 1953 and 1977, derived from a Yale University campus map c. 1980.** RAMSA/ Yale University Library, Manuscripts and Archives.

■ Residential colleges, 1921–40

■ Other new buildings, 1923–32

■ Significant Modernist buildings, 1953–77

Saarinen intended that the path and courts of Morse and Stiles would remain open to the public. Saarinen was also driven by a sense that new buildings ought to explore experimental technologies. He developed a system of exterior walls consisting of rubblestone bonded by sprayed gunite, the effect of which recalled Frank Lloyd Wright's Taliesin West more than anything hitherto seen at Yale. Wags would refer to the result as Taliesin West Haven.

Prompted by the advent of coeducation in 1969, Yale again set out to add two additional residential colleges. A Yale-owned site at the corner of Grove Street and Whitney Avenue was identified, and the firm Mitchell/Giurgola was selected from among eight to ten architects proposed for consideration. Though designs by Romaldo Giurgola (1920–2016) were submitted in 1972, the project stalled due to escalating costs and a failure of diplomacy between the university and the city, quashing further discussion of expansion for the foreseeable future. Had the two residential colleges been built as designed, they would have departed starkly from their predecessors in both the choice of building material — exposed reinforced concrete, reflecting the Brutalist aesthetics of their time — and the even more critical issues of massing, scale, and typology, as Giurgola seemed unwilling or unable to transfer Rogers's subtlety and spatial variety into a modern idiom.

With Modernist architectural principles widely upended in the 1970s and 1980s, Yale gradually reawakened to the value of its own architectural heritage, prompted in part by architectural historian and alumnus Vincent Scully's (BA 1940, MA 1947, PhD 1949) writing and teaching about issues of urbanism and style. Under the leadership of President (1986–1992) Benno C. Schmidt Jr., who had Michael McKinnell (1935–) as his principal architectural advisor, Yale began a return to the Collegiate Gothic, principally on Science Hill, in the form of the Bass Center for Molecular & Structural Biology (Kallmann

Gothic Yale: Scholastic Ideal and Urban Type

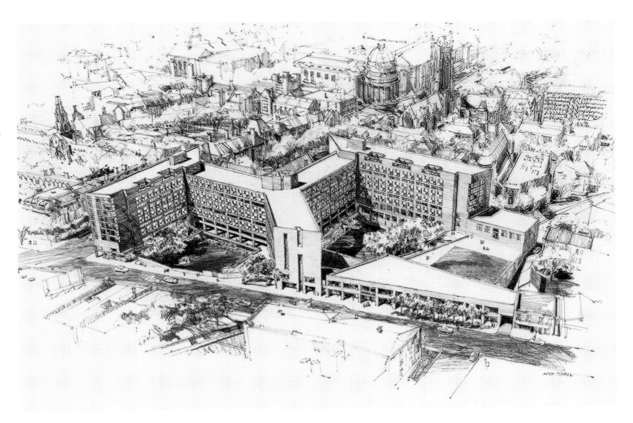

McKinnell & Wood, 1993), and more strongly with an addition to the Peabody Museum, the Class of 1954 Environmental Science Center (David M. Schwarz Architects, 2001), which fully embraced the Gothic of its host building. Schmidt also initiated a plan, carried out by his successor, President (1993–2013) Richard C. Levin (following the interim presidency of Howard R. Lamar), to restore the residential colleges, most of them sixty years old and falling into decrepitude owing to deferred maintenance. Between 1998 and 2011, building systems were upgraded, new circulation routes were opened through old walls, and new shared amenities were added.

President Levin also proposed a potential expansion of Yale College in 1998 to meet vastly increased demand for admission. But this proposal remained confidential until February 2007, when Levin felt confident enough to appoint a study group to advise him and the Yale Corporation on "the implications of potentially adding two new residential colleges on the site bounded by Prospect, Sachem, and Canal Streets (the Prospect-Sachem Triangle)," according to the group's report submitted one year later. The study group's two committees met regularly throughout 2007, interviewing numerous faculty and administrators and hosting five student forums, gathering valuable information that would serve as a detailed brief for our planning and design process. The Yale Corporation voted to proceed with expansion in June 2008, and in September of that year invited us to prepare the designs for the two new colleges.

The commission, Levin says, played to our firm's "two sweet spots, residential and collegiate architecture." To assure the social parity of the new residential colleges, and sensitive to students' lukewarm regard for the Modernist architecture of Morse and Stiles Colleges, the university directed us to adopt the quadrangular planning and one of the two stylistic idioms of the Rogers-era colleges. Because these first ten residential colleges, though essentially alike in underlying structure and plan, are almost evenly split between the Georgian and

Gothic styles, Yale left open for discussion the question of which style would be more suitable, pending analysis of cost and other factors. Style was less of an issue for Alice J. Raucher, Yale's senior architect and major projects planner from 2007 to 2015, who says, "Yale's campus is so extraordinary that any new buildings must be good, well-proportioned, well-detailed, and well-crafted buildings that can inspire — regardless of the style or period in which they're built."

Yet the issue of architectural style inevitably elicited strong opinions in the Yale community and beyond. Almost immediately, students expressed mixed views in response to the prospect of a new addition to the campus in a traditional style. In a guest column in the *Yale Daily News* published September 8, 2008, titled, "Stern offers elegance over absurdity," Nathan Harden, a senior, cheered the decision, stating, "For many, traditional architecture is part of what makes Yale special." A counterargument, "Stern should trade luxury for novelty," was delivered by sophomore Ryan Caro in the pages of the same publication on September 15, 2008, asserting that "a return to the architecture of yore only signals a longing for the Yale of the 1930s: a finishing school for the wealthy, white, Protestant sons of elite prep schools," and "recreating the past only encourages students to sit around idly applauding themselves for being accepted into the Ivy League."

We studied both Gothic and Georgian options for the new residential colleges as part of our concept design work in 2008, discussed more fully in Chapter 4. The seeming appeal of the Georgian style, at least to some parties involved, was that its flatter facades would prove less expensive to build. Preliminary cost analyses revealed both styles to be achievable within budget, a conclusion reaffirmed by Yale's comparison of the costs of several residential academic buildings in Connecticut that our firm had recently designed: two Georgian residence halls at the Hotchkiss School and a brick-and-stone Gothic addition to a residence hall designed by James Gamble Rogers at the Taft School.

With the financial equation balanced, we made a strong case for the Gothic, because it is the dominant style of the central campus and much of the science campus. Also, on a practical level, we knew that the Gothic language would be more flexible and forgiving of the irregularities in plan and elevation that would inevitably result from designing on the triangular site chosen for the new colleges. As Rogers himself noted to the president of Northwestern University in a letter of October 9, 1930, the Gothic "does not demand the symmetry that Georgian has to have."

Students developed their own rationale. In an op-ed in the *Yale Daily News* from April 7, 2013, Brendan Bashin-Sullivan, a sophomore, allowed that "the Yale Gothic campus" was something like a forgery of its Oxbridge counterpart, yet "a forgery of intense, scrupulous sincerity, a forgery with nearly a century of history of its own." Echoing the evolved views of William Harlan Hale from 1959, Bashin-Sullivan wrote that Yale's Gothic architecture "is transforming, with the passage of time, from imitation to original. And so we treat the campus with a peculiar mix of derision, humor, and affection: 'Hey, it's a fake, but it's our fake and it's not going anywhere.'"

In the spirit of such "scrupulous sincerity" as well as "humor and affection," which encapsulates the legacy of James Gamble Rogers at Yale, we welcomed the opportunity to enter into a conversation across time with the existing architecture of the campus. The language best able to facilitate that conversation, to our minds, was Gothic.

The Prospect-Sachem Triangle:
Between Two Cultures

Yale College and Sheffield Scientific School,
separated by only a few streets,
were two separate countries on the same planet.

LOOMIS HAVEMEYER
Sheff Days and Ways, 1958

An editorial in the *Yale Daily News*, published on February 22, 2008, tentatively endorsed President Richard C. Levin's proposal to build two additional residential colleges, but it acknowledged widespread student skepticism about the site designated for expansion:

> The chosen location—across the street from a graveyard, around the corner from, well, virtually nothing—could prove disastrous for the geographical and cultural cohesion of Yale College. That much is true: it could. But, if executed well, the extension of the undergraduate campus could achieve what is otherwise impossible—namely, the integration of Science Hill and the advent of new spaces that we direly need, and have needed for some time.

The proposed site, known as the Prospect-Sachem Triangle, did not seem to students to be part of Yale. A poll of 362 Yale undergraduates conducted earlier that month by the student-run daily newspaper found that only one in four students supported the expansion plan, with the most frequent complaint having to do with the seemingly remote location of the proposed colleges, just south of Science Hill. The distance represented at most a leisurely ten-minute walk north from the central Cross Campus quadrangle, but many perceived it as a long trek. "You would have thought it was Siberia to listen to some of the students' comments," recalls Laura Cruickshank, Yale's university planner from 2005 to 2013, who received student feedback at town hall-style meetings and survey responses leading up to the expansion.

The fact that students had no trouble getting to hockey games at Ingalls Rink, adjacent to the proposed site at the northwest corner of Prospect and Sachem Streets, suggested that the griping may have been partly related to undergraduate preference for courses in the humanities over required science courses. But even science majors deemed the site remote from the campus core, according to the 2008 report of the study group appointed by President Levin to consider the new residential colleges. The report further asserted that Science Hill offered "few attractions to lift the spirit"—no cafés, no evening dining centers, no late-night convenience or food outlets, no theater or rehearsal space, no athletic facilities except the hockey rink—and that "its isolation, underlined by its relative social emptiness, has been a serious problem for the university, because it has seemed to convey the sense that the sciences are somehow less valued."

Benjamin Franklin and Pauli Murray Colleges are built within the triangular site bounded by Prospect Street to the east, Sachem Street to the north, and Canal Street and the Farmington Canal Heritage Greenway, a sunken former canal and rail corridor transformed into a bike trail in 2003, to the southwest. The site is separated from the historic campus core by the Grove Street Cemetery, established in 1796, which borders the site across Canal Street. The wedge-shaped parcel chosen for the new colleges was never absorbed into nearby Science Hill, nor was it part of the nineteenth-century Hillhouse residential and academic quarter to the east. Hosting a cobbled-together assortment of structures and parking lots, and lacking a clear focus or relationship to its surroundings, the site was unrecognizable as Yale territory.

Seen in another light, however, Prospect-Sachem Triangle held latent importance as a potential physical link between the humanities-oriented core and the sciences. By bringing more than 900 resident undergraduates as well as faculty and visitors to the site, Yale moved to bridge the gap between what British scientist and novelist C. P. Snow (1905–1980) characterized in the 1950s as the "two cultures" of modern intellectual life, the humanities and the sciences, a schism embedded in Yale's institutional structure since the founding of the Sheffield Scientific School in 1847, which operated nearly autonomously until 1920 and was not formally disbanded until 1956. The gulf to be overcome was also a physical one, since the scientific school developed its own campus to the north of Yale's historic center. Indeed, the 2008 study group report stated, "as the University commits itself to enhancing the sciences and engineering, and as it constructs more buildings on Science Hill, it must expand the idea of what constitutes the central campus" to create a "unified whole" stretching from Chapel Street to the top of Science Hill.

During the nineteenth century, the Prospect-Sachem Triangle was developed with private residences of varying styles. Several prominent houses along Sachem Street, including the Eaton House (c. 1865) at the corner of Prospect Street, aspired to the gentility of Hillhouse Avenue, while an 1835 Greek Revival house anchored eight smaller lots facing Prospect Street and Prospect Place in the lower tip of the triangle. Over time, especially after the turn of the twentieth century, the site increasingly accommodated Sheffield student housing and programs amid the private homes. A three-story Georgian house at 124 Prospect Street, erected in 1907 and later named Brewster Hall, served initially as a fraternity house for "Sheff" students, then as a dormitory, and later as offices of the Yale political science department. A masonry house owned by Berzelius, a Sheff secret society corresponding to Yale's Skull and Bones, Scroll and Key, and Wolf's Head societies, stood a few doors down Prospect Street within the triangle.

Academic buildings began to impinge upon the site in the early twentieth century. Hammond Metallurgical Laboratory (W. Gedney Beatty, 1904), built for metallurgical research, contained an imposing machine hall as well as classrooms and offices behind a brick and limestone facade. The most memorable feature of the building, which fronted Mansfield Street and backed onto the canal-turned-railway, may have been its copper cornice surmounted by a hammer motif. The Berkeley Divinity School, an independent entity, found a suitable home in the Prospect-Sachem Triangle in 1928 when it moved to New Haven from Middletown, Connecticut. The leaders of this Episcopal seminary valued not only the site's proximity to Yale, including the Yale Divinity School, whose new quadrangle (Delano & Aldrich, 1932) was located further north on Prospect Street, but also its proximity to adjacent industrial and working-class neighborhoods, offering seminarians a glimpse of urban reality.

The Berkeley Divinity School acquired the former Eaton house and several others for use as dormitories. It also gave Prospect Street a dose of lackluster Modernism in the form of Urban Hall (Douglas Orr, 1957), enclosing a library, classrooms, and offices behind a primitive glass curtain wall and flat brick screen. In 1951 the seminary enlarged and converted a nineteenth-century carriage house on the site into a chapel. After Berkeley merged with the Yale Divinity School in 1971, the chapel was transformed and expanded to create Donaldson Commons (Herbert S. Newman, 1978), a dining hall for the School of Management recently established across Prospect Street.

By this time, the engineers had decamped from Hammond Metallurgical Laboratory to the Becton Engineering and Applied Science Center (Marcel

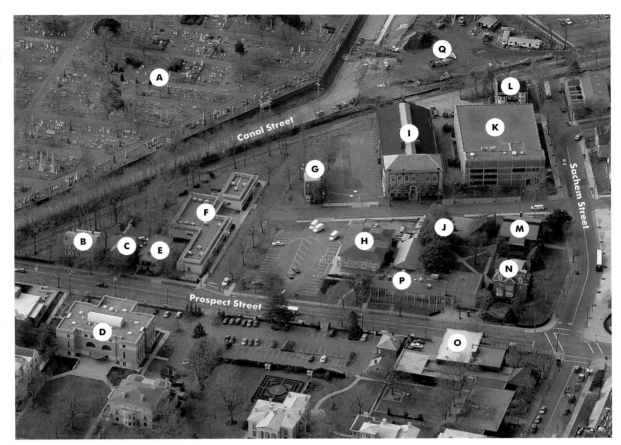

2.1. **Aerial view of the Prospect-Sachem Triangle, future site of Benjamin Franklin and Pauli Murray Colleges. Photograph 2006.** Yale University Office of Facilities.

A Grove Street Cemetery
B 88 Prospect
C 94 Prospect
D Henry R. Luce Hall
E 100 Prospect
F Prospect Place Modular Building
G 4 Mansfield
H Brewster Hall
I Hammond Metallurgical Laboratory
J Donaldson Commons
K Seeley G. Mudd Library
L 70 Sachem
M 80 Sachem
N Eaton House
O Founders Hall
P Urban Hall
Q Yale Health Center (under construction)

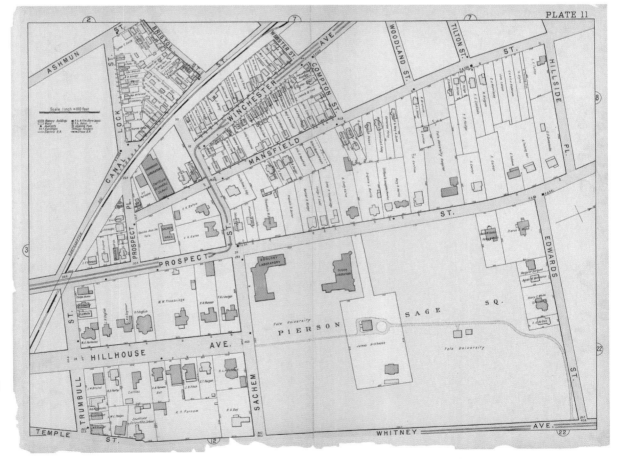

2.2. **Plate II of the 1911 Atlas of New Haven showing the Prospect-Sachem Triangle at middle left.** The New Haven Museum.

2.3. **Residence of Professor Daniel C. Eaton (architect unknown, c. 1865), acquired in the 1920s by the Berkeley Divinity School. View looking southwest from Sachem Street. Photograph 1936.** The New Haven Museum.

Breuer and Associates, 1970), and Hammond's voluminous interior became the sculpture studio of the Yale School of Art, which in turn relocated in 2008 to a new building on Edgewood Avenue designed by KieranTimberlake. Yale adapted former residences on the site to other uses, such as a two-story house at the western end of Sachem Street that served temporarily as a Yale police station. A Modernist brick residential building by Sherwood, Mills and Smith (1976) on Sachem Street was converted to academic use in the early 2000s.

The most prominent subsequent additions to the Prospect-Sachem Triangle were the Seeley G. Mudd Library (Roth and Moore, 1982), a brick-and-concrete structure at Mansfield and Sachem Streets that housed government documents and specialized research collections, and the provisional yet remarkable Prospect Place Modular Building (Centerbrook Architects and Planners, 2002), a temporary swing space for the political science department, composed of twenty-one factory-made units stacked and configured into three bars, clad in corrugated steel and slashed with ribbon windows. By the turn of the twenty-first century, all the buildings on the site belonged to Yale and were used for academic purposes. That was a key factor in receiving municipal permission to proceed with building the new residential colleges, and a key difference from Yale's failed effort to build residential colleges in the 1970s on a site that the city viewed as having commercial potential.

Yale's efforts to use architecture to connect its liberal arts and science programs predate the planning of Benjamin Franklin and Pauli Murray Colleges by more than a century. Starting in 1902, the Bicentennial Buildings provided shared dining and concert halls as well as a crucial circulation hinge between Yale College territory and that of the Sheffield Scientific School, with the Memorial Rotunda at the intersection of College, Prospect, and Grove Streets. A more substantial and systematic attempt at campus unification was made in 1919 by John Russell Pope, who criticized the "haphazardly placed buildings that should have been more reasonably designed with reference to one another," reflecting the eclectic results of Yale's prodigious and frequently donor-driven building

2.4. **Brewster Hall (attributed to Phillip Corbin, 1907) with Hammond Metallurgical Laboratory (W. Gedney Beatty, 1904) in background looking northwest. Photograph 2008.** RAMSA.

2.5. **Hammond Metallurgical Laboratory (W. Gedney Beatty, 1904). Photograph 1918.** Yale University Library, Manuscripts and Archives. Image no. 6470.

2.6. **Hammond Metallurgical Laboratory (W. Gedney Beatty, 1904). Photograph 2008.** RAMSA.

2.7. **Donaldson Commons (Herbert S. Newman, 1978). Photograph 2008.** RAMSA.

2.8. **Becton Engineering and Applied Science Center (Marcel Breuer and Associates, 1970). Photograph Michael Marsland, 2012.** Yale University Office of Public Affairs and Communications.

activities of the late nineteenth and early twentieth centuries, which had proceeded without an overall planning strategy.

To bring order to the chaos and to connect the central and science campuses, Pope proposed to blaze new axial connections through Yale and New Haven. First, a mid-block connection between the Old Campus quadrangle and the new proposed Cross Campus would be opened by knocking down Durfee Hall. Second, an enlarged east–west axis (including and expanding south of Wall Street) would become the backbone of a monumental Cross Campus, terminating in a broad new plaza about where Silliman College now stands, conceived as a knuckle between New Haven's Nine Square grid and the rotated grid to the north. The third proposed axis was a southern extension of Hillhouse Avenue joining the proposed new plaza. In Pope's plan, Prospect Street is treated as an edge, not a spine; the Prospect-Sachem Triangle remains marginal to the plan and literally recedes into the mist in Otto R. Eggers's renderings. Pope pictured the development of Science Hill as a kind of magnification of the Old Campus, with partially enclosed quadrangles around the perimeter defining a vast shared open space in the center.

2.11. Yale University perspective drawing of proposed development (John Russell Pope, 1919; Otto R. Eggers, delineator). John Russell Pope and Otto R. Eggers, *Yale University: A Plan for Its Future Building* (New York: The Cheltenham Press, 1919). Reprinted in Royal Cortissoz, *The Architecture of John Russell Pope* v. 1 (New York: Helburn, 1924), plate 30.

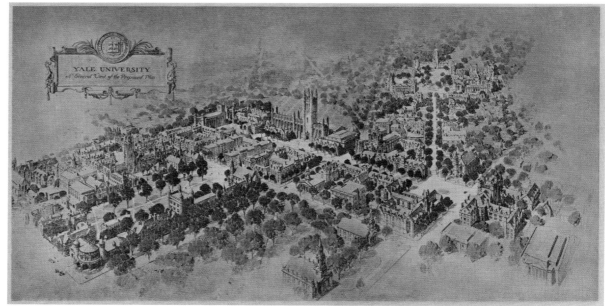

2.12. Yale University perspective drawings of proposed development (John Russell Pope, 1919; Otto R. Eggers, delineator). John Russell Pope and Otto R. Eggers, *Yale University: A Plan for Its Future Building* (New York: The Cheltenham Press, 1919). Reprinted in Royal Cortissoz, *The Architecture of John Russell Pope* v. 1 (New York: Helburn, 1924), plates 26 and 32.

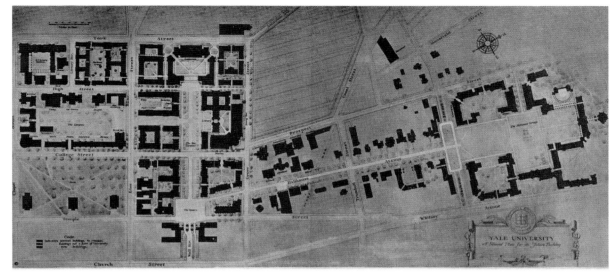

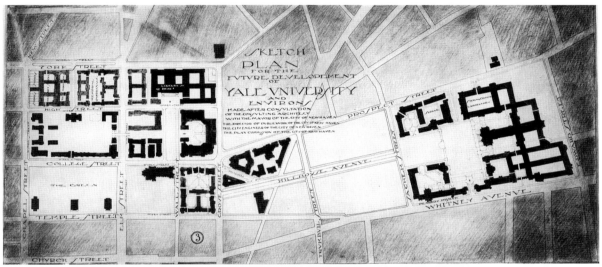

Pope's comprehensive proposal went unrealized after three leading architects—Bertram G. Goodhue (1869–1924), William Adams Delano (1874–1960), and Paul Philippe Cret (1876–1945)—submitted a tepid review to the trustees in February 1920. Their letter praised Pope's overall study as "in itself a work of art" thanks in part to the drawings by Eggers (1882–1964) but urged against the most transformative aspects of the plan. In November of that year, after the trustees appointed James Gamble Rogers as consulting architect, Pope's totalizing approach to planning lost out to a more incremental approach. Rogers adapted some of Pope's ideas (especially a truncated Cross Campus) but dropped the most sweeping parts of the proposed axial connections that would have required significant demolition and called for more intimately scaled quadrangles on Science Hill. With the construction of Silliman College in 1940, Pope's proposed connecting node at the base of an extended Hillhouse Avenue was blocked, imparting greater importance to Prospect Street and the Prospect-Sachem Triangle for purposes of campus-making.

Post–World War II developments along Prospect Street did little to help bridge the two cultures, with the exception of Saarinen's Ingalls Rink, the swooping "whale" at the corner of Prospect and Sachem Streets, which created a much-needed attraction near Science Hill. Two out of the three nineteenth-century Sheffield buildings designed by J. Cleaveland Cady, "the row of magnificent

2.15. Ingalls Rink (Eero Saarinen, 1958). View from southeast. Photograph c. 1960. Yale University Library, Manuscripts and Archives. Image no. 1575.

2.16. Sheffield Scientific School. View south along Prospect Street with Grove Street Cemetery to the right. From left to right: Non-affiliated private residence; Sheffield Chemical Laboratory (J. Cleaveland Cady, 1894–95; now Arthur K. Watson Hall); North Sheffield Hall (J. Cleaveland Cady, 1872–73; demolished 1967); and Winchester Hall (J. Cleaveland Cady, 1892, demolished 1967). Photograph 1901. Library of Congress Prints and Photographs Division, Detroit Publishing Company.

utilitarian cubes," as historian Patrick Pinnell calls them, were demolished in 1967 to make way for the pedestrian-unfriendly Becton Center. Only the former Sheffield Chemical Laboratory was granted a reprieve, renovated by Roth and Moore in 1986 and rechristened Arthur K. Watson Hall.

Postwar buildings on Science Hill, such as the mediocre Gibbs Laboratory (Paul Schweikher, 1955; demolished 2017) and the far more impressive Kline Biology Tower (1964–65) and Kline Chemistry Laboratory (1963–65) by Philip Johnson (1906–2005), seemed initially to defy quadrangular planning. More recent buildings — such as the 1993 Bass Center for Molecular & Structural Biology; Kroon Hall (Hopkins Architects with Centerbrook Architects and Planners, 2009); and the forthcoming Yale Science Building (Pelli Clarke Pelli Architects, 2019) — have combined with the older buildings to define a series of partially enclosed science quadrangles, even if these lack the scalar subtleties of their counterparts from the Rogers era.

A comprehensive study from 2000, "Yale University: A Framework for Campus Planning," prepared by Cooper Robertson, turned the university's attention to the Prospect-Sachem Triangle, the development of which, the study points out, would make Prospect Street "a more active pedestrian corridor between the Core and Science Hill." Without explicitly designating the use of

2.17. **Gibbs Laboratory (Paul Schweikher, 1955; demolished 2017). Photograph c. 1958.** Yale University Library, Manuscripts and Archives. Image no. 1183.

2.18. **Kline Biology Tower (Philip Johnson, 1963–65). View from northeast. Photograph Michael Marsland, 2012.** Yale University Office of Public Affairs and Communications.

2.19. **Kroon Hall (Hopkins Architecture with Centerbrook Architects and Planners, 2009). View from Sachem's Wood. Photograph 2017.** RAMSA.

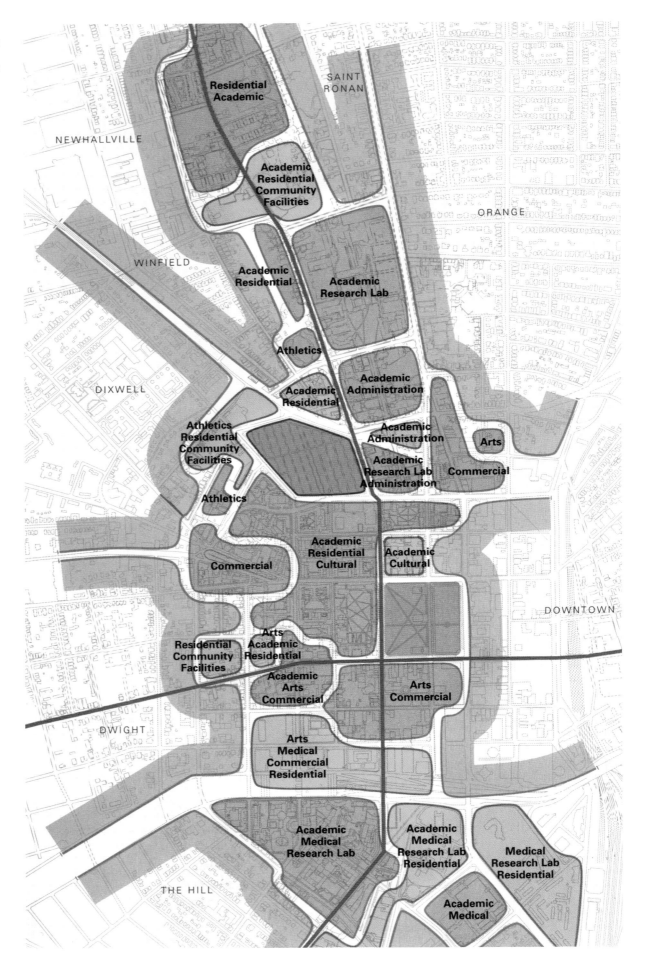

2.20. **Recommended campus use diagram (Cooper Robertson, 2000).** Richard C. Levin and Cooper Robertson, *Yale University: A Framework for Campus Planning* (New Haven: Yale University Press, 2000), 92.

▓ Existing uses
▓ Proposed uses

The Prospect-Sachem Triangle: Between Two Cultures

the site for new residential colleges, the plan identified it as an "opportunity area" primed for academic and residential redevelopment. The preliminary redevelopment framework suggested that some existing buildings, notably Hammond Hall (as it was known after it ceased being a laboratory) and Mudd Library, might remain in place. It also called for stronger east–west connections across the Greenway.

Cooper Robertson presented a new Yale campus map as part of the framework, substituting the standard north–south orientation for the east–west orientation historically preferred by Yale cartographers. The result emphasized the elongated proportions of the campus within New Haven: about two miles "tall" measured south-to-north, but only a fraction of that distance measured east-to-west, leading Vincent Scully to use a corporeal metaphor by describing this spatial condition as "a thin vertical body, stretching from the School of Medicine to the Divinity School and almost cut in half at the kidneys by Grove Street Cemetery . . . Yale is attenuated, rickety, with shaky connections." The redevelopment of the Prospect-Sachem Triangle thus emerged as a key strategic step in strengthening the campus fabric at a critical point of weakness.

In a follow-up study, Cooper Robertson identified the Prospect-Sachem Triangle as the most promising site for new residential colleges. Other sites were investigated—near the School of Music, near the Hall of Graduate Studies, and on Ashmun Street—but these were found to be either too small or too awkwardly configured to support the necessary program. The study concluded that the Prospect-Sachem site, though hitherto seen as peripheral, could have a transformative effect by bringing a critical mass of student residents to the area.

In 2003 Robert A.M. Stern acted as advisor to Yale College senior Jennifer Bernell, who undertook a remarkably prescient design for the colleges on the site later chosen for expansion, employing courtyard planning and contextually appropriate scale and facade design. Ironically, Cooper Robertson partner Jaquelin T. Robertson (1933–), serving as the William B. and Charlotte Shepherd Davenport Visiting Professor of Architectural Design at the Yale School of Architecture in fall 2004, assigned students the task of designing new residential colleges on a site along the east side of Whitney Avenue and on another along Crown Street.

A 2006 development agreement between Yale and the City of New Haven established the terms of a mutually beneficial exchange. Yale obtained the right to develop two generously sized quadrangles on the Prospect-Sachem Triangle site, incorporating portions of three streets ceded by the city: Prospect Place, the southernmost block of Mansfield Street, and the dead-end tip of Sachem Street west of Winchester Avenue. In return, Yale pledged to create east–west public walkways across the site and the Farmington Canal Heritage Greenway, as requested by Mayor John DeStefano Jr. and City Planner Karyn Gilvarg; and to contribute roughly $10 million to improving streets and sidewalks in the area; rebuilding pedestrian and vehicle bridges over the Greenway at Temple Street, Hillhouse Avenue, and Prospect Street; extending the Greenway beneath those bridges through the Yale campus to Temple Street; and the expansion of a nearby public space, Ella B. Scantlebury Park.

In February 2007, when President Levin appointed committees to provide advice on the implications of potentially adding two residential colleges on the Prospect-Sachem Triangle site, he indicated that Mudd Library would probably be conserved and renovated, according to the group's 2008 report. However,

2.21. **Jennifer Bernell (BA 2003), senior thesis, design for new residential colleges at Yale, 2003.** Jennifer Bernell.

feasibility studies undertaken prior to our involvement concluded that it would be difficult if not impossible to incorporate either Mudd Library or Hammond Hall into the new residential colleges while accommodating all the required programmatic elements at a contextually appropriate building scale. Our team came to the same conclusion upon further review. As former Yale planner Laura Cruickshank recalls, "We really, genuinely tried to make it work [to retrofit Mudd or Hammond], but in the end, to keep either building would have been the tail wagging the dog. It just couldn't all fit." Yale also intended that part of the site be left open for a cultural or academic "third building" independent of the two colleges, facing outward in a gesture of urban engagement. To this end a 17,000-square-foot space was left available for a future nonresidential building at the northeast corner of the Prospect-Sachem Triangle, though no plans have been made to date.

The planning and design process proceeded with close and constant attention to stakeholder demands. In the words of Yale architect and planner Alice Raucher, "We had input at every level of constituents. There were committees composed of deans and heads of colleges, student focused committees, steering committees, and executive committees. There were numerous meetings with the broader New Haven community, and we presented to the city administration at various stages in the approval process."

At the outset of our work, we were inspired not only by the long-running quest to strengthen the north–south link between the core and Science Hill, but also by the possibility, as suggested by Cooper Robertson in 2000, of completing a new east–west pedestrian link around the north side of the cemetery — formerly a desolate and potentially dangerous place — to connect the Payne Whitney Gymnasium with Science Hill. The revitalization of this northwest corner of the campus began when a shuttered commercial laundry complex was on the verge of being sold to an asbestos-removal company, prompting Yale to step in and acquire the land for more salubrious uses with the backing of New Haven Alderwoman Grace Gibbs and the local community board, the Dixwell Enterprise Community Management Team.

The Rose Center (William Rawn Associates, 2006), built on the former site of the laundry, serving both the university and the neighborhood with a

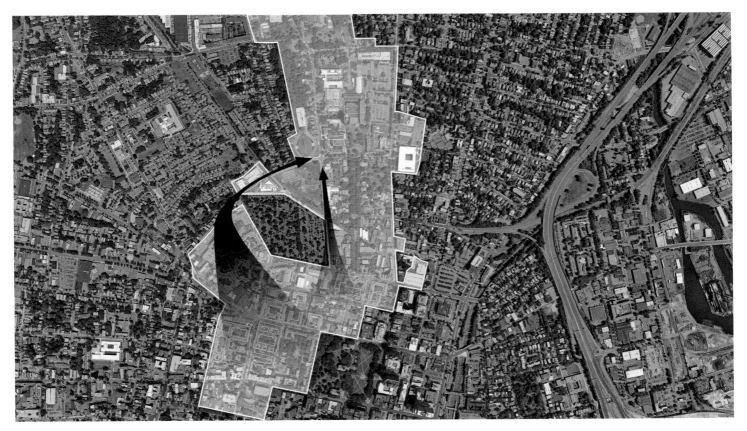

2.22. **Diagram of new circulation opportunities. Presentation drawing, 2017.** RAMSA.

glass-walled Yale police station and community learning center, created a beacon of safety at the corner of Lock, Ashmun, and Bristol Streets, the northwest corner of the cemetery. Further extending the new pedestrian-friendly route along the north side of the cemetery, the Yale Health Center (Mack Scogin Merrill Elam Architects, 2010), facing Lock Street and the Farmington Canal Heritage Greenway opposite Pauli Murray College, brought increased activity to the area in the course of serving thousands of Yale affiliates and offering clinical services, such as blood-pressure screenings, to local community members. The two new at-grade Greenway crossings, stipulated in the 2006 development agreement, allow pedestrians to cross from Science Hill and the residential colleges to the health center, the gym, Baker Hall, Morse and Stiles Colleges, and other points west of the cemetery.

Slightly farther afield, the urban fabric of the Dixwell neighborhood has been stabilized and revitalized with Monterey Place (Fletcher Thompson, 1994–2001), a Hope VI development of low-rise detached housing that replaced the unsuccessful Elm Haven public housing development (Douglas Orr, 1939–40; extended 1960). Bruce D. Alexander, Yale's Vice President for New Haven and State Affairs and Campus Development, involved since 1998, says that the renewed northwest corner is "a very good example of the university's effort to create neighborhood partnerships." Matthew Nemerson, New Haven's economic development administrator, told the *Yale Daily News* on April 7, 2017, "The whole sweep from Dixwell [Avenue] to Prospect [Street] has seen a great deal of investment over 25 years," so that the arrival of the new student population would not bring about a drastic change "because the change has already come."

Moreover, according to Alexander, Yale does not intend to alter the intact residential area due north of Benjamin Franklin and Pauli Murray Colleges—"an all-American neighborhood," as he calls it, praising its diverse mix of

2.23. **Elm Haven housing development, aerial view. Photograph 1958.** The New Haven Museum, New Haven Redevelopment Agency Photograph Collection.

2.24. **Monterey Place housing development, aerial view. Photograph c. 1995.** Blades and Goven LLC.

2.25. **Yale Health Center (Mack Scogin Merrill Elam Architects, 2010). Photograph 2010.** Mack Scogin Merrill Elam Architects.

2.26. **Malone Center (Pelli Clarke Pelli Architects, 2005). Photograph Jeff Goldberg, 2005.** Esto.

2.27. **Yale Center for Engineering Innovation and Design (Charney Architects, 2012) in Becton Center. Photograph 2013.** Yale Center for Engineering Innovation and Design.

2.28. **77 Prospect Street, Institution for Social and Policy Studies (Charney Architects, 2009). Addition to the former Wolf's Head Society Building (McKim, Mead & White, 1885). Photograph Robert Perron, 2009.** Charney Architects.

socioeconomic and racial groups and Yale- and non-Yale-affiliated residents. The university has reinvested in the maintenance and upkeep of houses it owns in the area, such as those along Mansfield Street, and continues redevelopment efforts further north at Science Park, a collection of abandoned industrial buildings being repurposed for a mix of new uses.

Attempting to address the impermeability of the Grove Street Cemetery, the 2008 study group report encouraged placing an additional gate on the north side of the cemetery and also recommended "that a portion of the cemetery's historic wall on Prospect Street be replaced with a beautiful wrought-iron fence so as to open the cemetery to view and reduce the sense of a forbidding walled-off enclosure that acts as a geographical barrier." The cemetery's Standing Committee of the Properties rejected the idea of a second gate before we began design, but at the request of Charles D. Ellis, a former Yale Corporation member who also served on the cemetery's Standing Committee, we explored the possibility of replacing some portions of the stone wall along the west side of Prospect Street with cast-iron fencing between existing stone piers to match the 1845 fence along the Grove Street frontage. The proposal, sponsored by Ellis, spurred six months of internal debate, but was withdrawn in October, 2009, in light of concerns from burial plot owners about noise intrusions.

As an alternative, the sidewalk along the cemetery wall on the west side of Prospect Street was refurbished and the adjacent strip planted with ground cover

2.29. **Rosenkranz Hall (Koetter Kim & Associates, 2009). Photograph 2013.** Koetter Kim & Associates.

and maple trees. "We had to get past the point where everyone felt tortured to walk to Science Hill," says Edward P. Bass, trustee of the Yale Corporation from 2001 to 2013, Senior Fellow of the Yale Corporation from 2011 to 2013, and member of the Yale Buildings and Grounds Committee from 2001 to present, who helped fund the work.

In addition, Yale took action to improve the built fabric along the east side of Prospect Street, fulfilling the 2008 study group's recommendation for "enhancing the buildings leading up to the proposed new colleges in order to improve the physical and psychological accessibility of the area." The completion of the Malone Center (Pelli Clarke Pelli Architects, 2005), home of the biomedical engineering department, established a new identity for the corner of Prospect and Trumbull Streets. The ground floor of Breuer's hulking Becton Center was transformed in 2012 into the Center for Engineering Innovation and Design, an 8,700-square-foot design-and-fabrication lab open twenty-four hours a day and, importantly, visible from the street through its glass wall. A forty-four-seat ground-floor café, which opened in 2013, further enlivened the street level.

Then, on the block facing Benjamin Franklin and Pauli Murray Colleges across Prospect Street, the crow-step-gabled former Wolf's Head Society building (McKim, Mead & White, 1885) was renovated and added to by Charney Architects in 2006 for Yale's Institution for Social and Policy Studies. Rosenkranz Hall (Koetter Kim & Associates, 2009) restored the street wall that had been compromised by the reclusive Luce Hall (Edward Larrabee Barnes, 1994), and matched the familiar four-story scale of many successful Yale buildings. Taken together, these new developments give Prospect Street a character and scale that it never had before, assuring a continuous and pedestrian-friendly urban fabric leading up to Science Hill. Even the southern end of Science Hill itself has become more hospitable in recent years, with new landscape elements designed by Laurie Olin knitting together the spaces between buildings and along the streets. This is just the beginning of what current President Peter Salovey describes as a comprehensive building and planning effort to make the historically fragmented northern part of the campus "feel like an integrated whole" while allowing "the town and the campus to flow into each other."

No longer does the Prospect-Sachem Triangle have a provisional or leftover quality. On the contrary, it now constitutes a place, recognizably a part of Yale, providing a crucial new link in the campus geography.

Design: From the Inside Out

Variation in the colleges creates an atmosphere of friendly competition that allows most Yale students to believe that their college is the best. Yale … cannot allow the new colleges to be seen as poor cousins to the older twelve.

Report of the Study Group to Consider New Residential Colleges, February 2008

Residential colleges work as social and intellectual incubators within the larger milieu of Yale College and the still-larger university. Each one is a semi-autonomous, multiuse community, in effect a "novel institution intermediate between a dormitory and the true English college," in the words of Yale historian George Wilson Pierson. Embracing a mix of public and private spaces, the essential elements of these academic villages reflect what James Gamble Rogers and Yale officials observed of the colleges at Oxford, Cambridge, and St. Andrews in Scotland in spring 1927, during a research trip that served as a secret feasibility study of sorts for creating residential colleges at Yale.

Rogers, in a 1927 memo informed by his review of premier British colleges coupled with his deep knowledge of Yale, suggested a "dividing up of the undergraduate department into a number of units," creating up to fifteen residential colleges of 150 to 250 students, each equipped with a dining hall, a commons room, a library, a comfortable suite for the faculty head, and additional rooms for visiting graduates or guests. He further emphasized that the population of each college "should be a collection of students studying various subjects," so that students could learn from one another and the "friction" of different disciplines. However, Rogers foresaw "very grave" challenges involved in implementing such a system at Yale, in connection with both the building of new colleges and the need to win over academic and alumni groups who held the bonds of class-year sacred above all and therefore resisted the idea of smaller, multi-year communities.

Those challenges were overcome by fall 1933, when Yale sophomores, juniors, and seniors moved into the first seven residential colleges, all but one designed by Rogers himself, each accommodating the variety of uses outlined in his 1927 memo. Social and academic spaces generally surround the largest quadrangle of each college, creating a public square or green frequently traversed by college residents and visitors. Additionally, the residence of the head of college—titled, until 2016, the *master*, in the Oxbridge tradition—is frequently paired with offices for the head and the dean. From that point on, incoming first-year students lived together on the Old Campus quadrangle, sharing room blocks with other first-years assigned to their college and still establishing traditional class-year solidarity. Almost a century later, the programmatic building blocks of the residential colleges are little changed, though they have been expanded to include a wider variety of recreational spaces and accessible, gender-neutral housing accommodations.

Each of Yale's fourteen residential colleges, Benjamin Franklin and Pauli Murray among them, houses a heterogeneous population of 250 to 450 undergraduate students plus faculty, fellows, and visiting guests. While the colleges emulate the residential and social structure of Oxbridge precedents, they reject the English college-based tutorial system, instead deferring to the university-wide educational approach adopted in the nineteenth century on the model of German research universities. Yale was not the first American university to attempt to import some version of Oxbridge, but it met with more stable success than others, such as Princeton, which adopted a residential college plan in 1906 and then, under pressure from conservative factions, dropped it in 1907, only to embrace it once again in 1982.

Given the higher costs associated with the construction and operation of residential colleges compared to conventional dormitories, the decision to build additional residential colleges in the twenty-first century speaks volumes about the importance of the colleges to the nature of undergraduate education and everyday life. President Levin considered residential colleges a crucial link within the "nested communities" that define undergraduate life at Yale: the residential suite, the entryway, the residential college, Yale College, and Yale University. Levin was backed in his conviction by the university's governing board, the Yale Corporation, led by Roland W. Betts (BA 1968), who helped propel the development of Benjamin Franklin and Pauli Murray Colleges as Senior Fellow of the Yale Corporation from 2003 to 2011 and chair of its Buildings and Grounds Committee from 2001 to 2011. To Betts, the residential colleges are "the secret to Yale."

The significant cost and complexity of the 1998–2011 renovations for the twelve existing colleges signaled that Yale was reinvesting in its cherished residential college model at a time when many other undergraduate institutions were moving toward apartments with kitchens and private bedrooms for all four years. Penelope Laurans, senior adviser at the university, who held a variety of academic and administrative roles including admissions from 1973 to 2016 and was head of Jonathan Edwards College from 2009 to 2016, notes that the residential college model "is consistent with the university's philosophy of education of the whole person that depends, as well, on students' extracurricular engagements and on their learning to live in a small community with a heterogeneous group of people."

Our original brief for designing two new residential colleges was to provide housing for a total of 850 (later increased to 904) students, of which 720 would satisfy expanded enrollment in Yale College and the rest would accommodate the "decompression" of other, overcrowded colleges. In addition, each of the new colleges would need a quadrangle large enough to accommodate 900-person tents for commencement-related ceremonies, and spaces to accommodate the myriad social and academic activities that are crucial to their success. Interior architecture and design, furniture, and finishes were also part of our scope.

As realized, Benjamin Franklin and Pauli Murray Colleges each have 452 student beds grouped in varying types of suites, a house for the head of college, three-bedroom apartments for each respective college dean and fellow, and single-bedroom accommodations for two graduate affiliates and visiting guests. Each college has its own dining hall and adjacent servery, a student common

3.1. **Program pie chart, concept design, 2008.** RAMSA.

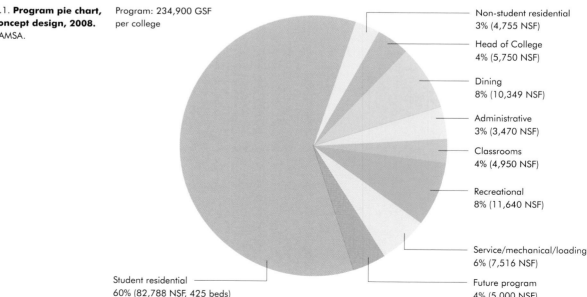

Program: 234,900 GSF per college

Non-student residential
3% (4,755 NSF)

Head of College
4% (5,750 NSF)

Dining
8% (10,349 NSF)

Administrative
3% (3,470 NSF)

Classrooms
4% (4,950 NSF)

Recreational
8% (11,640 NSF)

Service/mechanical/loading
6% (7,516 NSF)

Future program
4% (5,000 NSF)

Student residential
60% (82,788 NSF, 425 beds)

Design: From the Inside Out

3.2. Analysis of programmatic adjacencies in the first twelve residential colleges, concept design, 2008. RAMSA.

- Head of College house
- Administrative
- Dining hall
- Common room
- Library

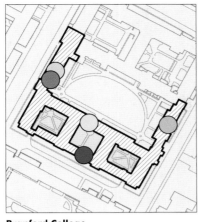

Branford College

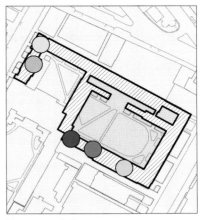

Saybrook College

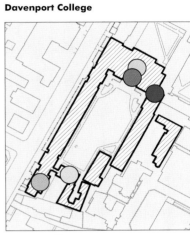

Davenport College

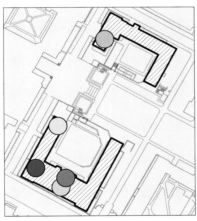

Jonathan Edwards College

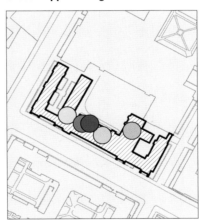

Grace Hopper College

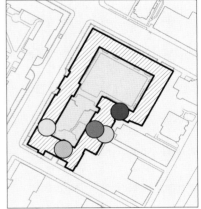

Pierson College

Berkeley College

Trumbull College

Timothy Dwight College

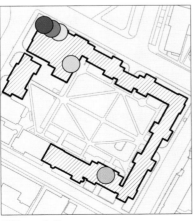

Silliman College

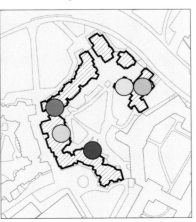

Morse College

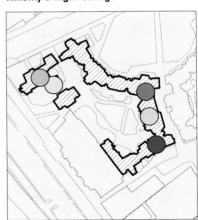

Ezra Stiles College

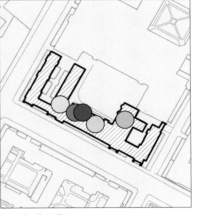

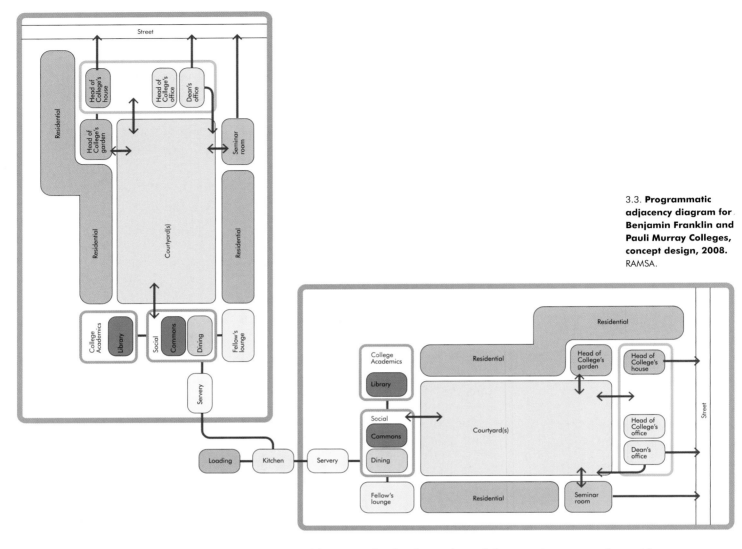

3.3. **Programmatic adjacency diagram for Benjamin Franklin and Pauli Murray Colleges, concept design, 2008.** RAMSA.

room, a library, and a faculty and special events lounge, and provides access to shared academic and recreation spaces on the lower level. Benjamin Franklin and Pauli Murray Colleges together enclose nine courtyards, and occupy a combined area of 531,953 gross square feet on a 6.7-acre site, adding roughly three percent to the university's existing footprint.

Conceived as fraternal twins, the two colleges are equal in their accommodations but different in character, inviting students to discover the unique qualities of each. Their combined population is to accrue from the two hundred incoming first-year students assigned at random each year, just as in the other twelve colleges, with exceptions only for students who request to live in the same residential college in which a family member previously lived or currently lives as an undergraduate. In addition, more than four hundred students secured rooms in the two new colleges through a transfer application and suite selection process completed in March 2017, in which students were permitted to apply in groups with peers from any of the existing colleges, then assigned randomly to either Benjamin Franklin or Pauli Murray College before entering a room draw.

Given the complexity of the program and the constraints of the triangular site, we embarked on a two-track design process, simultaneously working from the *inside out* — figuring out how to distribute the many interrelated program components — and from the *outside in*, as discussed in Chapter 4, using a massing strategy and developing architectural features that drew from precedents and responded to specific conditions of the site and New Haven's urban context. This dual trajectory mirrored the thinking of James Gamble Rogers who, in presenting his conceptual design for the Memorial Quadrangle in 1917, employed two key pieces of architectural representation: one was a precise architectural drawing of an entryway module, the residential unit that would form the functional backbone of the complex, consisting of a pair of two-bedroom suites accessed from a central stair hall with shared bathroom. The other was a detailed plaster model of the overall scheme, conveying a stirring impression of the place from the outside in.

Informing the design from the inside out, the major form-generators of Benjamin Franklin and Pauli Murray Colleges were, first, the residential modules based on Yale's time-honored "entryway" system; second, the shared food service and loading facilities; third, the social spaces clustered around the dining halls; and fourth, the location and internal organization of other key elements, such as the head of college house. The need to create connections and adjacencies drove the planning process, with all the major social spaces gathered around the main quadrangle of each college. Our process of inside-out design entailed careful study of precedents to ensure that the new colleges equaled or even surpassed their predecessors in fulfilling program requirements. We continually endeavored to turn the constraints of the site and code requirements into new opportunities to enhance character through design. Through modeling and

3.4. **Memorial Quadrangle (James Gamble Rogers, 1917–21) unit plan from initial design presentation.** Yale University Library, Manuscripts and Archives. Architectural drawings and maps of Yale University buildings and grounds, c. 1728–1990 (inclusive). Image no. 4530.

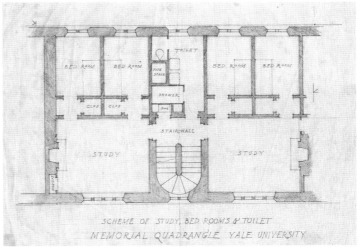

3.5. **Memorial Quadrangle (James Gamble Rogers, 1917–21) plaster model from initial design presentation. Photograph James S. Hedden, 1919.** Yale University Library, Manuscripts and Archives. Photographs of Memorial Quadrangle, Yale University, by James S. Hedden, 1917–22 (inclusive). Image no. 681.

drawing at several scales, we investigated different options for the development of all interior spaces, from libraries and dining halls to student suites.

The entryway system, crucial to undergraduate social exchange, denotes the arrangement of residential units stacked around separate stair halls and entries, contrasting with typical dormitories organized around corridors. It reflects the customary arrangement at Oxford and Cambridge but is rare among American colleges. It was adopted first by Harvard College in the 1600s, then by Yale in its first New Haven building, the 1717 College House, with three stair entries spaced evenly along its 170-foot-wide elevation. Incorporating the same idea, the five dormitories of the Brick Row each had two stair halls penetrating front-to-back through the approximately 100-by-40-foot floorplates.

A refinement was introduced between the first of these four-story dormitories, Connecticut Hall (President Thomas Clap, Francis Letort, and Thomas Bills, 1750–53), in which each entry served four double rooms on each floor; and the second one, Union Hall (John Trumbull and James Hillhouse, 1793–94; demolished 1893), later known as South College, which, though outwardly similar to the first, combined the formerly separate doubles into suites "consisting of a large common parlor & two bedrooms, serving as studies also," as Trumbull noted on his 1792 plan (see fig. 1.4). The use of suites expanded student living space, reduced construction costs by eliminating redundant walls and chimneys, and helped mitigate the seasonal extremes of heat and cold on either side of the building.

3.6. **Connecticut Hall (President Thomas Clap, Francis Letort, and Thomas Bills, 1750–53) plan showing double rooms. Drawn February 1934 by Palmer Johnson for the Historic American Buildings Survey.** Library of Congress Prints and Photographs Division, Historic American Buildings Survey.

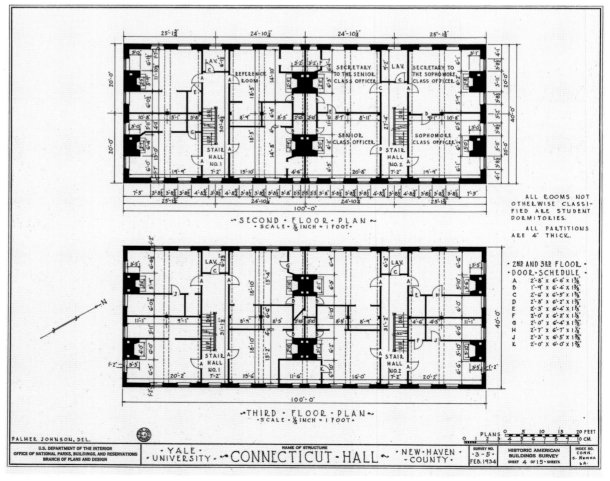

The entryways, meanwhile, proved to be socially significant, encouraging students to form relationships and sometimes clubs with the occupants of other rooms sharing the same stairway. A vertical hierarchy emerged as seniors typically took the second floor, juniors the third, and sophomores and freshmen endured either the climb to the top or the humidity of the ground level. The third and fourth dormitories of the row, Berkeley Hall, also known as North Middle College (1801; demolished 1895) and North College (1820; demolished 1901), maintained basically the same configuration of entryways and suites, as did the Divinity College (1835; demolished 1869), the fifth and final residential hall of the row.

Notably, the entryways of the Brick Row opened to both the front and back of the buildings, creating permeable and semipublic throughways from College Street to the landscaped grounds within the College Square. This permeability would vanish by the end of the nineteenth century as the Brick Row was demolished in stages, beginning in 1869, and replaced by predominantly fortress-inspired buildings to form the enclosed quadrangle known today as the Old Campus. Each of the new dormitories facing the New Haven Green carried forward the entryway system, with three to six individual stair halls dividing each building into smaller social units. The key difference was that the post–Civil War entryways open only to the new quadrangle, not to the street, with the lone exception of Vanderbilt Hall.

3.7. **Vanderbilt Hall (Charles C. Haight, 1894) plan, designed with six residential entryways distributed around the courtyard facing Chapel Street. It was the lone exception to the inward-facing orientation of Old Campus dormitories after the Civil War.**
Yale University, Manuscripts and Archives. Architectural drawings and maps of Yale University buildings and grounds, c. 1728–1990 (inclusive).

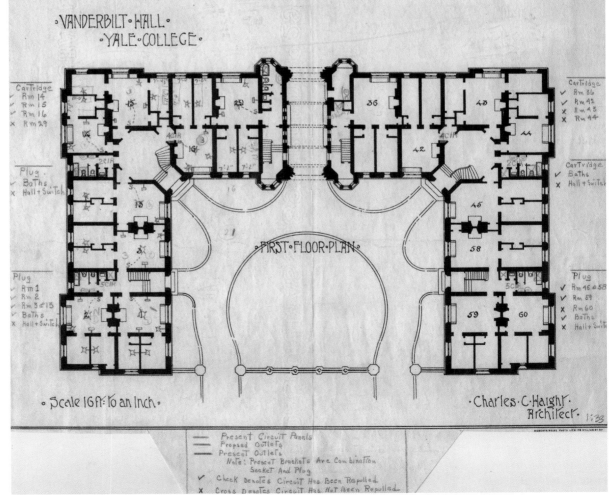

These newer, larger dormitories abandoned much of the Puritan austerity of an earlier era. Vanderbilt Hall, notably plush, introduced features such as steam heat, electric lighting, and decorative trim in a bid to lure wealthy students back onto campus from private boarding houses to which they had increasingly gravitated in the Gilded Age. A more worldly generation of students, in turn, responded with sophisticated interior decoration of their rooms, some of which were professionally photographed.

The inward-turned entryways of the Old Campus became an essential ingredient in Rogers's Memorial Quadrangle, originally designed to house 630 students, composed of buildings ranging from two to five stories in height excluding towers. Rogers's decision to adopt the traditional entryway system was not based on sentiment but on a sense of efficacy: its "many advantages for safety and convenience were so apparent that it was considered almost a requirement," according to *The Architectural Record* of February 1918. The plan's apparent "convenience" lay in the congenial results of suites spanning the full width of the building, from street to court or court to court, thereby providing natural ventilation in warm weather and balanced heat distribution in the winter.

The plan for the Memorial Quadrangle comprised a variety of suites consisting usually of a study and two bedrooms (though some had one or three), interspersed with 130 non-suite single bedrooms, all in all providing an agreeable mix of social and personal space. The "safety" of the Quadrangle's entryway system, by the standards of its own day, lay in the use of fire-resistant masonry walls, extending from basement to roof, separating the rooms of one entry module from the next, together with masonry stairways linked in the attic by "fireproof" passages and steel doors to provide emergency egress. Bathrooms were located in the stair hall, providing easy access to cleaning staff without invasion of privacy.

Subsequently the residential college system expanded on the spatial and social patterns established in the Memorial Quadrangle by adopting courtyards and entryways but adding dining halls, libraries, and common rooms grouped together in a social nucleus, along with offices and living accommodations for faculty. Ten such colleges were opened between 1933 and 1940 through a combination of new construction and conversion of existing dormitories, including the remodeling of the Memorial Quadrangle itself. Saarinen's Morse and Stiles Colleges, opened in 1962 to accommodate a postwar surge in enrollment, kept the entryway system but eliminated the traditional suite system in favor of mostly single-person bedrooms. The change was made in response to student complaints of overcrowding and lack of privacy in the existing colleges, but the resulting lack of social contact within these halls ultimately made them less popular. In addition, to satisfy new safety requirements demanding two means of egress for each resident, the bathrooms were pressed into double duty as hall corridors, an arrangement that turned out to be problematic after Yale College became coeducational in 1969.

Renovations to Morse and Stiles Colleges completed in 2011 by KieranTimberlake addressed this shortcoming by reinstating suites and reconfigured bathrooms within the existing structure. All other residential colleges were also refurbished in the preceding decade, requiring the addition of fire doors between suites, which was considered an acceptable solution to the two means of egress required by life safety codes. As a response to the Americans with Disabilities Act (ADA) of 1990, each existing college was provided with

3.8. **Durfee Hall
(Russell Sturgis Jr.,
1871) unidentified stu-
dent room. Photograph
c. 1871.** Yale University
Library, Manuscripts and
Archives. *Yale College "A
Sketch of Its History"* by
William L. Kingsley. Image
no. 10305.

3.9. **Lawrance Hall
(Russell Sturgis Jr.,
1885–86), Henry
Hallan Tweedy's room.
Photograph 1889.**
Yale University Library,
Manuscript and Archives.

3.10. **Vanderbilt Hall
(Charles C. Haight,
1894) unidenti-
fied student room.
Photograph c. 1900.**
Yale University Library,
Manuscripts and Archives.
Yale University buildings
and grounds photographs,
1716–2004 (inclusive).
Image no. 2258.

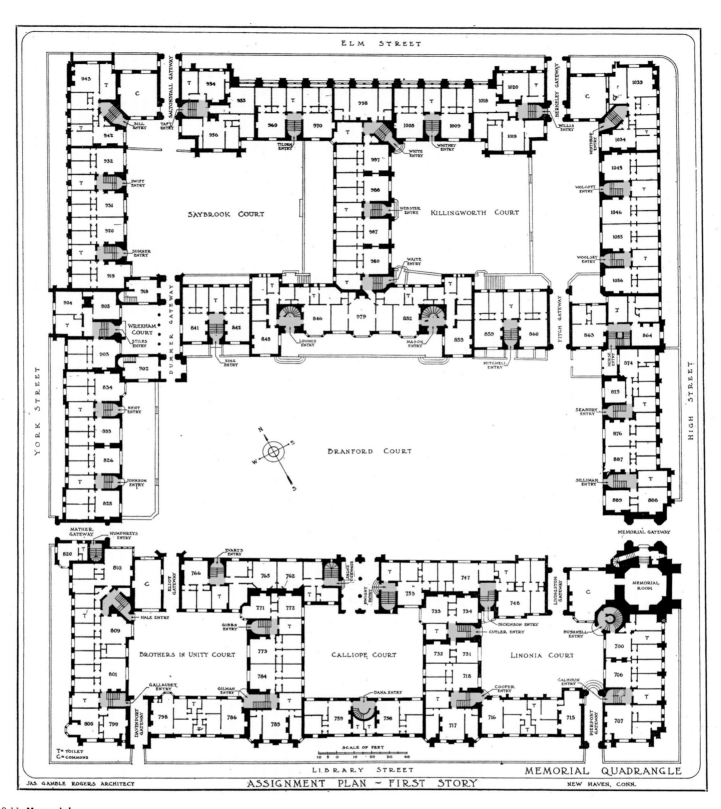

3.11. **Memorial Quadrangle (James Gamble Rogers, 1917–21), plan with entryways highlighted.**
James Gamble Rogers, "The Harkness Memorial Quadrangle, Yale University," *Architecture* v. 44, n. 4 (October 1921): plate 154 / RAMSA.

accessible rooms, but regrettably the stair-dependent entryway system meant these rooms could only be located on the ground floor of each college, thereby compromising overall social integration.

Increasingly stringent life safety and access standards meant that incorporating the entryway system into Benjamin Franklin and Pauli Murray Colleges, as Yale leaders and the 2008 study group report maintained was necessary to achieve parity with the existing colleges, added considerable complexity to the project. Fire codes mandating two means of egress from any point in the building could no longer be solved by Saarinen's hallway bathroom arrangement, nor was it acceptable in a new building to replicate the strategy pursued in the renovation of the Rogers-era colleges, namely adding an exit through the neighboring suite. Finally, the need to provide barrier-free access to all facilities would require many more elevators than in a conventional corridor-plan building of comparable size.

These requirements and their budgetary implications had been daunting enough to cause Princeton to abandon its customary use of vertical entries in its newest residential college, Whitman College (Demetri Porphyrios, 2007), which we visited as we began our design work. Despite an elaborate Gothic design reflecting Oxbridge precedents and Princeton's own architectural legacy, Whitman's student rooms are accessed from conventional double-loaded corridors, resulting in the loss of entryway-based social groups and creating a wider floorplate, which in turn led the steeply pitched roofs to appear conspicuously massive relative to those of Princeton's earlier Gothic-inspired residence halls.

To reconcile the traditional entry arrangement with today's rigorous life safety and accessibility requirements, we developed a *double entryway* module with an abbreviated corridor on each floor connected to two stairways and an elevator. (The use of the twenty-two passenger elevators is limited to residents and visitors who cannot take the stairs.) Larger, floor-through suites housing four to six students are found at either end of the module, with two-person suites, single rooms, and shared bathrooms strung along the middle. The doubling of stair access on each floor for emergency egress revisits the century-old plan of the Memorial Quadrangle, in which each stairway was connected to the next adjacent stairway by a "fireproof" passage but only at the attic level.

This plan, particularly the use of floor-through suites, allows floorplates to measure only 35.5 feet wide from street facade to courtyard facade, respectably close to the 33-foot width that is typical of the interwar colleges, meaning that daylight penetrates easily through the interiors, and the sloping roofs do not grow overly tall. The paired entryway system also reduces the area consumed by hall corridors while enlarging the corresponding social unit, so that the community that formerly sprung up around a single stair hall is modestly expanded to the community whose comings and goings revolve around two linked entryways. Students interviewed about this potential change prior to its formal adoption responded favorably, imagining that the doubled entryways would enliven their vertical neighborhood without sacrificing its intimacy.

Suites consist of a common room (typically 260 square feet) and various combinations of single-bed (114 square feet) and two-bed (202 square feet) rooms with 8-foot-6-inch-high ceilings based on a 9-foot-4-inch floor-to-floor distance similar to the Rogers-era colleges. The most common living unit remains the four-person suite or "quad," accounting for one-third of the housing in Benjamin Franklin and Pauli Murray Colleges. Upperclass students can also

3.12. Historic entryway residential modules. RAMSA.

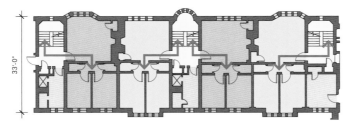

Typical Floor

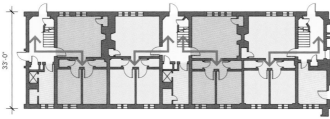

Ground Floor

3.13. Renovated entryway residential modules. RAMSA.

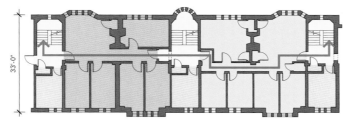

Typical Floor

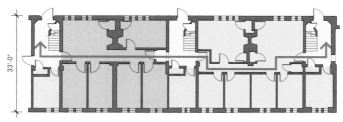

Ground Floor

3.14. Modified entryway residential modules designed for Benjamin Franklin and Pauli Murray Colleges. RAMSA.

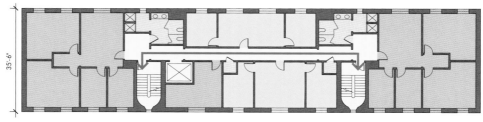

Typical Floor

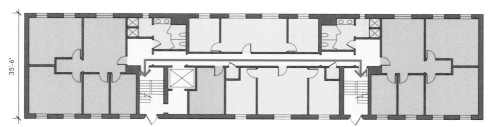

Ground Floor

Design: From the Inside Out

3.15. **Typical four-single-bedroom suite diagrams. Presentation drawing, 2017.** RAMSA.

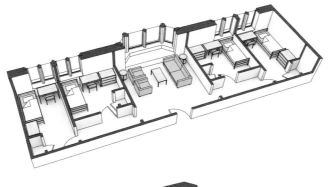

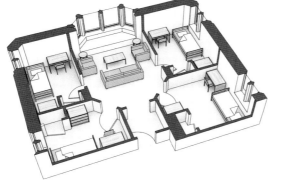

3.16. **Typical six-single-bedroom suite diagram. Presentation drawing, 2017.** RAMSA.

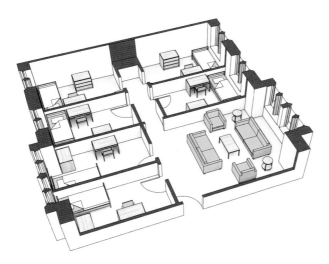

3.17. **Special seven-single-bedroom suite diagram in south tower of Benjamin Franklin College overlooking the main campus. Presentation drawing, 2017.** RAMSA.

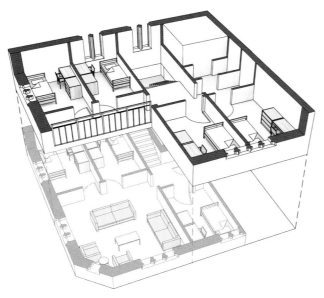

apply to live in double, triple, quintet, sextet, and even a few septet and octet suites — or in one of the 77 non-suite singles also intended for first-year counselors or students who go abroad for one semester. Rather than allot each of the two new colleges an identical assortment of suite types, the plan gently differentiates them based on efficiencies established through site and plan analysis, with the side effect of helping to establish each college's respective character. Pauli Murray College offers more non-suite singles and quintet suites than Benjamin Franklin College; while Benjamin Franklin College offers more of everything else, notably septet and octet suites.

Adding to the variety is the fact that certain suites have unique floorplans and views, joining a long tradition of eccentric — and eccentrically named — undergraduate suites such as Branford College's four-person "God Quad," Saybrook's dozen-person "12-Pack," Grace Hopper's (formerly Calhoun's) "Book World," and Davenport's "Cottage," which function as social hubs or "party suites" and in some cases require would-be occupant groups to win an intramural election. Benjamin Franklin and Pauli Murray Colleges have their own prized suites, though Yale is moving away from the notion of "party suites." The most spectacular is probably a duplex septet suite in Benjamin Franklin College, nestled into the tower at the southern tip of the site, with a double-height living room and seven single bedrooms. Additional octet suites line the hypotenuse of the small triangular courtyards, overlooking intimate courtyards on one side and the Farmington Canal Heritage Greenway on the other. At the northern end of the site, the elevated planted courtyard above the loading dock of Pauli Murray College — bisected by a residential building into two microcourts — serves as the focal point for several distinctive suites including a duplex, evoking the unique situation of Pierson College's Lower Court.

Although nonrepetition was a design goal for James Gamble Rogers, it is even more pronounced in our design, owing to the triangular shape of the site that forces building modules to meet at nonorthogonal angles. As our modified entry module confronted the realities of the site, we soon realized that direct repetition would be all but impossible, and we took to calling our prototypical plan diagram the "fantasy bar." The actual hall and suite configurations diverged into numerous variations on the type, fostering a sense of individuality throughout the colleges, while room sizes and finishes were held to a consistent standard to ensure parity. The irregular massing of the buildings even alters the relationship of a stairwell to the floor plan at different levels, so that a single stairway may be paired with more than one other stairway along its flight, and may serve multiple entryway modules.

As the design process unfolded, we took advantage of two specific conditions to reduce building costs and enliven the colleges both inside and out. One was programmatic: the fact that Yale desired to excavate the entire footprint of the building's basement level to maximize efficiency, even though our early designs accommodated all of the social and recreational spaces on that level, as well as the required connections between the colleges, within a smaller proposed excavation area. The second condition was topographic: the site drops almost a full story in elevation as it slopes down toward the cemetery, effectively transforming the lower level along the Greenway into the ground level.

Taking advantage of this change in elevation, we placed a total of forty-three student rooms on the western edge of the lower level of both colleges, providing occupants with views of the bicycle path and planted meadow

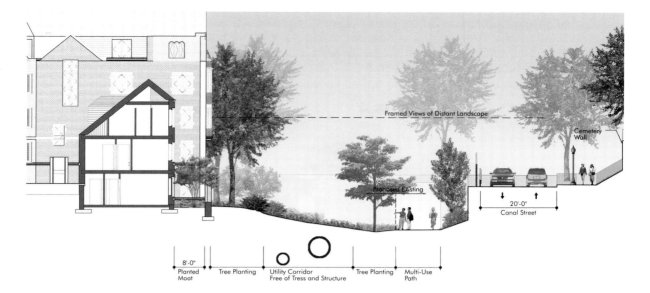

Framed Views of Distant Landscape

Cemetery Wall

Proposed Existing

20'-0"
Canal Street

8'-0"
Planted
Moat

Tree Planting

Utility Corridor
Free of Tress and Structure

Tree Planting

Multi-Use
Path

landscape. This design move saved the cost of building more above-ground suites, dovetailing with our desire for the building mass to step down toward the Greenway. The active facade also heightened the sense of vitality and safety for passersby, and it put student residential spaces in close proximity to lower-level social areas. An added benefit was the reduced depth of excavation, since the residential areas need not sit as deeply in the ground as the adjacent basement social areas, which require higher ceiling heights and more overhead clearance for piping and mechanical equipment.

The issue of housing first-year students received special consideration in the 2008 study group report. Since the introduction of the residential college system in 1933, most Yale first-year students had lived together with other first-years assigned to the same college in dormitories on the Old Campus, before migrating to their residential colleges as sophomores. Since the 1960s, however, the size of the incoming class has exceeded the capacity of the Old Campus, leading to a perennially controversial solution that locates incoming students assigned to the largest colleges — Silliman, Timothy Dwight, and now Benjamin Franklin and Pauli Murray — within their college's own quadrangle.

"Partisans of the Old Campus experience have difficulty imagining Yale without it," the 2008 study group report noted, based on interviews with students and alumni who cherished the relationships they formed with other first-years and the "magical spirit" they associated with the space where they lived during their introductory year at Yale. However, the report also found that students and alumni of Silliman and Timothy Dwight "swear loyally by their experience of having lived as freshmen alongside students from other years. They praise their early integration in a small community: the advantages of making and developing friendships across classes, the opportunity to have easier access during freshman year to their master and dean," and other benefits.

This contrarian view lent support to the plan to house the two hundred first-year members of Benjamin Franklin and Pauli Murray Colleges within the colleges themselves. Still, to encourage first-year residents of Benjamin Franklin and Pauli Murray to get to know one another, first-year suites are clustered together in specific wings, preserving both a modicum of the immersive first-year Old Campus experience and the independence of upperclassmen who have already begun to form their own friendships and living preferences. The first-year suites do not differ significantly from the others, however, so that this arrangement can be modified in the future.

As developed through the design process in 2009 and 2010, most suite common rooms were provided with bay windows, where a window bench complements the seating group. Student rooms have operable steel casement windows and stained white-oak strip flooring. White-oak trim accentuates the windows, doors, and bases. Since the building systems are vertically piped, not horizontally ducted, the ceiling could simply be the structural concrete slab finished with a skim coat of plaster, saving the cost of a dropped ceiling. Although student furniture adheres to the standard pieces used in all the Yale residential colleges for ease of maintenance, all rooms are designed to accommodate at least two possible furniture configurations. We also designed a custom light fixture for the student rooms that cost less and, we thought, complemented the design better than available stock fixtures. At once characteristic and economical, our fixture has a specially designed pattern derived from the Yale *Y*. An aesthetically similar and equally efficient custom-designed sconce illuminates the seventy-six entryway stairs.

All 176 bathrooms are designed to be gender-flexible, which means that they can be assigned to women, men, or both. In practice this means that there are no urinals and showers have lockable doors. Showers and water closets use low-flow water conservation technology, and all bathrooms are arranged

3.19. **Early options for custom-designed student room light fixtures featuring a Yale Y pattern. Photograph September 28, 2012.** RAMSA.

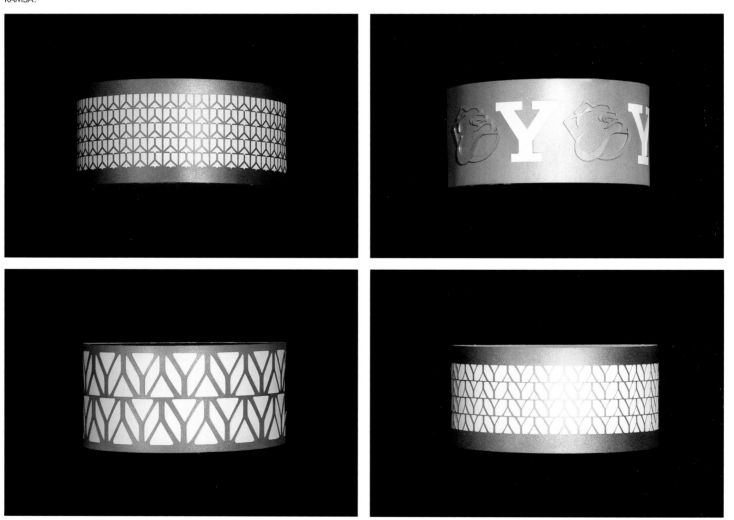

to provide a person in a wheelchair with access to toilets, sinks, and showers. Several suites are equipped with electrically operated doors, and there are several single-person bathrooms sprinkled throughout the plan, intended especially for use by students who, for a variety of reasons, may require such privacy. These accommodations are meant to secure equal dignity and comfort for all students, removing barriers to their inclusion in the community. Benjamin Franklin and Pauli Murray Colleges thus establish a new paradigm for inclusive design at Yale.

After we completed construction documents in 2012, Yale decided to increase the combined capacity of the two colleges from 850 to 904 without changing the building dimensions, a move intended to reduce per-capita costs. As a result, the intended combined college membership rose to 936, since some juniors and seniors choose to live off-campus or study abroad. This added density required us to modify the floor plan and convert single-occupancy rooms, yielding additional variety in the suite plans and, as a bonus, additional cost savings by reducing the number of in-suite corridors in need of full ventilation and hence simplifying mechanical systems. From an architectural perspective, the redesign exercise was akin to altering an existing building, since the location of structural columns, windows, and corridors was considered fixed. In effect, Benjamin Franklin and Pauli Murray Colleges were "renovated" before they were even built, an interesting early proof of the concept that they could also be flexible enough to accommodate changes and possible future renovations.

After the entryway module, the next most important inside-out form-generator for the new colleges was the provision of food services. First, in keeping with the need for parity with the existing residential colleges, Yale stipulated that Benjamin Franklin and Pauli Murray Colleges each needed their own distinctive dining hall with adjacent servery, an area for preparing and serving food. Second, to improve staffing and service efficiency, Yale requested a shared kitchen to serve both colleges, an idea first embraced by Saarinen at Morse and Stiles Colleges, and subsequently implemented in the renovation of several other residential college pairs in the 1990s. Third, a covered loading dock, connected to the kitchen and other service facilities, would improve the efficiency of delivery and waste removal activities while screening the surrounding neighborhood and faculty and student rooms from the associated noise of these activities. This loading dock represented something new and different for Yale, where other dining facilities in the central campus area operate, somewhat painfully, without one, leading to traffic disruptions and noise complaints.

In October 2008 we analyzed the interconnected problems of locating and concealing the loading dock and the shared kitchen through a series of diagrammatic studies and test-fit scenarios. Given that trucks had to enter the site from Sachem Street on the north so as not to block traffic on Prospect Street, we evaluated options for placing the loading dock either at grade or underground. The shared kitchen, if it was going to connect across the required east–west walkway and emergency vehicle path between the two colleges, would have to be located either below ground or in a bridge spanning the path, reminiscent of the Yale Art Gallery's bridge over High Street (Egerton Swartwout, 1928), with or without one of the two dining halls similarly elevated in such a bridge. These predesign studies proceeded in parallel with the "outside-in" exercises of determining the carrying capacity of the site, distributing building masses across the site, and testing courtyard shapes and sizes to create conceptual plans.

After reviewing the opportunities and constraints of each of the many options with our counterparts in Yale's planning office, it was determined that the one that made the most sense was to place the loading dock—a four-bay, 9,700-square-foot space accommodating up to twenty-four truck deliveries per day, developed with consultant Jonathan Parker of Kleinfelder—in a ground-level enclosure on Sachem Street, configured so that the space needed to allow the turning of trucks would not unduly constrain the planning of the courtyards and residential areas of Pauli Murray College. At the same time, the 4,400-square-foot shared kitchen was assigned a spot beneath Prospect Walk, directly between the two colleges, with access to each dining hall's servery by way of service elevators and dedicated underground service corridors that connect to the loading dock without crossing the separate residential circulation corridors.

Although the basic distribution of these functional elements was established in the concept or predesign phase, subsequent client feedback and cost analysis spurred several important refinements of the massing and some of the more innovative features of our layouts. In one key example, we came to recognize an interesting design opportunity in the flat roof of the loading dock, which we had intended as an open roof garden facing Sachem Street. The client's concerns about student safety and our ensuing discussion about the necessary height of an enclosure for this roof garden led us to the more radical idea of wrapping student residences completely around it, creating two microcourts accessed by a covered exterior stair. This change in massing allowed us to improve the quality and uniqueness of the residential suites as well as to enlarge the college's central court by increasing the density of rooms over the loading dock.

A second refinement during the schematic design phase saw the shared kitchen pushed northward from beneath Prospect Walk, to the basement of the south wing of Pauli Murray College, forming an L-shaped connection with the two serveries, saving excavation costs and simplifying coordination with buried utilities while retaining the service advantages of the previous design concept. This adjusted location also allowed for easier concealment of kitchen venting through a prominent chimney at the southwest corner of Pauli Murray College's center court.

Once we knew where the kitchen and dining halls would be located, straddling Prospect Walk with recourse to tunnels rather than bridges, we still needed a more detailed understanding of the required capacity, given the expected additional demand on dining resources from students and professors on Science Hill. For guidance we analyzed the dining halls and serveries of the twelve existing colleges and those of Princeton's Whitman, Rockefeller, and Mathey Colleges, which we had visited together with Yale representatives. Through the design process we developed a close working rapport with Rafi Taherian, associate vice president of Yale Hospitality, who has earned recognition for putting sustainability and wellness at the center of Yale's dining operations.

Simultaneously we undertook an elaborate comparative study of Yale and other colleges and universities in collaboration with our food service consultant, Cini-Little, to test assumptions about dining hall capacity and to identify factors unique to Yale's dining culture. The study found that Yale students tended to linger longer over meals than students at other colleges. This meant less of a rush for service and suggested the need for more space devoted to seating. The dining halls would have to accommodate several annual banquets to mark

3.20. **Early diagrams showing food service and loading sequence options, concept design, 2008.** RAMSA.

Utility Legend

▦ Utilities to remain, very difficult to cross

- - Upgraded utility lines, easy to cross

Legend

▦ Second floor

▦ Ground floor

▦ Basement floor

Option 1

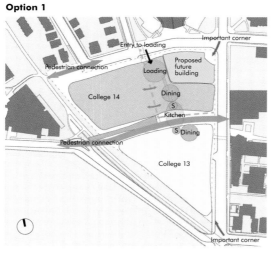

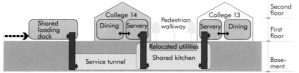

Option 2

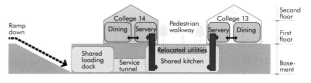

Option 3

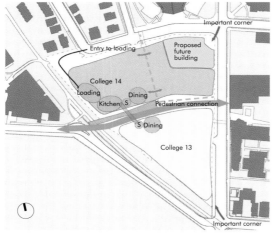

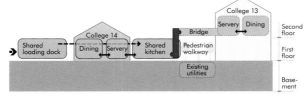

Option 4

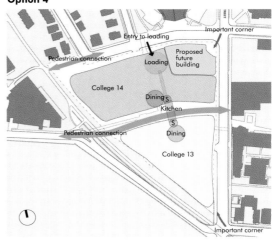

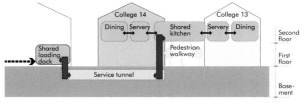

91

3.21. **Section through loading dock and microcourt, schematic design, 2009.** RAMSA.

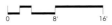

Loading dock

3.22. **Scale of micro-courts is similar to Pierson College's Lower Court. Photograph Robert A.M. Stern, September 16, 2000.** RAMSA.

special occasions as well as the more typical meals in which students and faculty seat themselves in informal groups.

Identical in program but different in character, the dining halls of Benjamin Franklin and Pauli Murray Colleges each provide seating for approximately 300, and both are configured with the servery at one end and a large fireplace at the other. With larger capacities than most of the other residential colleges, the new dining halls combine a main central space with more intimate spaces along the periphery. This retains a sense of scale in the main space in keeping with the historic colleges, while also accommodating more seating — similar in effect to the small booths and side spaces at Timothy Dwight College, the window alcoves and end bays at Saybrook College, the articulated end bay at Silliman College, and the ancillary spaces at Trumbull and Grace Hopper Colleges.

The Benjamin Franklin College dining hall, 4,250 square feet in area, has a series of six intimate alcoves facing south into the quadrangle, each seating sixteen to twenty people, as well as recessed seating niches within the north-facing floor-to-ceiling window bays. The main space is defined by a 33-foot-high barrel-vaulted acoustic plaster ceiling embellished with molding, from which are suspended three large custom-designed chandeliers. Drawing loosely from those in the Berkeley College dining hall, these consist of two concentric wrought-iron cable-stayed rings with thirty-five cylindrical lights in each fixture. Classically inspired doorways and window openings are articulated by simplified pilasters, molding, and architraves.

The 3,500-square-foot dining hall of Pauli Murray College has different proportions and character: its main hall, capped by a 36-foot-tall tray ceiling, adjoins a secondary dining room that seats up to sixty students, providing a change of scale. The main space is lit by five south-facing round-arched windows and eight custom-designed wrought-iron chandeliers inspired by those in Trumbull College, but vertically proportioned and composed of a central cylindrical lamp surrounded by two stacked rings of eight smaller cylindrical lamps. Both dining halls have 6-inch-wide stained red-oak flooring.

Furniture and fixture selection and design for the social spaces and head of college houses was a monumental undertaking, given the many different types of spaces and our desire to make sure that each college would be distinct in character. We approached the task much in the same way we approached the architectural design, starting first with extensive research of precedents at Yale and comparable institutions on both sides of the Atlantic, and then focusing on Arts and Crafts, Georgian, and early-twentieth-century Scandinavian design. Among the furnishings we designed are the tables and chairs for each college's dining hall: X-leg trestle dining tables and ladder-back chairs for Pauli Murray College, and for Benjamin Franklin College, dining tables with slender double-column legs and oak-and-leather chairs with minimalist openwork arched backs. By project's end we wrote 960 unique specifications for selected carpets, furniture, fabrics, decorative lighting, and window coverings. The challenge of lighting was met by a combination of custom fixtures that were designed to be mass-produced (for the student rooms) or unique (for the dining hall chandeliers), and stock luminaires.

Additional social spaces pinwheel around the dining halls on both the ground and second levels. Adjoining the dining halls at ground level are the 1,000-square-foot common rooms, typically available for informal student

3.23. Timothy Dwight College dining hall. Photograph 1935.
Yale University Library, Manuscript and Archives. Pictures of Timothy Dwight College, Yale University, 1934–38 (inclusive). Image no. 42998.

3.24. Berkeley College dining hall. Photograph 1964.
Yale University Library, Manuscript and Archives. Yale events and activities photographs, 1852–2003 (inclusive). Image no. 10190088.

3.25. Berkeley College dining hall. Photograph 1969.
Yale University Library, Manuscript and Archives. Pictures of student life at Yale, 1779–1988 (inclusive). Image no. 10187111.

meetings and studying at the discretion of the head of college. The Marx-Better Common Room in Pauli Murray College beckons like a lantern, visible from Prospect Street on axis with Prospect Walk, defined by its stone-trimmed arched windows. The Millstone Common Room in Benjamin Franklin College addresses Prospect Walk from the canal path, animating this otherwise calm elevation with its large alcove windows.

The two common rooms, facing one another across Prospect Walk, provide students with a flexible, lounge-like environment with the added attraction of active gas fireplaces. Furnishings include comfortable sofas and chairs, some of which, in the Marx-Better Common Room, are contemporary reinterpretations of original furniture from Yale's Linonia and Brothers Reading Rooms. The Millstone Common Room contains furnishings by Sir Edwin Lutyens and custom pieces inspired by Mogens Koch and Ole Wanscher. One level above each common room is a fellows' lounge, a faculty-oriented version of the same concept, reserved for special dinners and

95

3.28. Dining hall and servery comparisons of existing colleges, concept design, 2009. RAMSA.

Berkeley College

422 Members
232 Beds
182 Chairs

Dining hall: 2,832 Sq. Ft.
Seating area only:
2,404 Sq. Ft.
Servery: 1,415 Sq. Ft.

Total space between
dining and servery:
14'-10"

Sq. Ft./person
15.6 13.2

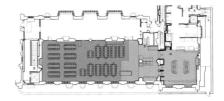

Saybrook College

477 Members
287 Beds
205 Chairs

Dining hall: 2,641 Sq. Ft.
Seating area only:
2,542 Sq. Ft.
Servery: 1,285 Sq. Ft.

Total space between
dining and servery:
9'-0"

Sq. Ft./person
12.9 12.4

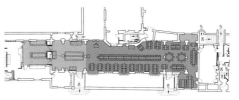

Grace Hopper College

426 Members
234 Beds
170 Chairs

Dining hall: 3,198 Sq. Ft.
Seating area only:
3,198 Sq. Ft.
Servery: 950 Sq. Ft.

Total space between
dining and servery:
12'-4"

Sq. Ft./person
18.8 18.8

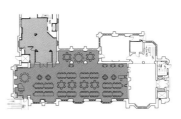

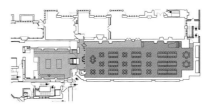

Jonathan Edwards College

419 Members
218 Beds
154 Chairs

Dining hall: 2,849 Sq. Ft.
Seating area only:
2,409 Sq. Ft.
Servery: 786 Sq. Ft.

Total space between
dining and servery:
8'-0"

Sq. Ft./person
18.5 15.6

Davenport College

434 Members
284 Beds
200 Chairs

Dining hall: 3,065 Sq. Ft.
Seating area only:
2,772 Sq. Ft.
Servery: 1,274 Sq. Ft.

Total space between
dining and servery:
10'-2"

Sq. Ft./person
15.3 13.9

Morse & Stiles Colleges

877 Members
500 Beds
343 Chairs

Dining hall: 5,913 Sq. Ft.
Seating area only:
5,273 Sq. Ft.
Servery: 1,034 Sq. Ft.

Total space between
dining and servery:
3'-6"

Sq. Ft./person
17.2 15.4

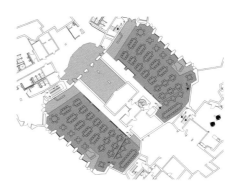

Pierson College

485 Members
309 Beds
184 Chairs

Dining hall: 3,025 Sq. Ft.
Seating area only:
3,025 Sq. Ft.
Servery: 1,017 Sq. Ft.

Total space between
dining and servery:
12'-8"

Sq. Ft./person
16.4 16.4

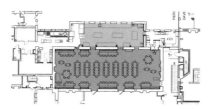

Trumbull College

397 Members
211 Beds
180 Chairs

Dining hall: 3,215 Sq. Ft.
Seating area only:
3,215 Sq. Ft.
Servery: 1,024 Sq. Ft.

Total space between
dining and servery:
13'-0"

Sq. Ft./person
17.9 17.9

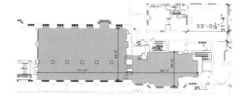

Silliman College

436 Members
402 Beds
272 Chairs

Dining hall: 4,083 Sq. Ft.
Seating area only:
3,222 Sq. Ft.
Servery: 1,958 Sq. Ft.

Total space between
dining and servery:
12'-4"

Sq. Ft./person
15.0 12.2

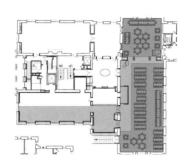

Branford College

458 Members
265 Beds
175 Chairs

Dining hall: 2,572 Sq. Ft.
Seating area only:
2,187 Sq. Ft.
Servery: 976 Sq. Ft.

Total space between
dining and servery:
9'-6"

Sq. Ft./person
14.7 12.5

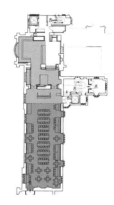

Timothy Dwight College

379 Members
323 Beds
207 Chairs (common
room inc.)

Dining hall:
3,500 Sq. Ft.
Seating area only:
3,221 Sq. Ft.
Servery: 1,222 Sq. Ft.

Total space between
dining and servery:
6'-0"

Sq. Ft./person
16.9 15.6

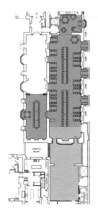

97

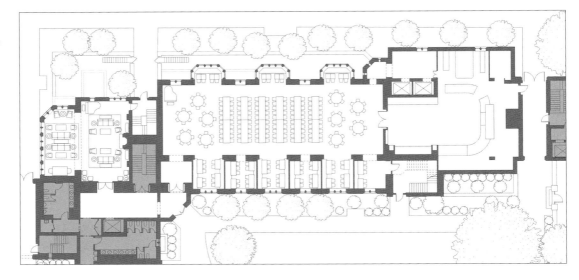

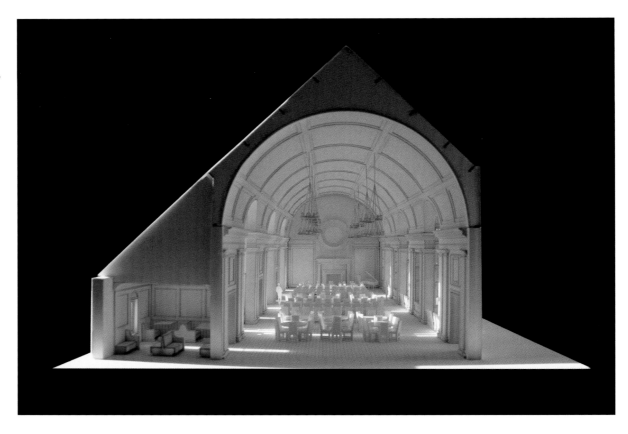

3.31. **Pauli Murray College dining hall and Marx-Better Common Room plan, schematic design, 2010.** RAMSA.

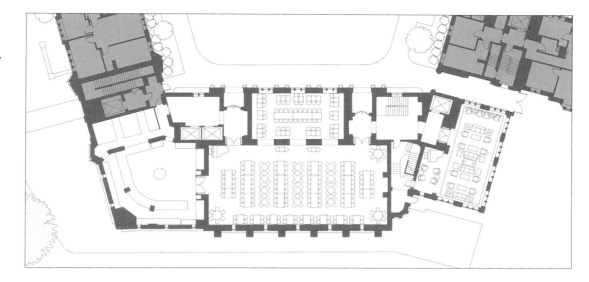

3.32. **Pauli Murray College dining hall model, schematic design. Photograph March 25, 2010.** RAMSA.

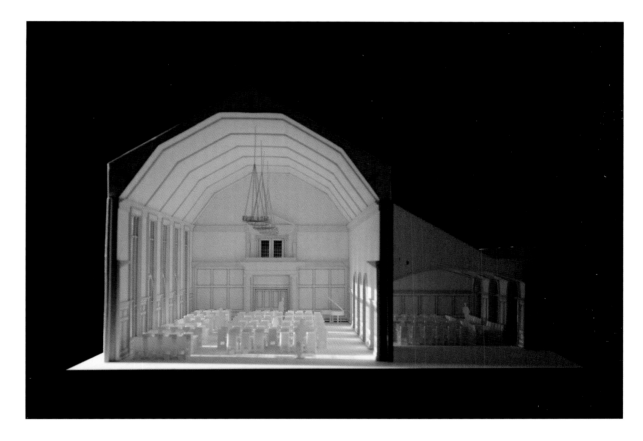

meetings. Each fellows' lounge—Franke Fellows' Lounge in Pauli Murray College and Selin Fellows' Lounge in Benjamin Franklin College—consists of a flexible dining room and exterior terrace facing its counterpart diagonally across Prospect Walk.

The next component that fell into place around the social nucleus of the dining halls was the pair of libraries, each enclosing about 2,000 square feet. Many of the preexisting residential college libraries are tucked away on the second floor, with one, at Trumbull College, notably located within the dining hall volume on a mezzanine overlook separated by a glass wall. Although this adjacency adds social vibrancy, noise from the dining hall regrettably infiltrates the library. For Benjamin Franklin and Pauli Murray Colleges, we embraced the social advantages of this configuration, designing two very different library spaces, each overlooking their respective dining halls through an interior window that solved the noise problem.

The Crown Library in Benjamin Franklin College, with its wood-paneled vaulted ceiling, pays homage to the Old Library at St. John's College, Cambridge University, and the library at Oxford's Corpus Christi College. The space is lined by intimate study nooks along the north and south sides, where built-in carrels, with integral shelving, receive natural light through mullioned windows set in molded wood jambs. A library table based on a design by the Arts and Crafts architect Philip Webb—made of wood from trees that were salvaged when the building site was cleared—is found in the adjoining conference room. The reading room of Benjamin Franklin College is anchored by the largest hand-knotted oriental carpet in the project, 48 by 15 feet, which took artisans in India a year to produce.

The Strickler Family Library in Pauli Murray College consists of several interconnected spaces: a main reading room above the servery, inspired by the living rooms of English country houses and particularly the work of Lutyens, adjoins two smaller library spaces stacked inside the base of Bass Tower, one at the same level as the main reading room and the other one level above. The main room centers on a circular oculus skylight accentuated by ring-shaped plaster molding, beneath which stands a large round work table also made from reclaimed wood. Externally, the 192-foot tower appears separate from the two-story pavilion containing the servery and library, but the interior connection creates a subtle slippage between use and expression—precisely the kind of sly complexity that Rogers was known for as he balanced practical and aesthetic concerns.

Additionally, Bass Tower, half of whose internal volume is occupied by required circulation functions, contains seminar rooms on the fourth, fifth, and sixth levels, and music practice rooms in the lower level, available to all students in Yale College. The crown of the tower is reserved for the potential installation of a set of manually operated change-ringing bells from the Whitechapel Bell Foundry in England. Change-ringing bells differ from carillon bells, such as those in Harkness Tower, in that they are rung by a group of ringers pulling ropes in a full circle, beginning from a bell-upward position, resulting in unique musical and rhythmic properties.

Below ground, the new colleges contain 118,000 square feet of social and academic space, providing a continuous network of passages to allow residents to move about in foul weather or late at night in casual attire according to the so-called "slipper rule." Some of these spaces are shared by the two colleges, namely the Juliet-type black-box Lighten Theater, art studios, music practice rooms, dance rehearsal rooms, a basketball court, a fitness room, and a student-run bike repair shop, requested by students, located conveniently adjacent to the Greenway cycling path. However, each college has its own distinct buttery, a student-operated late-night lounge and canteen, as well as a dedicated student kitchen, a meeting room, a TV lounge, and computer and laundry rooms. Seminar and tutoring rooms on the lower level are open to students from other colleges. Generally the design of basement levels is contemporary in character, in keeping with the strategy used in renovating the historic colleges. Designed with today's students in mind, many of the recreation spaces are flexible enough to be repurposed in the future if desired. There are even a few rooms left unfinished in anticipation of new programmatic uses as the communities develop their own identities.

The 10,000-square-foot houses built for each head of college had their own constraints and inside-out pressures. Their domestic function as the private quarters of the head of college is in fact secondary to their social role as the public face of the college, with the ground level designed for receptions and dinners that frequently bring outside guests together with members of the college. Opening both to the street and to the main quadrangle, the head of college houses come with specific requirements for access, circulation, and internal and external connections. They need to be contiguous with the student residential blocks but stand out with their two-story massing and prominent front doors opening to the street. In each house, interconnected living, dining, and gallery reception spaces open to a rear garden terrace at the edge of the college's principal courtyard, forming an open circuit designed to ensure that guests can mingle easily at a party and, in fine weather, can flow comfortably from inside to outside.

Each house's dining room accommodates a table that can comfortably seat fourteen and adjoins a catering kitchen. An adjacent family eat-in kitchen, connected to a back stair, allows everyday activities to take place simultaneously with formal events. Additionally, the ground-floor space accommodates a separate guest suite and a two-car garage, and connects to the college administrative suite. In essence the houses are microcosms of the programmatic and social complexities of planning the colleges as a whole, gathered together within one building that expresses itself as a single-family residence.

Yale directed us to make the Benjamin Franklin and Pauli Murray head of college houses a bit smaller than their predecessors, allocating more space for the areas dedicated to public functions and less to the private areas upstairs. In addition, these houses are the first to be fully accessible, both as required for public functions and to accommodate a disabled head of college or member of his or her family, something never before possible. We were also asked to improve the catering setup for delivery, preparation, and serving for functions large and small. The houses needed to have a decidedly less institutional character than any other space in the colleges, offering a sense of respite for students coming for everything from "teas" (afternoon lectures hosted in the living rooms, a longstanding tradition) to late-night study breaks during exam period. Our design goal was therefore both to accommodate and to express the important role that the head of college plays in the social dynamic and well-being of the college community.

The two houses are similar in plan, but each has a different character. In Pauli Murray College, the house is directly opposite the dining hall, centered

101

3.33. Library comparisons of existing colleges, schematic design, 2009. RAMSA.

Branford College

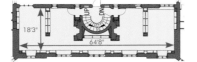

First floor plan

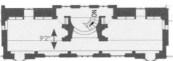

Second floor plan

Davenport College

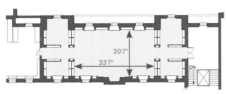

Second floor plan

Jonathan Edwards College

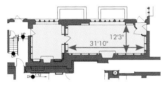

First floor plan

Trumbull College

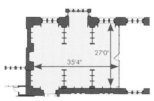

Second floor plan

Grace Hopper College

Second floor plan

Timothy Dwight College

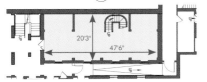

Second floor plan

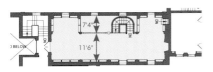

First floor plan

Pierson College

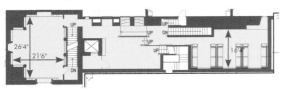

Second floor plan

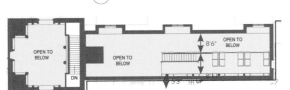

Third floor plan

Silliman College

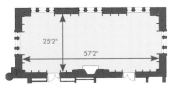

Third floor plan

Saybrook College

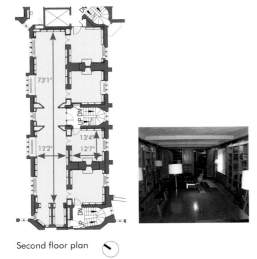

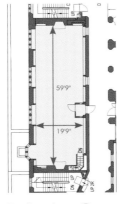

Second floor plan

Berkeley College

First floor plan

3.34. **Philip Webb's Rounton Grange side table, a precedent for the RAMSA-designed table in Crown Library, Benjamin Franklin College. Photograph c. 1887.** Webb Collection.

3.35. **Crown Library, Benjamin Franklin College, table design sketches.** RAMSA.

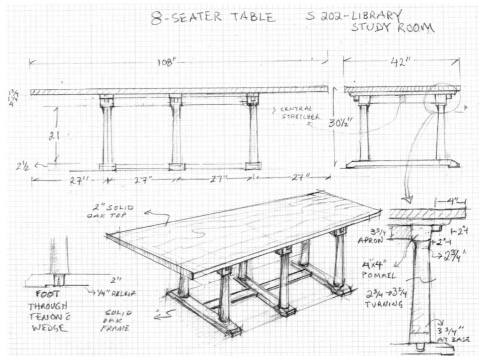

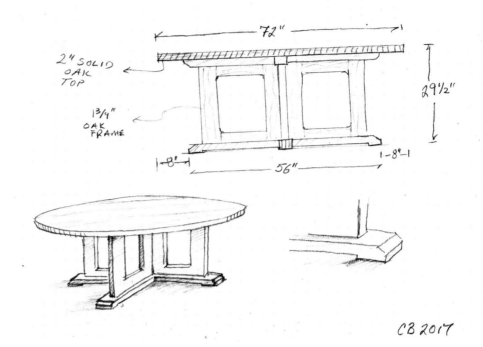

ROUND TABLE N 201 - LIBRARY

72"

2" SOLID OAK TOP

1 3/4" OAK FRAME

29 1/2"

8"

56"

1 - 8" - 1

CB 2017

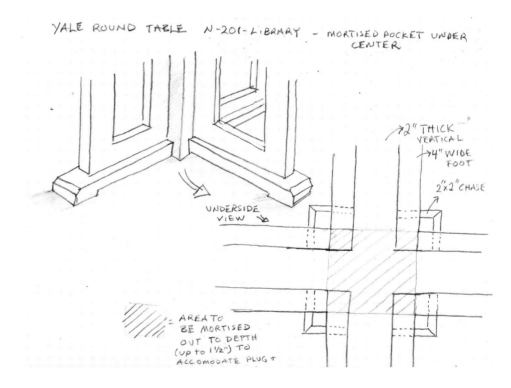

YALE ROUND TABLE N-201-LIBRARY - MORTISED POCKET UNDER CENTER

2" THICK VERTICAL

4" WIDE FOOT

2"x2" CHASE

UNDERSIDE VIEW

AREA TO BE MORTISED OUT TO DEPTH (UP TO 1 1/2") TO ACCOMODATE PLUG +

3.37. **Head of college house, Benjamin Franklin College, ground floor plan, design development, 2010.** RAMSA.

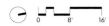

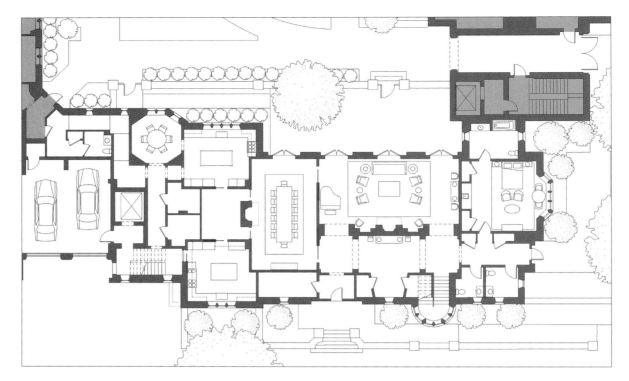

on Bekenstein Court, and the formality of its placement slightly broken by its asymmetrical massing and facade. The entry hall is broad and paneled in light wood, with a shallow-arched ceiling, and it leads to a rectangular living room with a fireplace at one end and a large window with a window seat flanked by two French doors, which lead to the terrace. The dining room is a Classical wood-paneled space drawing on various English country house precedents. The kitchen and catering kitchen face one another across the butler's pantry, with the family kitchen incorporating an island and dining table in a single space overlooking the terrace, main courtyard, and Bass Tower through a large bay window. Above this space, accessed by a back stair, is a small private family room with a tray ceiling that shares a similar view. Off the entry hall is a two-story stair hall with a sweeping, open stair that leads to the second-floor private living quarters and ground floor guest suite that defines the east side of the terrace. From the street side, the main entry door addresses the axis of Winchester Avenue, suggesting a link with the residential neighborhood to the north.

At Benjamin Franklin College, the head of college house also enjoys placement on Nyburg Baker Court, but in a much more informal arrangement cater-corner to the dining hall and adjacent to the main entrance from Prospect Walk. The details are decidedly more Gothic than at the Pauli Murray College house. A vaulted and paneled entry hall leads to a central living room with three French doors opening to the terrace, opposite a shallow fireplace inglenook with bookshelves. The adjacent dining room has little paneling but is instead defined by a central fireplace and a bold, geometric plaster ceiling. The kitchen and catering kitchen have a similar relationship as in the Pauli Murray College house, but this time the family kitchen and dining functions are separated, with family dining accommodated in a small octagonal breakfast room facing the courtyard.

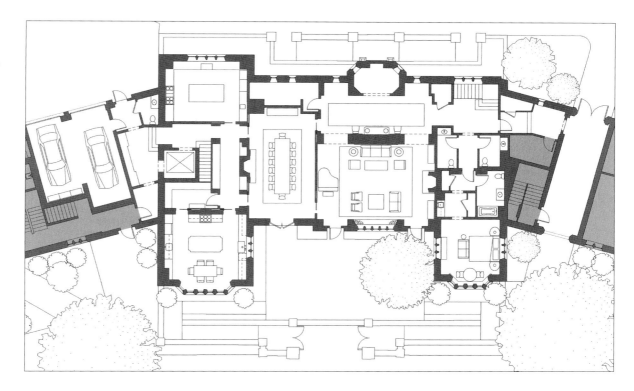

This house enjoys an additional surprise element: its corner location at Prospect Walk allows for a private, walled side garden. The siting of this house extends the grand residential neighborhood of upper Prospect Street south toward the main campus, while also marking the cross-axial connection to Hillhouse Avenue and its own collection of grand houses, including the Yale president's house.

There is additional housing for faculty within both Benjamin Franklin and Pauli Murray Colleges: apartments for a dean and a fellow in each college, as well as single-room accommodations for two graduate-affiliates (graduate students who assist the head of college), are located between the main courtyard and the secondary courtyard of each college. These are not expressed on the exterior but rather are tucked around the courtyards much like the student suites, although they enjoy a prominent location with views into multiple courtyards, enabling their residents to keep an eye out for excessive outbursts of undergraduate exuberance.

Interior details and the furniture also distinguish the two head of college houses. Decorative lighting is brass in the Pauli Murray College house, but nickel in its Benjamin Franklin College counterpart. Graphically bold patterns appear in the carpets of the Pauli Murray College house, while the carpets in that of Benjamin Franklin College have floral and botanical motifs, including a depiction of a walled garden, recalling the walled garden along Prospect Walk, in the carpet in the entry gallery. Elegant round-backed side chairs inspired by Kaare Klint are paired with a slim-armed contemporary sofa and lounge chairs in the Benjamin Franklin College head's living room, while the Pauli Murray College head's living room is furnished with curving Lutyens sofas counterbalanced with clean Modernist armchairs. The dining furniture is similarly varied: for Pauli

3.39. Interior design meeting. Clockwise from left: Christopher McIntire, Preston J. Gumberich, Leo Stevens, Lawrence Chabra, Robert A.M. Stern, Melissa DelVecchio. Photograph July 20, 2011. RAMSA.

3.40. Interior design meeting. Clockwise from left: Lawrence Chabra, Jennifer Stone, Kurt Glauber, Leo Stevens, Robert A.M. Stern. Photograph August, 9, 2011. RAMSA.

Design: From the Inside Out

Murray College, a custom table based on a Lutyens design is paired with simple chairs with upholstered seats and wooden backs; at Benjamin Franklin College, beneath a tracery ceiling in high-relief plaster, a Georgian-style table with book-matched walnut veneer is paired with Sheraton-style chairs with carved wood backs in the form of pointed arches.

The internal organization and design of Benjamin Franklin and Pauli Murray Colleges was driven by the pressures of use but also by the need to support the essential role that each residential college plays within Yale undergraduate life. However, this represents only half of the story of the design process, which simultaneously proceeded from the outside in to fulfill our mandate to make the new colleges visually connect with, and indeed embrace, Gothic Yale.

Design:
From the Outside In

You cannot design by reason,
though it is absolutely essential that your design,
when finished, should be reasonable.

JAMES GAMBLE ROGERS
The American Architect/The Architectural Review, 1921

Working from the *outside in*, we initiated the concept or predesign phase (September 2008–April 2009) by building a series of simplified scale models of the existing twelve residential colleges. Based on archival drawings, these models allowed us to study the massing and planning strategies employed by Rogers, Pope, and Saarinen, which informed our own responses to site and program. In the second stage—schematic design (May 2009–April 2010)—we further developed our concept, designing the major facade elements, balancing repetition and variation of each component type, grouping them into compositions reflective of the program behind, and exploring cladding materials, roof pitch, and character. The third stage—design development (May 2010–April 2011)—saw the full, detailed elaboration of architectural components, from gates and passageways to windows, light fixtures, and exterior ornament, to name just a few, and their integration with structural and mechanical systems. After that came construction documents (May 2011–March 2012), where all the detailed drawings and specifications required to construct the building were finalized and developed, including strategies for offsite fabrication or "prefabrication."

As Yale grappled with the consequences of the 2008 recession, the project schedule was strategically prolonged, incorporating a series of holds between design phases, most notably a fourteen-month hold after we completed construction documents. The project resumed in July 2013 and construction began in October 2014, as discussed in Chapter 5. The size of our team increased from about twelve people at the start of concept design to between twenty and thirty people throughout the design process—equivalent to the size of a medium-size architecture firm—ramping up briefly to around forty architects and designers just prior to the submission of construction documents on March 30, 2012.

At the outset of the design process, our concept study models of the existing residential colleges helped us to appreciate Rogers's clear, functionally driven massing on the one hand, and on the other the scenographic effects he achieved through irregular groupings and sequences that seem to speak to each other across courts, walkways, and streets. To meet capacity requirements, Rogers designed buildings as tall as five stories but always sited them to the north, with lower buildings to the south, allowing rays of the low winter sun into the courts. The artful arrangement of a pragmatically determined building mass, combining rational Beaux-Arts planning with varying building heights, thereby accommodating both the required density and the local climate and urban context of New Haven, was one of Rogers's great innovations beyond the Oxford and Cambridge models.

In order to better understand the organization and scale of the Yale campus and the urban context of the site of Benjamin Franklin and Pauli Murray Colleges, we gathered the individual historic college building models into a single, expansive model. This design tool allowed us to analyze the disposition of the existing residential colleges within the New Haven street grid, helping us to quickly identify opportunities for axial and visual connections with our site.

We began to determine the location and scale of three new towers with respect to sight lines, street crossings, and notable campus markers, first incorporating the 2008 proposal by President Levin's advisory committees for "creating some kind of highly visible tower or gateway" at the southern tip of the site, at the intersection of Prospect and Canal Streets, "in order to lessen the sense of distance" between the campus core and the new colleges. We projected a second tower rising near the intersection of Prospect Walk and the Farmington Canal

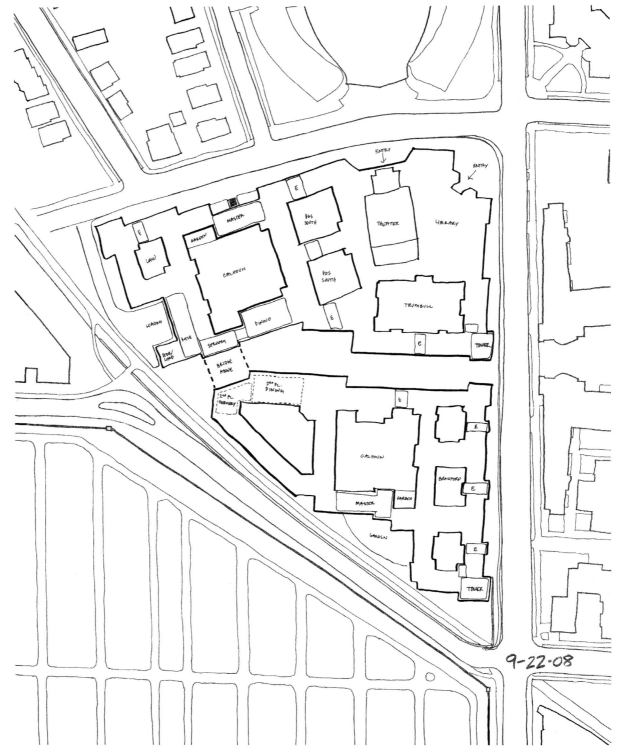

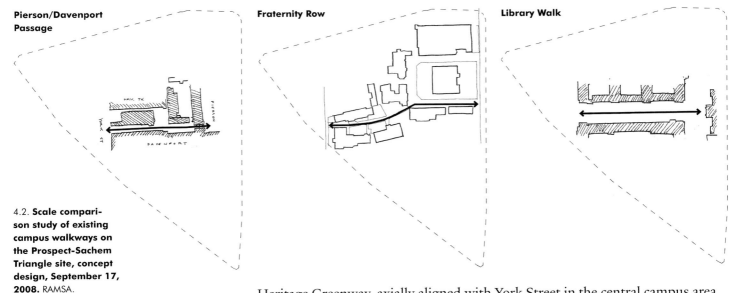

Pierson/Davenport Passage

Fraternity Row

Library Walk

4.2. **Scale comparison study of existing campus walkways on the Prospect-Sachem Triangle site, concept design, September 17, 2008.** RAMSA.

Heritage Greenway, axially aligned with York Street in the central campus area. A third tower was to mark the entrance to Prospect Walk from Prospect Street and also the principal entrance to Pauli Murray College. Although the towers were not yet designed, this first important step of establishing their approximate locations and massing helped convince doubters that the new colleges could be made to feel contiguous with the existing campus fabric and skyline and that the site was indeed closer to the historic core than many realized.

To further understand the scale and carrying capacity of our 6.7-acre site, as well as to explore different ways of apportioning it between the two colleges, we assembled prototype colleges by collaging courtyards and buildings from the Rogers-era colleges onto the Prospect-Sachem site. This exercise allowed us to develop our strategy for distributing open space and building mass across the site, based on the average number of beds accommodated per linear foot of building, which we knew from analyzing the existing residential colleges, and other inside-out pressures discussed in Chapter 3.

The basic site plan, consisting of one north and one south college bisected by an east–west pedestrian walk, was all but determined by Mayor John DeStefano Jr.'s request to conserve east–west circulation across the site, although in early studies we also explored whether one or both of the colleges might be split across the required pathway, similar to the way Berkeley College is split by the cross-campus mall. The form and proportions of the walkway between the two colleges, Prospect Walk—articulated in two segments that meet in a widened area near the middle—was informed by our study of existing walkways on campus. The bluestone-paved walk's longer (eastern) segment recalls the scale and atmosphere of historic Library Walk, a former street between the Memorial Quadrangle and Jonathan Edwards College that stands today as a quintessential Yale pedestrian path. This segment also approximates the length of the passage between Pierson and Davenport Colleges, while the shorter (western) segment opens wider as it meets the Farmington Canal Heritage Greenway to emphasize the public nature of the walkway. Taken as a whole, Prospect Walk's length and jagged trajectory evoke the path through Fraternity Row from York to Park Streets, and to some extent the path between Saarinen's Morse and Stiles Colleges, though without the steps up and down.

Using quick massing studies in sculptor's modeling clay (technically *plasticine*, of which our favorite is #2 Roma Plastilina) paired with transparent

4.3. **Massing studies in sculptor's modeling clay, concept design. Melissa DelVecchio and Robert A.M. Stern. Photograph October 1, 2008.** RAMSA.

4.4. **Massing studies in sculptor's modeling clay, concept design. Photograph October 1, 2008.** RAMSA.

overlays of the plans of the existing colleges used as scale references, we began to design the massing of Benjamin Franklin and Pauli Murray Colleges. As a practical and forgivingly imprecise design tool, clay lends itself to collaborative design sessions during which options can be developed and assessed quickly, and the process can be documented with photographs and video. Free-flowing design conversations occur around clay models in a way that they don't around a set of drawings, which can appear more fixed than they really are.

From the outset we embraced Rogers's massing strategy, keeping building heights lower along the south side of the courts and performing an extensive series of shadow studies to analyze solar exposure at different times of day throughout the year. This research shaped our approach to setting the heights of individual building masses and configuring them around variously sized courts. Buildings and voids alike were shaped by the combination of the limits of the triangular site, the program requirements developed from the inside out, and a desire to allow sunlight to reach the courtyards in all seasons.

4.5. Site model of the existing campus, concept design. Left to right: George de Brigard, Robert A.M. Stern, Melissa DelVecchio, Milton Hernandez. Photograph October 14, 2008. RAMSA.

4.6. Site model of the existing campus used to study the location and scale of three new towers with respect to sightlines, street crossings, and other notable campus markers, concept design. Photograph October 22, 2008. RAMSA.

Concurrently with these massing studies, we began to explore facade design options, wrapping placeholder Gothic and Georgian elevations around our three-dimensional models to suggest possible stylistic choices but principally to help our client understand the scale of the seemingly tiny study models and of the project as a whole. After cost analysis showed both Gothic and Georgian to be feasible within the budget, Yale embraced and approved our case to proceed in the Gothic style, as described at the end of Chapter 1, and we proceeded to develop options for a palette of facade materials combining brick and stone.

Although many imagine Gothic Yale as predominantly a stone campus — fulfilling the dictates of the second Timothy Dwight in 1871 — Rogers was in fact adept in mixing stone and brick, gradually increasing the proportion of brick as he moved outward from the historic core toward the edges of residential neighborhoods. The high pageantry in stone that encompasses the Memorial Quadrangle, Sterling Memorial Library, and the buildings of Sterling Memorial Library's monumental forecourt, adjacent to the Old Campus, gives way to brick

4.7. Preliminary elevations of Benjamin Franklin and Pauli Murray Colleges compared to the existing residential colleges, concept design, 2008. RAMSA.

Pierson & Davenport
Colleges West elevation

570 Ft.

Davenport College
North elevation

437 Ft.

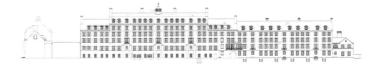

Silliman College
North elevation

413 Ft.

Pauli Murray College
South elevation

424 Ft.

Branford & Saybrook
Colleges West elevation

400 Ft.

Pauli Murray College
North elevation

405 Ft.

Branford & Saybrook
Colleges East elevation

400 Ft.

Benjamin Franklin College
North elevation

398 Ft.

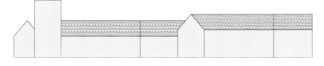

Branford College
South elevation

335 Ft.

Saybrook College
North elevation

335 Ft.

Benjamin Franklin College
Southwest elevation

362 Ft.

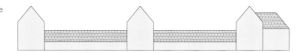

Design: From the Outside In

Trumbull College
South elevation

335 Ft.

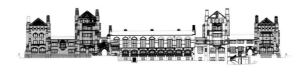

Benjamin Franklin College
East elevation

357 Ft.

Jonathan Edwards College
North elevation

335 Ft.

Silliman College
South elevation

332 Ft.

Timothy Dwight College
West elevation

329 Ft.

Pauli Murray College
West elevation

245 Ft.

Silliman College
East elevation

309 Ft.

Branford College
North elevation

273 Ft.

Jonathan Edwards College
West elevation

263 Ft.

Davenport College
South elevation

255 Ft.

Timothy Dwight College
North elevation

219 Ft.

4.8. **Shadow studies comparing Benjamin Franklin and Pauli Murray Colleges with Jonathan Edwards, Branford, and Saybrook Colleges during the spring and fall equinoxes and the summer and winter solstices, concept design, 2009.** RAMSA.

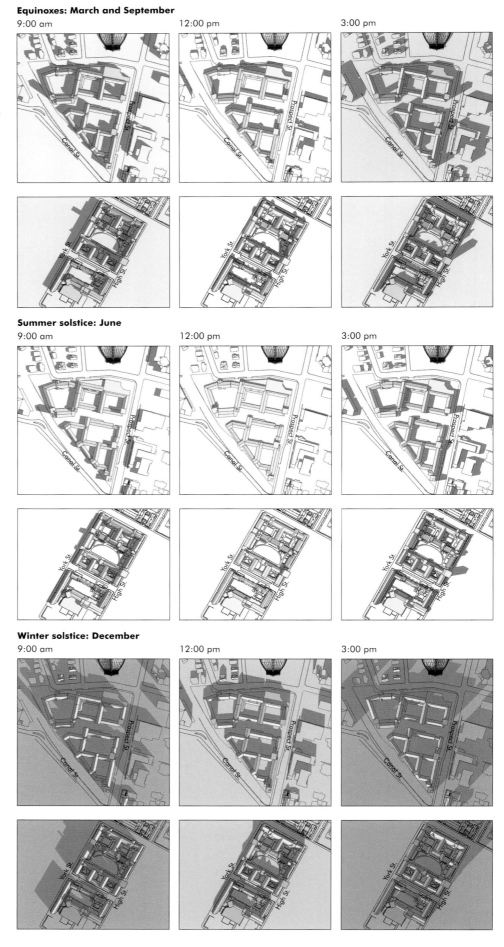

Equinoxes: March and September

9:00 am   12:00 pm   3:00 pm

Summer solstice: June

9:00 am   12:00 pm   3:00 pm

Winter solstice: December

9:00 am   12:00 pm   3:00 pm

Design: From the Outside In

facades along the perimeter buildings fronting Park Street to the west, Grove Street to the north, and Temple Street to the east, delineating a radial gradient of stone to brick.

Most intriguing from our point of view was the way in which Rogers feathered stone and brick together on several building facades to mediate this transition, as along York Street, where the west facade of Jonathan Edwards College shifts from entirely stone cladding at Library Walk to a predominantly brick facade as it nears Chapel Street. Similarly, a few blocks to the north, the York Street elevation of the Sterling Law Building transitions from stone at the intersection of Wall Street to mostly brick at the corner of Grove Street. And on the west side of York Street, the stone portico of the Hall of Graduate Studies gives way to the mostly brick facades of the large courtyard and tower.

Indeed, Rogers also favored brick cladding for many of his Gothic inner courts, taking advantage of its lower cost and more domestic character, starting with Linonia Court, a brick-and-stone enclave of Branford College set within the outwardly granite-clad Memorial Quadrangle. The courtyard facades of Grace Hopper (formerly Calhoun) College, designed by John Russell Pope, similarly combine brick and stone, which contrasted with the all-stone cladding of the street-facing facades. It was initially the courtyard facade of Jonathan Edwards College — containing 48 percent brick, 35 percent stone, and 17 percent glass — that served as our target combination of materials in the facades of Benjamin Franklin and Pauli Murray Colleges, but as our design progressed it moved closer to the proportions used in the north facade of the Sterling Law Building, closer to our site, which contains a higher percentage of brick. As is the case with the law school, all the moat walls of Benjamin Franklin and Pauli Murray Colleges were designed and realized in stone.

Considering the size and complexity of the project, an important step in the predesign phase was to create a pricing model based on our best guesses about levels of finish and detail for student rooms, social spaces, and most importantly for a building with extensive street and courtyard facades, the exterior surfaces. Each program area was assigned a budget and the projected costs were tracked at each phase of design, allowing Yale to benchmark the costs of this project relative to its other residential facilities, in keeping with the idea of parity. This was also the university's way of making sure that no single aspect of the project, such as the facades, was developed at the expense of another, like student rooms.

The landscape design concept for the new colleges came together with the preliminary planning, massing, and cladding strategies in the early months of 2009. Each college encloses a large quadrangle — rectangular at Benjamin Franklin and trapezoidal at Pauli Murray — measuring over 17,000 square feet, with plenty of open space in the middle to accommodate commencement-related ceremonies under a tent. In addition, there are a total of three medium-size courtyards, each 8,000 to 10,000 square feet, comparable in size to Saybrook Court in the Memorial Quadrangle. And Benjamin Franklin College has two smaller, 4,100-square-foot courtyards recalling the intimate scale of Linonia, Calliope, and Brothers-in-Unity Courts in the Memorial Quadrangle. These are, however, triangular in shape, following the diagonal cut of the Farmington Canal Heritage Greenway. It was only later that we hit upon the idea of developing the roof over the loading dock with additional floors of student suites, which not only freed up more area for the middle courtyard of Pauli Murray College

4.9. Jonathan Edwards College courtyard and York Street facades. Photographs November 7, 2008. RAMSA.

4.10. Sterling Law Building (James Gamble Rogers, 1931). Photograph Robert A.M. Stern, c. 1980s. RAMSA.

and resolved a safety issue, as discussed in Chapter 3, but also made it possible to create two elevated "secret gardens" or microcourts similar in scale to Lower Court at Pierson College, and accessible from a larger courtyard via a staircase.

The courts and street-facing walks and gardens of Benjamin Franklin and Pauli Murray Colleges were designed by OLIN, the Philadelphia-based landscape architecture firm that previously led the restoration of the Old Campus quadrangle as well as the courtyards of the existing colleges. Richard Newton, the partner-in-charge at OLIN, explains that the design approach was driven by a dual desire to channel the essential qualities of existing Yale courtyards and to work with the specific views and sequences created by the architecture of the new colleges. OLIN took inspiration from the tranquility and simplicity of the Yale landscapes designed by Beatrix Farrand (1872–1959), who directed the design and planting of the university's grounds from 1922 to 1945. With the center of each court given to open lawn, large trees were positioned to spread their canopies at some distance from the buildings, while less substantial understory plantings were confined to the perimeters, framing the architecture without hiding it. Bluestone paths were laid out orthogonally or diagonally across the courts to connect entryways and vaulted passageways.

OLIN also reprised Farrand's artful planting of the moats that surround the colleges, forming a porous and colorful screen of greenery visible from the street while providing privacy to rooms at grade and funneling light to basement areas below. Yale first adopted moats in the nineteenth century to buffer Farnam Hall from College Street, and subsequently Rogers and Farrand, who did not always agree on planting strategy, developed garden moats into a signature feature of the Memorial Quadrangle and subsequent residential colleges. The garden moats that surround Benjamin Franklin and Pauli Murray Colleges along Prospect Street and Sachem Street are typically 8 feet wide and 8 to 10 feet deep, and are fronted by a 3-foot-6-inch-or-taller stone wall depending on the grade. The moats become wider along Prospect Walk, but, along the Farmington Canal Heritage Greenway, give way to an iron grille set between brick piers with

4.12. The courtyards of Benjamin Franklin (south) and Pauli Murray (north) Colleges compared to the courtyards of the existing residential colleges, concept design, 2008.
RAMSA/OLIN.

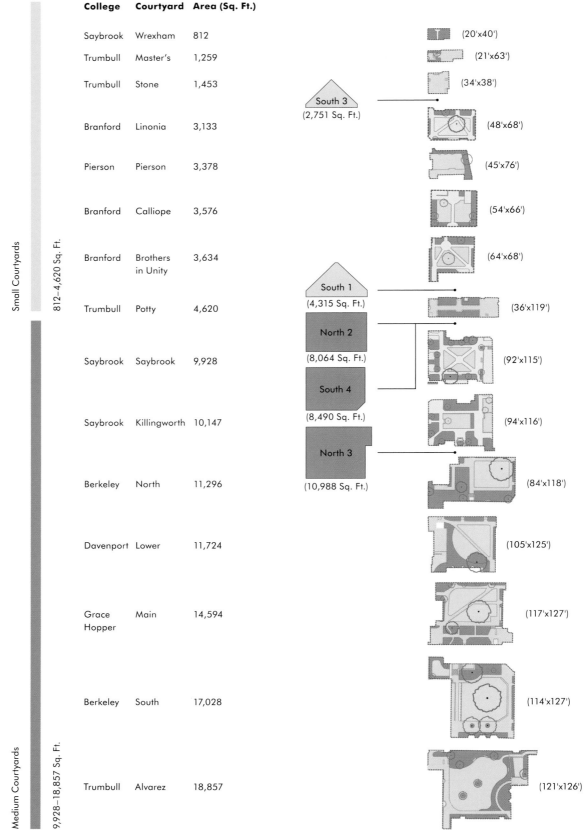

College	Courtyard	Area (Sq. Ft.)
Saybrook	Wrexham	812
Trumbull	Master's	1,259
Trumbull	Stone	1,453
Branford	Linonia	3,133
Pierson	Pierson	3,378
Branford	Calliope	3,576
Branford	Brothers in Unity	3,634
Trumbull	Potty	4,620
Saybrook	Saybrook	9,928
Saybrook	Killingworth	10,147
Berkeley	North	11,296
Davenport	Lower	11,724
Grace Hopper	Main	14,594
Berkeley	South	17,028
Trumbull	Alvarez	18,857

Small Courtyards — 812–4,620 Sq. Ft.

Medium Courtyards — 9,928–18,857 Sq. Ft.

(20'x40')
(21'x63')
(34'x38')

South 3
(2,751 Sq. Ft.)

(48'x68')
(45'x76')
(54'x66')
(64'x68')

South 1
(4,315 Sq. Ft.)

North 2
(8,064 Sq. Ft.)

South 4
(8,490 Sq. Ft.)

North 3
(10,988 Sq. Ft.)

(36'x119')
(92'x115')
(94'x116')
(84'x118')
(105'x125')
(117'x127')
(114'x127')
(121'x126')

College	Courtyard	Area (Sq. Ft.)
Jonathan Edwards	Main	20,878
Davenport	Kumbull	25,294
Timothy Dwight	Timothy Dwight	25,734
Pierson	Lower	812
Ezra Stiles	Stiles	26,983
Samuel F. B. Morse	Morse	30,770
Branford	Branford	34,138
Silliman	Silliman	70,498

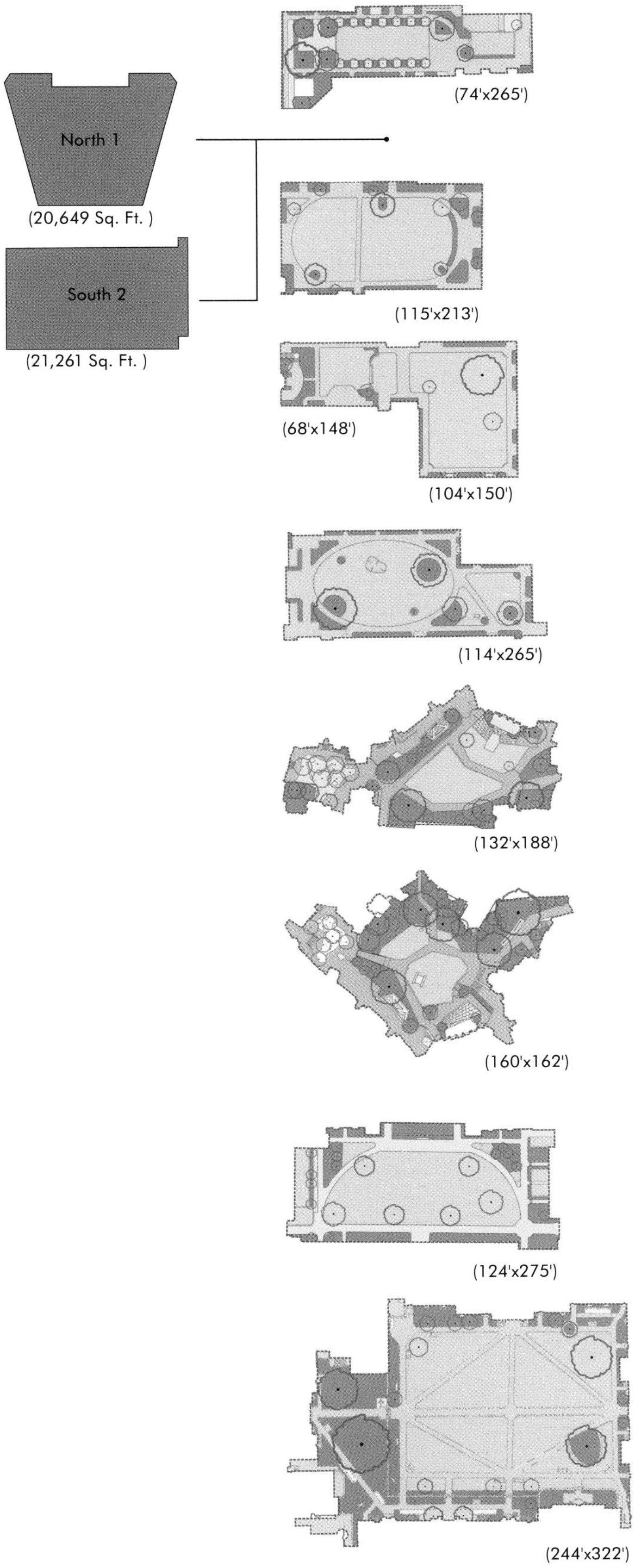

(74'x265')

North 1

(20,649 Sq. Ft.)

South 2

(21,261 Sq. Ft.)

(115'x213')

(68'x148')

(104'x150')

(114'x265')

(132'x188')

(160'x162')

(124'x275')

(244'x322')

Large Courtyards

20,878–70,498 Sq. Ft.

123

4.13. **Moat precedents. Photographs March–April, 2010.** RAMSA/OLIN.

Sterling Law Building, buttresses within moats

Branford College, moat entrance condition

Jonathan Edwards College, buttresses within moats

Branford College, moat along Library Walk

stone caps, which, in place of a moat, encloses plantings and confers privacy and security to the at-grade student rooms.

The refurbished Greenway itself, a 12-foot-wide multiuse path, is planted with a biodiverse meadow landscape for the stretch bordering the new residential colleges. OLIN and our firm also created improved urban connections: a new at-grade crossing over the Greenway from Prospect Walk to Lock Street, a new public staircase descending from the corner of Prospect and Trumbull Streets to the Greenway below, and improved sidewalks, lighting, and plantings along Prospect and Sachem Streets.

OLIN subsequently developed the landscape design concept to contribute to the individual characteristics of each courtyard. The south triangular courtyard of Benjamin Franklin College, for example, is planted with three species of birch (paper birch, gray birch, and river birch), each of which has slightly different habit and bark texture, while the adjacent triangular courtyard to the north is planted with trees that have contrasting leaf shapes, from the

4.14. **Landscape plan, schematic design, 2010.** RAMSA/OLIN.

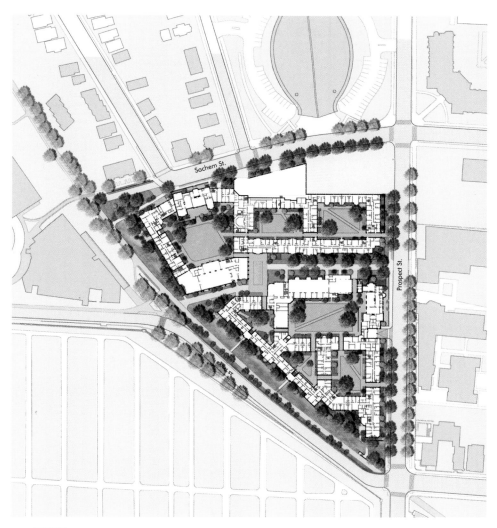

4.15. **Section through Prospect Walk showing moats, looking east, schematic design 2010.** RAMSA/OLIN.

10'-4" Moat   13'-10" Groundcover   15'-0" Prospect Walk   11'-11" Groundcover   8'-8" Moat

4.16. Material comparison of Benjamin Franklin and Jonathan Edwards Colleges, schematic design, 2010. RAMSA.

Schematic Design

Stone 28%
Brick 55%
Glazing 15%
Continuous dormer 2%

Benjamin Franklin College elevation along Prospect Street

Concept Design

Stone 30%
Brick 55%
Glazing 11%
Continuous dormer 4%

Benjamin Franklin College elevation along Prospect Street

Jonathan Edwards

Stone 48.5%
Brick 37%
Glazing 14.5%

Jonathan Edwards College elevation along York Street

heart-shaped-leaved katsura to the palmate-leaved horse chestnut. The bluestone pathways are complemented by granite setts (Belgian blocks) beneath the benches and bicycle racks, with a granite curb lining the perimeter of each courtyard.

As our architectural design work proceeded into schematic design in the spring of 2009, we reexamined the precedents we thought we knew so well, but this time through a more detailed lens, discovering nuances of type and variation. We looked carefully at window rhythms, for example, noting their relationship to the distribution of the residential and social spaces behind the facades. We also looked at the many types of dormers used on the Yale campus and their relationship to roof pitch and the rooms tucked within, well aware that on a group of buildings as large and complex as Benjamin Franklin and Pauli Murray Colleges, design decisions on these issues would have a significant cumulative cost impact. For example, our Vermont slate roofs have a relatively low pitch, rising 10 inches in height for every 12 inches in length—closer to Rogers's 1930s residential colleges such as Berkeley and Trumbull than to the more steeply pitched roofs of his earlier Memorial Quadrangle, and resulting in significant savings in roof area. Perhaps most importantly, our investigation of the Rogers-era residential colleges showed us how he compensated for cost-effective repetition of facade elements with strategically situated special moments in the dining halls, libraries, and head of college houses.

This analysis led us to develop a series of repeating elements for the design of student residential areas, while also introducing a variety of bay windows,

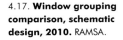

Jonathan Edwards College, York Street

Saybrook College, Elm Street

Benjamin Franklin College (proposed), Prospect Street

4.18. **Roof pitch and gable end comparison, schematic design, 2010.** RAMSA.

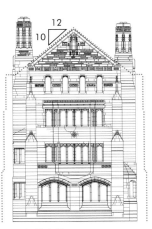

Trumbull College

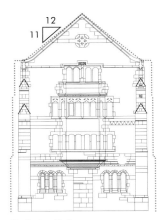

Berkeley College

Pauli Murray College (proposed)

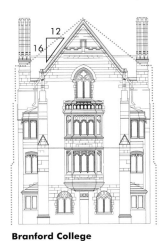

Branford College

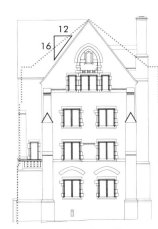

Jonathan Edwards College

Grace Hopper College

127

4.19. Executive Committee meeting, concept design. Left to right: Robert A.M. Stern, Lara Apelian, Melissa DelVecchio, Judith B. Krauss, Linda Koch Lorimer, J. Lloyd Suttle, Laura Cruikshank, Bruce D. Alexander, Graham S. Wyatt. Photograph October 20, 2008. RAMSA.

4.20. Yale President meeting, concept design. Left to right: Jennifer Stone, Melissa DelVecchio, Alice J. Raucher, Graham S. Wyatt, Bruce D. Alexander, Roland W. Betts, Laura Cruickshank, Richard C. Levin. Photograph December 1, 2008. RAMSA.

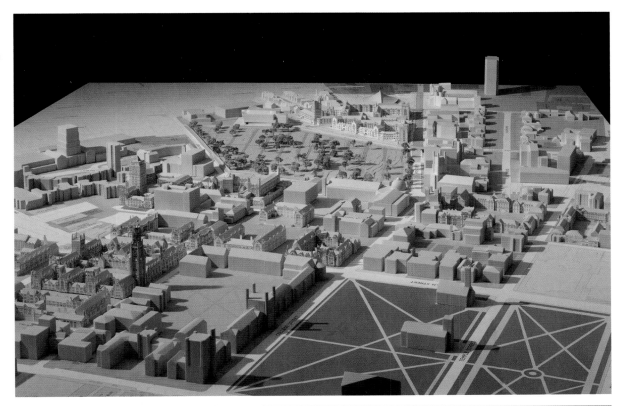

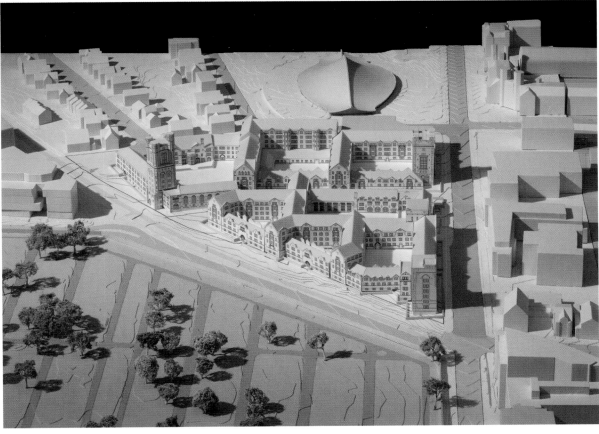

4.22. **View looking north from Prospect Street, concept design, February 15, 2009. Jeff Stikeman, delineator.** RAMSA.

4.23. **View looking north from Prospect Street, schematic design, August 4, 2010. Jeff Stikeman, delineator.** RAMSA.

4.24. **View looking northwest along Prospect Street, concept design, February 15, 2009. Jeff Stikeman, delineator.** RAMSA.

4.25. **View looking northwest along Prospect Street, schematic design, August 4, 2010. Jeff Stikeman, delineator.** RAMSA.

131

4.26. **View looking west from Prospect Walk, concept design, February 15, 2009. Jeff Stikeman, delineator.** RAMSA.

4.27. **View looking west from Prospect Walk, schematic design, August 4, 2010. Jeff Stikeman, delineator.** RAMSA.

4.28. View looking north from Farmington Canal Heritage Greenway, concept design, February 15, 2009. Jeff Stikeman, delineator. RAMSA.

4.29. View looking north from Farmington Canal Heritage Greenway, schematic design, August 4, 2010. Jeff Stikeman, delineator. RAMSA.

133

4.30. **Pauli Murray College Bekenstein Court, view looking southwest, concept design, February 15, 2009. Jeff Stikeman, delineator.** RAMSA.

4.31. **Pauli Murray College Bekenstein Court, view looking southwest, schematic design, August 4, 2010. Jeff Stikeman, delineator.** RAMSA.

Design: From the Outside In

4.32. **Pauli Murray College small court-yard, view looking southwest, concept design, February 15, 2009. Jeff Stikeman, delineator.** RAMSA.

4.33. **Pauli Murray College small court-yard, view looking southwest, schematic design, August 4, 2010. Jeff Stikeman, delineator.** RAMSA.

4.34. Benjamin Franklin College Nyburg Baker Court, view looking north-east, concept design, February 15, 2009. Jeff Stikeman, delineator. RAMSA.

4.35. Benjamin Franklin College Nyburg Baker Court, view looking north-east, schematic design, August 4, 2010. Jeff Stikeman, delineator. RAMSA.

4.36. Benjamin Franklin College triangular courtyard, view looking northwest, concept design, February 15, 2009. Jeff Stikeman, delineator. RAMSA.

4.37. Benjamin Franklin College triangular courtyard, view looking northwest, schematic design, August 4, 2010. Jeff Stikeman, delineator. RAMSA.

4.38. **Prospect Walk north elevation, schematic design, April 7, 2010.** RAMSA.

4.39. **Prospect Walk south elevation, schematic design, April 7, 2010.** RAMSA.

4.40. **Farmington Canal Heritage Greenway elevation, schematic design, April 7, 2010.** RAMSA.

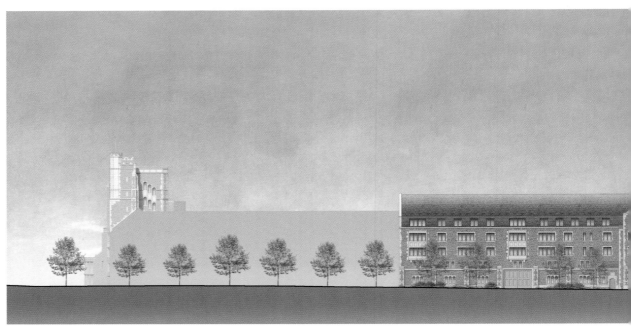

4.41. **Sachem Street elevation, schematic design, April 7, 2010.** RAMSA.

4.42. **Prospect Street elevation, schematic design, April 7, 2010.** RAMSA.

4.43. **North-south section, schematic design, April 7, 2010.** RAMSA.

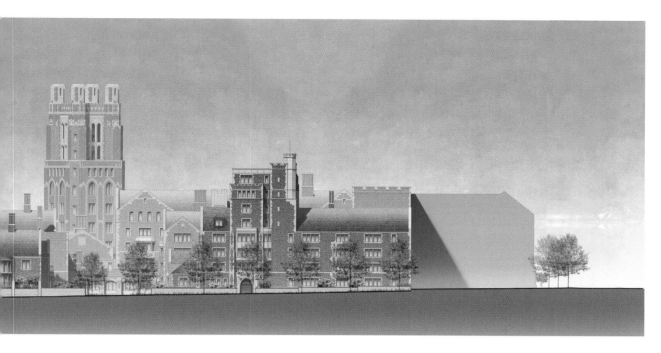

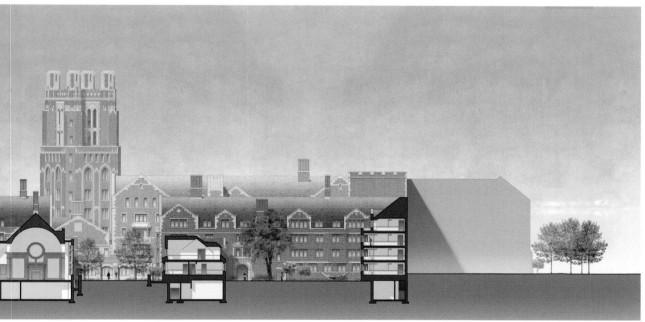

4.44. **University Council meeting, concept design. Photograph April 17, 2009.** RAMSA.

4.45. **Concept design unveiled to the public with a 1/32" = 1'-0" scale model at a presentation in Sterling Memorial Library. Photograph May 28, 2009.** RAMSA.

4.46. **Schematic design unveiled to the public with a 1/16" = 1'-0" scale model in Sterling Memorial Library. Photograph May 28, 2010.** RAMSA.

dormers, towers, and other features to differentiate the building masses and articulate each courtyard as an outdoor room with its own character. We followed Rogers's logic for labeling and referring to courtyards (letters A–G) and facades (buildings 1–27, followed by a directional marker), having stumbled upon the convenience of this system for communication among our design team and model shop staff. On May 28, 2009, our concept design was unveiled to the public in the form of a 1/32"=1'-0" scale model at a presentation in Sterling Memorial Library, and it was displayed at class reunions the following month.

During the lull in the project schedule for Benjamin Franklin and Pauli Murray Colleges, and through serendipity, we were invited to participate in a competition that gave us a reason to tour Oxford and Cambridge in depth with access granted to spaces not ordinarily open to the public. These visits during the spring and summer of 2009 helped us create a library of imagery that would be very difficult to obtain by only using published research materials. We thoroughly documented compositional elements, such as doorways and windows, but also details that Rogers had also likely tried to develop a familiarity with.

145

4.47. **Melissa DelVecchio and Robert A.M. Stern touring the University of Oxford with Magdalene Tower in the background. Photograph Graham S. Wyatt, June 1, 2009.** RAMSA.

4.48. **All Souls College, University of Oxford. Photograph April 13, 2009.** RAMSA.

4.49. **St Catherine's College, University of Oxford. Photograph April 14, 2009.** RAMSA.

4.50. **Keble College, University of Oxford. Photograph April 18, 2009.** RAMSA.

4.51. **Nuffield College, University of Oxford. Photograph April 18, 2009.** RAMSA.

4.52. **St Johns College, University of Oxford. Photograph April 15, 2009.** RAMSA.

4.53. **St Johns College, University of Oxford. Photograph April 15, 2009.** RAMSA.

4.54. **George de Brigard as scale figure at Lincoln College, University of Oxford. Photograph April 13, 2009.** RAMSA.

4.55. **Lincoln College, University of Oxford. Photograph April 13, 2009.** RAMSA.

4.56. **Corpus Christi College, University of Cambridge. Photograph April 15, 2009.** RAMSA.

4.57. **Pembroke College, University of Cambridge. Photograph April 18, 2009.** RAMSA.

4.58. **Peterhouse College, University of Cambridge. Photograph April 15, 2009.** RAMSA.

Design: From the Outside In

4.59. Trinity College, University of Cambridge. Photograph April 18, 2009. RAMSA.

4.60. Corpus Christi College, University of Cambridge. Photograph April 15, 2009. RAMSA.

4.61. Pembroke College, University of Cambridge. Photograph April 18, 2009. RAMSA.

4.62. Pembroke College, University of Cambridge. Photograph April 18, 2009. RAMSA.

4.63. Peterhouse College, University of Cambridge. Photograph April 15, 2009. RAMSA.

4.64. View from Melissa DelVecchio's guest room at Peterhouse College, University of Cambridge. Photograph April 18, 2009. RAMSA.

Structural engineering and interior planning played a role in shaping the schematic design, as we repeatedly adjusted the typical entryway module to fit the irregular shape and sloping contours of the site. The structural system, engineered by Massachusetts-based Weidlinger Associates (now part of New York–based Thornton Tomasetti), consists of cast-in-place flat concrete slabs with 4,000 concrete columns, continuous perimeter concrete edge beams, and concrete shear walls, maintaining a floor-to-floor distance of 9 feet 4 inches, similar to the earlier residential colleges.

The buildings of Benjamin Franklin and Pauli Murray Colleges, typically 35-1/2 feet wide, are supported by columns along their perimeter and also along their center. The option for a column-free span, though appealing for space planning, was found to be too costly, because it would have necessitated much thicker and more heavily reinforced concrete slabs. A third option, for an all-steel structural system, would have cost slightly less than either of the concrete slab options but was rejected because it would have required a much taller floor-to-floor height to achieve the same floor-to-ceiling height, thus jeopardizing our ability to work within a scale that was consistent with the older colleges and also because of the extra coordination and potential added costs that would have been required to arrange individual beams, penetrations, and joints within the irregularly situated buildings. A steel structure, however, was deemed optimal for the uppermost story, where, in areas, a subtle step in the facade creates a "continuous dormer," as seen on many of the Rogers-era colleges.

While most buildings are designed on a repeating structural grid with fixed distances between columns, Benjamin Franklin and Pauli Murray Colleges are designed with variably spaced columns whose locations were individually adjusted so as not to interrupt window bays and other architectural design features. The location of projecting windows and other facade elements was adjusted to the structural system where possible, but in effect the facade and structural design were synchronized, very laboriously, through the schematic design phase and into design development. Architectural design decisions were also affected by seismic requirements, which necessitate building substantial shear walls and lateral reinforcing in particular places.

Mechanical engineering, lighting, and sustainability consulting by BuroHappold Engineering resulted in the use of highly energy-efficient building systems, which are expected to earn the project a Leadership in Energy and Environmental Design (LEED) Gold rating from the US Green Building Council. Designing around these systems also presented a series of knotty coordination challenges that Rogers did not have to contend with in the 1930s. We set out to overcome those challenges while maintaining the charming and slightly diminutive scale of Rogers's work.

Building systems are configured according to what Denzil Gallagher, principal at BuroHappold, calls "an above and below approach," with ventilation equipment for residential suites located in the attic level, and the rest of the mechanical, electrical, and plumbing systems looped through the basement. In place of conventional forced air heating and cooling, student rooms are ventilated naturally via operable windows, and they are warmed and cooled by efficient radiant "valance" units that use hydronic technology to draw the ambient air across water-filled coils. The central air-conditioning system is to be activated only for the comfort of summer conference guests, leaving undergraduate residents on the same footing with their peers in other colleges — that is, without

A/C on hot spring and fall days, instead seeking comfort in shaded courtyards and air-conditioned common areas.

Conventional mechanical ventilation technology is used to heat and cool the hallways inside and outside the suites, as well as all the nonresidential areas, such as dining halls and performance spaces. The cost of this heating and cooling is reduced by an estimated 10 percent through the use of a closed-loop geothermal system engineered by Haley & Aldrich, taking advantage of the relatively steady temperature of groundwater to receive heat in the winter and expel heat in the summer via several dozen interconnected 400-foot-deep wells beneath the courtyards. Another active energy-saving feature is the heat-recovery system that preheats incoming fresh air using heat energy harnessed from exhaust air. Overall energy performance benefited from a precisely engineered insulated cavity wall construction and a multilayered roof assembly, which minimize thermal transfer. Efficient compact fluorescent and LED lighting fixtures are used throughout the residential and shared spaces as are water-conserving bathroom fixtures.

The circulation of steam and chilled water from Yale's central plant is controlled by a single efficient pump in the basement, with additional dedicated loops for domestic water, gas, electricity, data, security, sewer, and stormwater utilities. All these utilities are distributed horizontally along the basement corridors, rising vertically through strategically placed shafts whose locations were calibrated to protect structural integrity—meaning that the shafts must not penetrate the floor slabs within a certain distance of an edge, column, stairwell, or elevator shaft, leaving precious few options in buildings that are typically only 35-1/2 feet wide.

The reliance on vertical piping rather than horizontal ductwork on the residential floors parallels the use of separate vertical entryways instead of horizontal corridors for resident circulation, yielding unique cost benefits. Perhaps the greatest benefit was that the floor-to-ceiling height of student rooms is undiminished by utilities, so that the ceiling itself is nothing more than the structural slab, finished with skim-coated plaster. But just as the layouts of the residential modules deviated from the prototypical or "fantasy bar" configuration discussed in Chapter 3, the layout of building systems, given the irregular shape of the site and irregular column grid, involved similarly atypical configurations in plan and section.

Three-dimensional digital modeling was key to the design process in conjunction with hand drawing and physical modeling. Beginning in the schematic design phase, at Yale's request, we moved the project from a conventional computer-aided design (CAD) platform to a more innovative Building Information Modeling (BIM) platform, Autodesk Revit, representing a fundamental shift in our methodology of design, documentation, and coordination. Unlike CAD systems in which the drawing elements are two-dimensional graphical abstractions (points, lines, planes), a BIM model's elements are architectural (column, floor, window, etc.), requiring the designer not to "draw" by means of lines, but instead to "build" each component in three dimensions to form a wall or roof, which allows for the production of two-dimensional, three-dimensional, isometric, and perspective drawings and views. A BIM workflow uses shared databases and virtual three-dimensional models to streamline coordination and visualize the relationships between complex pieces and systems, highlighting potential conflicts or gaps that might otherwise go unnoticed until later in the process.

Our office had previously completed only one project using Revit, so the change of software platforms on this large and highly complicated project presented a major challenge and also a major opportunity. We were eager to take advantage of Revit's ability to process all drawings as quantifiable data, yielding efficient calculations related to components, costs, and scheduling, with the added bonus of visualization of complex elements. To train our staff in Revit and its shared databases, we used the prototypical entryway module, which not only helped us to determine the best modeling strategies but also gave us the opportunity to test the structure and mechanical systems discussed above.

The overall digital model, containing the huge amount of data required to coordinate the half-million-gross-square-foot Gothic building complex, soon ballooned into what was likely the largest single Revit model produced to date, largely because the complex massing and program made it difficult to divide into multiple linked digital models. We could only divide our work across four models—a Pauli Murray College model, a Benjamin Franklin College model, and a corresponding interior model for each (which only held interior elevations and details). Still, these models were unwieldy multigigabyte files. Simultaneously, we found ourselves constrained by the limits of software and hardware, at times waiting up to twenty minutes to open or save the shared file—a difficult situation in a software based on synchronized data. This was solved by investment in more powerful computers for our staff and the use of an intra-office desktop chat system and a team wiki to coordinate work among team members and share modeling strategies.

Phillip G. Bernstein (BA 1979, MArch 1983), who has lectured on professional practice at the Yale School of Architecture since 1989 and served as vice president of strategic relations at Autodesk from 2000 to 2016, stepped in to help address these challenges. He recalls that Revit's capacity as a digital modeling tool was "emerging" and "not very mature" when design work began in 2008. "The software was not designed in anticipation of the creation of this incredibly elaborate and precisely orchestrated Gothic building. Bob basically summoned me and said, 'This better work,'" Bernstein said, referring to his ambassadorial role in facilitating the use of Revit on the new colleges. Autodesk embraced the Yale project as an important proof-of-concept for its tool and took the unusual step of providing direct access to software engineers to ensure its successful application. "Can you imagine if you could pick up the phone and call the design studio at Honda and say, 'I'm having trouble with this turn signal?'" Bernstein asked rhetorically. "But we didn't hear a lot of whining," he noted with respect to RAMSA. "They were incredibly disciplined." Revit proved exceptionally helpful as we managed information about components such as windows and doors, allowing us, as one example, to create filters to visualize and quickly assess if fire doors were properly located amid the 1,900 total interior doors.

A number of masonry components, such as the passageways and window surrounds, were too geometrically complex to be modeled in Revit (at least in the version available in 2009), so we also turned to Digital Project, the parametric software specially designed by Gehry Technologies to model complex forms. We also enlisted the assistance of Gehry Technologies, the developer of the software, as a consultant to support our team's efforts to master specific modeling techniques and coordination challenges, including the complex analysis required for the prefabrication of Bass Tower. The software allowed us to study Gothic profiles in hand drawings and then test and modify them for different

4.65. **Pauli Murray College view of Autodesk Revit digital model showing exterior, structural, and mechanical systems, 2012.** RAMSA.

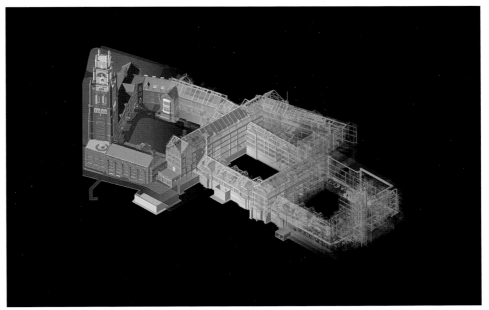

4.66. **Pauli Murray College door data visualization in Autodesk Revit, 2012.** RAMSA.

4.67. **Benjamin Franklin and Pauli Murray Colleges window data visualization showing components modeled in Gehry Technologies Digital Project to supplement Autodesk Revit model, 2012.** RAMSA.

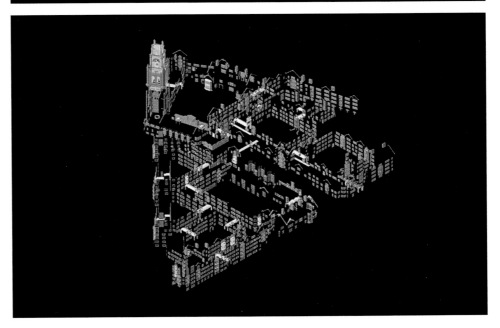

situations, helping us coordinate the application of more than 600 stone profiles. Additionally, the two-dimensional drawings generated from the Digital Project model were more legible, more subtly delineated, and more data-efficient than the drawings produced from the Revit model. When the complex component geometries were finalized, we integrated the Digital Project models back into the overall Revit building information model.

To initiate the design development phase, with the goal of reaching the level of detail achieved by Rogers, our team undertook a rigorous process of research and documentation. Returning again to the architectural richness of the Yale campus but this time in more detail, each member of the team was asked to research, analyze, and photograph a different component of the buildings and consider how it was deployed by Rogers and Pope. For example, we documented many types of buttresses found at gable ends, dozens of variations of wood doors set within stone archways and lintels, and the various uses of crenellation and coping near the roof. These studies were compiled in a seventy-five-page book, which became a lasting resource to the team even through construction. We worked hard to tease from the design of each element its role in the composition of a college and, by extension, its role in the physical identity of Yale's campus.

This advanced phase of design required study at a larger scale and a higher resolution of detail, and our working models accordingly grew in size and scale. In one of the "war rooms" in our New York office, we built a 1/4"=1'-0" scale model as a design tool, which dwarfed the earlier 1/16"=1'-0" scale, schematic design model by a factor of four. This 20-foot-long model kept thirty people working together effectively, with each team member assigned a courtyard or portion of a building within the overall composition and charged with design and modelmaking responsibilities within that zone. The continuously evolving physical model allowed us to work through a vast array of design issues and to communicate about complex spatial decisions with our clients in considerable specificity, which would have been difficult by any other means. Holes cut in the center of each of the principal courtyards and other locations — openings referred to colloquially as the "Bob holes" — allowed designers and clients to see the courtyards in their entirety in a way no hand drawing or digital model would have permitted. The physical model also helped us refine the digital model, since difficulties encountered while modeling in cardboard often led us to discover an underlying coordination issue buried somewhere in the digital model.

Street and courtyard elevations consist primarily of molded, hand-set brick in a tricolor blend, accented with rustic buff Indiana limestone and Weymouth granite ashlar blocks and quoins, composed in a manner reminiscent of the brick-and-stone Gothic precedents. Limestone trim, in hundreds of varying shapes and sizes, is used to form the pointed buttress caps, the flush or profiled detailing surrounding wood exterior doors and passageway entrances, and many ornamental elements. Cast stone forms the repeating copings and parapets, window surrounds, and ornament. This versatile material offered the benefits of strength, economy, customization, and, in the case of repeating elements, speed of fabrication, as Rogers must have appreciated when he used it to form the window surrounds of Jonathan Edwards College and various facade elements in the 1920s Fraternity Row buildings at Yale.

The distribution of limestone and granite accents throughout the extensive street and courtyard facades may appear casual but was, in fact, carefully mapped piece by piece in all of our elevation drawings, with stone details

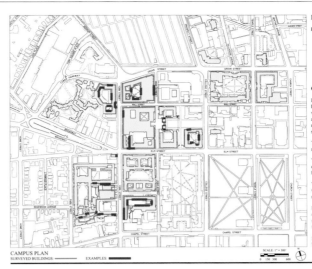

4.68. **Detail precedents of brickwork and stonework, design development, May 18, 2010.** RAMSA.

BRICKWORK AND STONEWORK

Rebecca Atkin and George de Brigard

- Coursing, patterns and detailing
- Integration with stone
- Unfamiliar uses
- Copings, frames, sill
- Changes in plane
- Ornament, patterns

CONCLUSIONS

Running, flemish and garden flemish are the most frequently used bond patterns in the buildings surveyed. Coursing is supplemented with detailed or contrasting patterns in the wall field, gables tops and stringcourses. The patterns are sometimes random elements mixed within the wall field, sometimes closely integrated with stone surrounds, and sometimes the focal point of a wall.

The use of a wider range of brick colors is coupled with a wider range of brick patterns. Walls of fewer colors have less patterning.

The use of shaped brick was very limited and almost exclusively employed at window surrounds. Relief in the brick was achieved by the use of projecting and recessing brick units or courses.

Yale's buildings present a great variety of stone profiles, often within the same facade. Coping at gables, for example, changes in response to location, height, neighboring material, etc.

Exterior walls change plane at the water table and, often, at a belt course. Simple profiles are used in most instances; it is the wall section that matters, not the stone band. This is not documented in the SD set.

Stone is used much more strategically in the existing buildings. Not every change of plane is fully surrounded by stone.

CAMPUS PLAN
SURVEYED BUILDINGS: EXAMPLES:

SCALE: 1" = 300'
0   150 300   600

DD DETAIL PRECEDENTS
YALE'S EXISTING BUILDINGS

BRICKWORK
MAY 18, 2010

NEW RESIDENTIAL COLLEGES
YALE UNIVERSITY
ROBERT A.M. STERN ARCHITECTS

FLEMISH GARDEN BOND WITH DIAGONALS
CALHOUN COLLEGE

RUNNING BOND ON THE DIAGONAL
PIERSON COLLEGE

MIXED BRICK PATTERNS
HALL OF GRADUATE STUDIES

BRICK PATTERNS
BRICKWORK
MAY 18, 2010

DD DETAIL PRECEDENTS
YALE'S EXISTING BUILDINGS

NEW RESIDENTIAL COLLEGES
YALE UNIVERSITY
ROBERT A.M. STERN ARCHITECTS

LOW-PROFILE COPING
JONATHAN EDWARDS COLLEGE

HIGH-PROFILE COPING
JONATHAN EDWARDS COLLEGE

NO COPING, QUOINING
ROSE ALUMNI HOUSE

FLUSH STRINGCOURSE
STERLING LAW BUILDING

FLUSH AND PROFILED STRINGCOURSES
LANGROCK BUILDING

FLUSH AND PROFILED STRINGCOURSES
CALHOUN COLLEGE

COPING AND BELT COURSES
BRICKWORK AND STONEWORK
MAY 18, 2010

DD DETAIL PRECEDENTS
YALE'S EXISTING BUILDINGS

NEW RESIDENTIAL COLLEGES
YALE UNIVERSITY
ROBERT A.M. STERN ARCHITECTS

4.69. Detail precedents of decorative stone elements, design development, May 18, 2010. RAMSA.

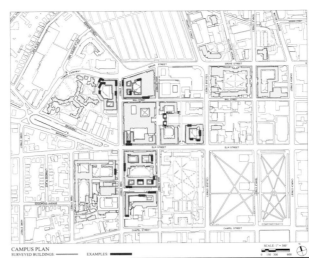

DECORATIVE STONE ELEMENTS

Jon Kelly
- Applied decorative elements
- Detailing projecting from the façade (including buttresses)
- Transition of materials
- Carved elements, etc

CONCLUSIONS

Decorative stone elements help give Yale its unique character. Not only do they aid in the differentiating one building from another, they also announce and separate the courtyard spaces within each complex. The location of decorative stone elements can be seen in four major categories:
- Massing and Structure (Towers, Buttresses, and Crenellation)
- Entry Procession (Passageways and Main Entrances)
- Opening Embellishment (Door and Window Surrounds)
- Facade Treatment (Relief, Descriptive Elements, Patterns)

Economically speaking, it is most logical to place these elements in areas of high pedestrian foot traffic, and indeed the intricate details around passageways and doorways speak to this methodology. Many of Yale's decorative stone elements, however, are located high up or in areas that are generally overlooked. This helps give each building its unique quirkiness, and makes each courtyard a space to be slowly discovered and cherished by its residents.

CAMPUS PLAN
SURVEYED BUILDINGS: ——— EXAMPLES: ———

SCALE: 1" = 300'
0   150   300   600

DD DETAIL PRECEDENTS
YALE'S EXISTING BUILDINGS

DECORATIVE STONE ELEMENTS
MAY 18, 2010

NEW RESIDENTIAL COLLEGES
YALE UNIVERSITY
ROBERT A.M. STERN ARCHITECTS

TOWER (HARKNESS)
BRANFORD COLLEGE

TOWER
HALL OF GRADUATE STUDIES

TOWER DETAIL
STERLING LAW BUILDING

TOWER DETAIL
SAYBROOK COLLEGE

CRENELLATION
BRANFORD COLLEGE

CRENELLATION
CALHOUN COLLEGE

BUTTRESS
CALHOUN COLLEGE

BUTTRESS
HALL OF GRADUATE STUDIES

BUTTRESS
HALL OF GRADUATE STUDIES

BUTTRESS
JONATHAN EDWARDS COLLEGE

BUTTRESS
TRUMBULL COLLEGE

BUTTRESS
STERLING LAW BUILDING

DD DETAIL PRECEDENTS
YALE'S EXISTING BUILDINGS

DECORATIVE STONE ELEMENTS
MAY 18, 2010

NEW RESIDENTIAL COLLEGES
YALE UNIVERSITY
ROBERT A.M. STERN ARCHITECTS

DOOR SURROUND
SAYBROOK COLLEGE

DOOR SURROUND
CALHOUN COLLEGE

BAY WINDOW
TRUMBULL COLLEGE

WINDOW SURROUND
HALL OF GRADUATE STUDIES

WIINDOW SURROUND
JONATHAN EDWARDS COLLEGE

WINDOW SURROUND
STERLING LAW BUILDING

BAY WINDOW AND DOOR SURROUND
CALHOUN COLLEGE

WINDOW SURROUND
HALL OF GRADUATE STUDIES

DD DETAIL PRECEDENTS
YALE'S EXISTING BUILDINGS

DECORATIVE STONE ELEMENTS
MAY 18, 2010

NEW RESIDENTIAL COLLEGES
YALE UNIVERSITY
ROBERT A.M. STERN ARCHITECTS

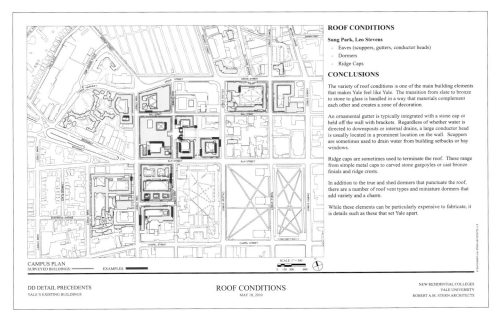

ROOF CONDITIONS

Sung Park, Leo Stevens

- Eaves (scuppers, gutters, conductor heads)
- Dormers
- Ridge Caps

CONCLUSIONS

The variety of roof conditions is one of the main building elements that makes Yale feel like Yale. The transition from slate to bronze to stone to glass is handled in a way that materials complement each other and creates a zone of decoration.

An ornamental gutter is typically integrated with a stone cap or held off the wall with brackets. Regardless of whether water is directed to downspouts or internal drains, a large conductor head is usually located in a prominent location on the wall. Scuppers are sometimes used to drain water from building setbacks or bay windows.

Ridge caps are sometimes used to terminate the roof. These range from simple metal caps to carved stone gargoyles or cast bronze finials and ridge crests.

In addition to the true and shed dormers that punctuate the roof, there are a number of roof vent types and miniature dormers that add variety and a charm.

While these elements can be particularly expensive to fabricate, it is details such as these that set Yale apart.

CAMPUS PLAN
SURVEYED BUILDINGS: ——— EXAMPLES: ———

SCALE: 1" = 300'
0 150 300   600

DD DETAIL PRECEDENTS
YALE'S EXISTING BUILDINGS

ROOF CONDITIONS
MAY 18, 2010

NEW RESIDENTIAL COLLEGES
YALE UNIVERSITY
ROBERT A.M. STERN ARCHITECTS

GUTTER BOX AND OVERFLOW SCUPPER
BERKELEY COLLEGE

GUTTER AT DORMER
BERKELEY COLLEGE

EAVE AT COPPER ROOF
TRUMBULL COLLEGE

GUTTER AND STRAP
BERKELEY COLLEGE

GUTTER BOX
HALL OF GRADUATE STUDIES

GUTTER BOX
BERKELEY COLLEGE

DD DETAIL PRECEDENTS
YALE'S EXISTING BUILDINGS

ROOF CONDITIONS
MAY 18, 2010

NEW RESIDENTIAL COLLEGES
YALE UNIVERSITY
ROBERT A.M. STERN ARCHITECTS

CONDUCTOR HEADS
DAVENPORT COLLEGE

CALHOUN COLLEGE

HALL OF GRADUATE STUDIES

CALHOUN COLLEGE

CALHOUN COLLEGE

CALHOUN COLLEGE

CALHOUN COLLEGE

CALHOUN COLLEGE

YALE DAILY NEWS

DAVENPORT COLLEGE (YALE HERALD)

HALL OF GRADUATE STUDIES

JONATHAN EDWARDS COLLEGE

DD DETAIL PRECEDENTS
YALE'S EXISTING BUILDINGS

ROOF CONDITIONS
MAY 18, 2010

NEW RESIDENTIAL COLLEGES
YALE UNIVERSITY
ROBERT A.M. STERN ARCHITECTS

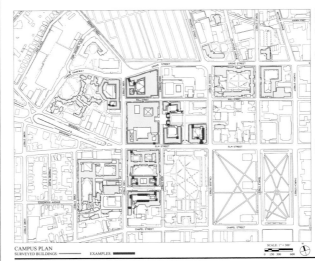

PASSAGEWAYS, GATES & ENTRYWAY DOORS

William West

CONCLUSIONS

- Compared to the current design, the colleges surveyed exhibit a greater variety in depth, width, and height of passageways.
- In passageways, vaulting in both brick and stone is common; however, there are also examples of simple vaults and coffered ceiling that remain harmonious with the Gothic style.
- Within a given courtyard, repetition and alternation of basic entryway door types is common.
- Courtyard and passageway entryway doors ways appear to form distinct sub-types. Passageway doors are more commonly peaked, and have more stone detail in order relate to vaulting.

From the colleges surveyed, the following design challenges for passageways in the new colleges are apparent:

- Negotiating accessibility requirements with the desire for deep door surrounds, especially in passageways
- Finding cost- and space-efficient designs for vaulting
- Providing integrated treatment for modern hardware such as call boxes, sprinkler heads, and card readers

CAMPUS PLAN
SURVEYED BUILDINGS: ▬▬▬ EXAMPLES: ▬▬▬

SCALE: 1" = 300'
0 150 300 600

DD DETAIL PRECEDENTS
YALE'S EXISTING BUILDINGS

PASSAGEWAYS, GATES & ENTRYWAY DOORS
MAY 18, 2010

NEW RESIDENTIAL COLLEGES
YALE UNIVERSITY
ROBERT A.M. STERN ARCHITECTS

ELIOT GATEWAY
BRANFORD COLLEGE

PASSAGE TO GROVE STREET
STIRLING LAW BUILDING

ELM STREET GATE
TRUMBULL COLLEGE

PASSAGE TO CROSS CAMPUS
CALHOUN COLLEGE

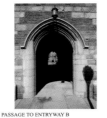
PASSAGE TO ENTRYWAY B
JONATHAN EDWARDS COLLEGE

PIERPONT GATEWAY
BRANFORD COLLEGE

ARCHWAY TO NW COURT
STIRLING LAW BUILDING

ELM STREET GATE
CALHOUN COLLEGE

DD DETAIL PRECEDENTS
YALE'S EXISTING BUILDINGS

PASSAGEWAYS—ARCHES
MAY 18, 2010

NEW RESIDENTIAL COLLEGES
YALE UNIVERSITY
ROBERT A.M. STERN ARCHITECTS

ENTRYWAY I
BERKELEY COLLEGE

ENTRYWAY M
BRANFORD COLLEGE

ENTRYWAY G
CALHOUN COLLEGE

ENTRYWAY A
HALL OF GRADUATE STUDIES

ENTRYWAY B
HALL OF GRADUATE STUDIES

ENTRYWAY C
BRANFORD COLLEGE

ENTRYWAY D
BRANFORD COLLEGE

ENTRYWAY P
BRANFORD COLLEGE

ENTRYWAY E
CALHOUN COLLEGE

ENTRYWAY C
BERKELEY COLLEGE

ENTRYWAY B
JONATHAN EDWARDS COLLEGE

ENTRYWAY G
BERKELEY COLLEGE

DD DETAIL PRECEDENTS
YALE'S EXISTING BUILDINGS

ENTRYWAY DOORS—GENERAL VARIATION
MAY 18, 2010

NEW RESIDENTIAL COLLEGES
YALE UNIVERSITY
ROBERT A.M. STERN ARCHITECTS

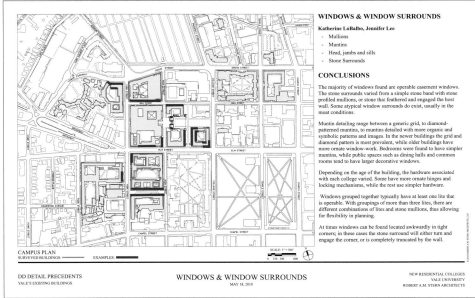

WINDOWS & WINDOW SURROUNDS

Katherine LoBalbo, Jennifer Lee
- Mullions
- Muntins
- Head, jambs and sills
- Stone Surrounds

CONCLUSIONS

The majority of windows found are operable casement windows. The stone surrounds varied from a simple stone band with stone profiled mullions, or stone that feathered and engaged the host wall. Some atypical window surrounds do exist, usually in the moat conditions.

Muntin detailing range between a generic grid, to diamond-patterned muntins, to muntins detailed with more organic and symbolic patterns and images. In the newer buildings the grid and diamond pattern is most prevalent, while older buildings have more ornate window-work. Bedrooms were found to have simpler muntins, while public spaces such as dining halls and common rooms tend to have larger decorative windows.

Depending on the age of the building, the hardware associated with each college varied. Some have more ornate hinges and locking mechanisms, while the rest use simpler hardware.

Windows grouped together typically have at least one lite that is operable. With groupings of more than three lites, there are different combinations of lites and stone mullions, thus allowing for flexibility in planning.

At times windows can be found located awkwardly in tight corners; in these cases the stone surround will either turn and engage the corner, or is completely truncated by the wall.

CAMPUS PLAN
SURVEYED BUILDINGS: EXAMPLES:

SCALE: 1" = 300'
0 150 300 600

DD DETAIL PRECEDENTS
YALE'S EXISTING BUILDINGS

WINDOWS & WINDOW SURROUNDS
MAY 18, 2010

NEW RESIDENTIAL COLLEGES
YALE UNIVERSITY
ROBERT A.M. STERN ARCHITECTS

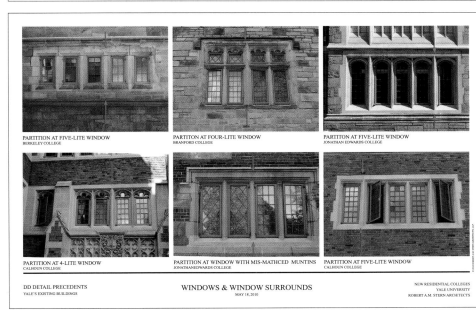

PARTITION AT FIVE-LITE WINDOW
BERKELEY COLLEGE

PARTITON AT FOUR-LITE WINDOW
BRANFORD COLLEGE

PARTITON AT FIVE-LITE WINDOW
JONATHAN EDWARDS COLLEGE

PARTITION AT 4-LITE WINDOW
CALHOUN COLLEGE

PARTITION AT WINDOW WITH MIS-MATHCED MUNTINS
JONATHANEDWARDS COLLEGE

PARTITION AT FIVE-LITE WINDOW
CALHOUN COLLEGE

DD DETAIL PRECEDENTS
YALE'S EXISTING BUILDINGS

WINDOWS & WINDOW SURROUNDS
MAY 18, 2010

NEW RESIDENTIAL COLLEGES
YALE UNIVERSITY
ROBERT A.M. STERN ARCHITECTS

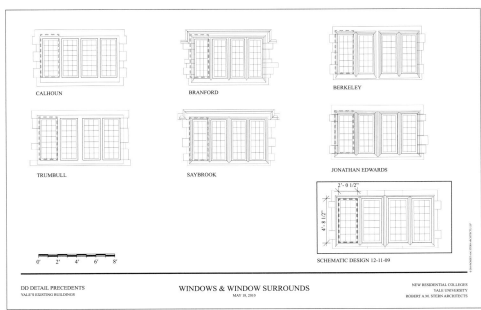

CALHOUN

BRANFORD

BERKELEY

TRUMBULL

SAYBROOK

JONATHAN EDWARDS

2'- 0 1/2"

4'- 8 1/2"

SCHEMATIC DESIGN 12-11-09

0' 2' 4' 6' 8'

DD DETAIL PRECEDENTS
YALE'S EXISTING BUILDINGS

WINDOWS & WINDOW SURROUNDS
MAY 18, 2010

NEW RESIDENTIAL COLLEGES
YALE UNIVERSITY
ROBERT A.M. STERN ARCHITECTS

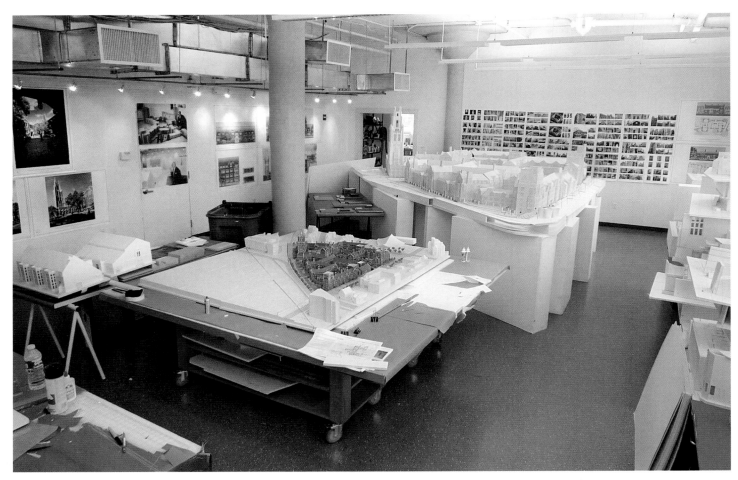

4.73. **"War room" in RAMSA's office. Left to right: Benjamin Franklin College dining hall model, Pauli Murray College dining hall model, schematic design model, design development model. Photograph October 2, 2011.** RAMSA.

4.74. **Schematic design model, 1/16" = 1'-0" scale. Photograph April 7, 2010.** RAMSA.

4.75. **Design development model, 1/4" = 1'-0" scale model, with Anya Grant. Photograph September 15, 2010.** RAMSA.

4.76. **Robert A.M. Stern peering through a "Bob hole" in the design development model. Photograph July 20, 2010.** RAMSA.

4.77. **Robert A.M. Stern peering through a "Bob hole" in the design development model. Left to right: Asdren Matashi, Kurt Glauber, Jonathan Kelly, Melissa DelVecchio, Tanya Lee, Jennifer Bailey, Leo Stevens. Photograph September 14, 2010.** RAMSA.

4.78. **Edward P. Bass peering through a "Bob hole" in the design development model with Bass Tower in background. Photograph September 22, 2011.** RAMSA.

4.79. **Pauli Murray
College dining hall,
north elevation
sketches, design devel-
opment, 2010.** RAMSA.

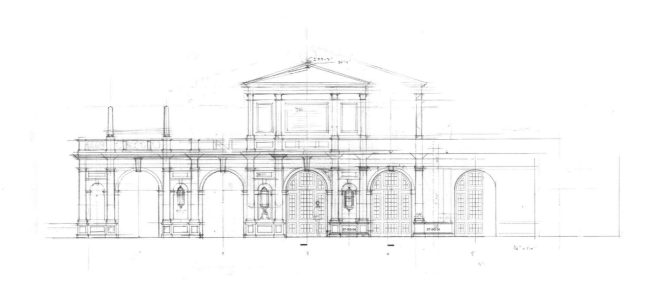

4.80. **Entry into Benjamin Franklin College's triangular courtyard from Farmington Canal Heritage Greenway**, sketch, design development, 2010. RAMSA.

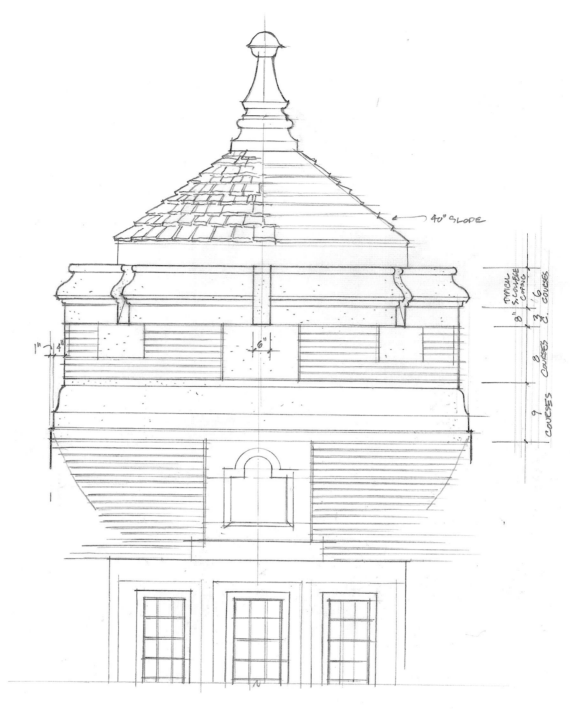

40° SLOPE

TYPICAL S. COURSE COPING

8" 3' 6
8" COURSES 2 COURSES
8" COURSES

9 COURSES

1" 4"

6"

STONE PROFILES
BLG 18 · TURRET
½"= 1'-0"   126.12

Design: From the Outside In

4.82. **Entry off of Benjamin Franklin College Nyburg Baker Court, sketch, construction documents, 2012.** RAMSA.

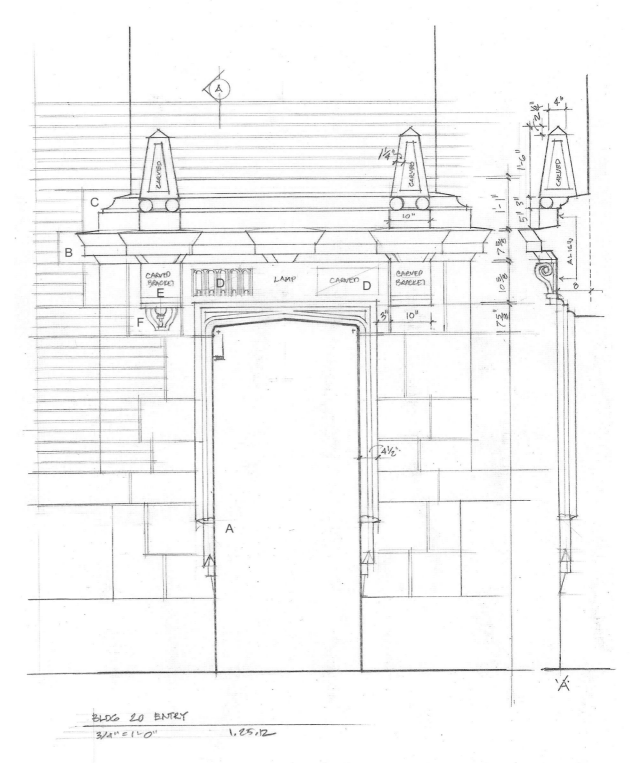

BLDG 20 ENTRY
3/4" = 1'-0"   1.25.12

4.83. Eero Saarinen with model of Morse and Stiles Colleges. Photograph 1959.
Yale University Library, Manuscripts and Archives. Eero Saarinen collection, 1880–2004 (inclusive). Image no. 295.

4.84. Robert A.M. Stern channeling Eero Saarinen with model of Benjamin Franklin and Pauli Murray Colleges. Photograph September 14, 2010. RAMSA.

typically concentrated at the base, corners, and moat walls. The 123 specified sizes of ashlar and quoins all correspond to the modular proportions of the standard-sized face brick, which is set in a Flemish garden bond. To subtly distinguish one college from the other, Benjamin Franklin College is endowed with a greater quantity of decorative brickwork, while Pauli Murray in turn has more decorative stonework.

Entryway doors, most accessed from the courtyards, are of solid oak with iron strapping set within varying stone archways and jambs. Although their depth was limited by accessibility requirements that Rogers did not have to consider, they nonetheless evoke Gothic precedents. Metal-and-glass lighting fixtures inspired by those from the Rogers era, some of which were procured from the same suppliers used by Rogers, also help define the individual character of each courtyard and entryway.

In the earlier colleges, Rogers frequently grouped two or more windows together in a row to bring more daylight inside. We studied the proportions of the individual windows and groups, the stone surrounds, the partitions between windows, and the patterns of lead came between panes, concluding that window design epitomized the balance of repetition and variation characteristic of Gothic Yale.

We aimed to achieve a similar balance in the facades of Benjamin Franklin and Pauli Murray Colleges, which contain 4,282 steel-framed windows consisting of 129 different types, three-quarters of which are operable casements.

Design: From the Outside In

Repeating window types, including one rectangular unit that accounts for 58 percent of all the windows, appear in varying rhythms of one, two, three, or four adjacent units, wrapping around projecting bays or set within flat walls, and interspersed with many other types including narrower, diagonally camed windows. Using Digital Project to group variable elements into *families* or types, we created a design variation kit containing numerous component options, from which the designer working with each individual facade elevation would select coordinated head, sill, and jamb elements.

Our analysis of the roof designs of the Rogers-era Gothic colleges focused on the vertical transition from graduated standard slate roofing, to lead-coated copper gutters (in our buildings, these are reinterpreted in zinc) and to other ornamental metalwork, including profiled or flush stone coping and quoining along the upper part of the facade — all characterized by variation within a consistent architectural language. The gabled roofscapes were enlivened by details, such as ridge caps and scuppers, several types of dormers, and sculpturally articulated chimneys that are engaged with the elevation face, recessed along the sloping roof, or straddling the ridgeline.

Punctuating the roofscape of Benjamin Franklin and Pauli Murray Colleges, forty-five chimneys with nineteen different formal variations impart a distinctive look and feel to various buildings and courtyards. Thirty-three conceal the air-handling vents and louvers that typically litter the roofs of modern buildings, six serve fireplace hearths, and another six are purely decorative. The chimneys' aesthetic aspect was important because the roofscape is the primary view from many of the upper-level rooms, something called to our attention by architect Thomas H. Beeby (1941– ; MArch 1965), a longstanding member of the university's buildings and grounds committee and dean of the Yale School of Architecture, 1985–92. A strong advocate for our design, Beeby reviewed our progress at each milestone and took a particular interest in policing our roofscape.

For the roofing itself, we specified a multihued palette of natural-cleft slates comprising four variants of blue-green and plum-purple, some of which are "unfading" and others of which will weather over time to a neutral tone, complementing the similarly multihued face brick and the pale facade masonry. On the lower buildings, where the roof is more visible from the ground, the slates are graduated, increasing substantially from 1/4 inch thick and 12 inches long at the ridge to 1 inch thick and 24 inches long at the eaves, giving a greater sense of texture and scale. But on buildings at least three stories high, to control cost, we specified the consistent use of 3/8-inch-thick slates. These slates also clad the vertical faces of the "continuous dormer" areas between the gabled dormers, which animate the roof profile and are accented with limestone and granite quoining near their peaks. The transition from roof to facade is further mediated by zinc-coated drip edges, zinc gutters and downspouts, and cast-stone coping.

The three towers incorporate some of the most important design features of the colleges. Their designs were developed over many iterations throughout the course of a year or so and are not modeled on specific precedents, although we took inspiration from Rogers's towers at Yale and work elsewhere including his Colgate Rochester Crozer Divinity School. We also looked farther afield to buildings at Oxford and Cambridge, church towers by Nicholas Hawksmoor, and buildings by Sir Edwin Lutyens and Bertram G. Goodhue, among others. By far the tallest of the three is Edward P. Bass Tower, which at 192 feet is similar in height to the towers of Rogers's Hall of Graduate Studies and Pope's Payne Whitney Gymnasium, a result of Yale selecting the middle of three height options that we proposed.

Bass Tower steps back significantly as it rises from the lower half, containing classroom and library spaces, to the future belfry and the ornamental crown accentuated with corner finials, a profile that is very English in its quirkiness. Its footprint and lower shaft contours were determined in part by the need to include two stairs and an elevator serving the usable levels. By contrast, Harkness Tower — containing only the carillon rooms accessible via a narrow, winding stair above the memorial chapel at its base — tapers gradually, almost imperceptibly, toward its octagonal crown. On the other hand, the Hall of Graduate Studies Tower, filled with usable spaces, rises in a nearly undiminished shaft to its pyramidal crown. The arched openings and corner finials of Bass Tower bear a certain resemblance to those of the Hawksmoor-designed tower of St. Michael, Cornhill — a medieval parish church in the City of London that was rebuilt in the late seventeenth and early eighteenth centries — but the deeply setback crown of our tower more aptly recalls Hawksmoor's towers of the London churches of St. Anne's Limehouse, St. George in the East, and Christ Church Spitalfields.

4.85. **Robert A.M. Stern with tower study models. Photograph June 21, 2010.** RAMSA.

4.86. **Tower study models. Photograph October 2, 2011.** RAMSA.

4.87. Tower height comparisons, schematic design, 2010. Bass Tower proposed heights compared to other Yale towers' heights above sea level. RAMSA.

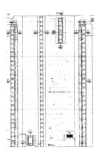

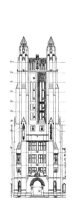

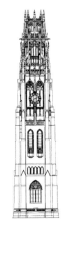

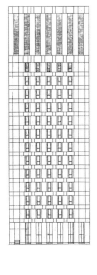

Option 1

Option 2

Option 3

Morse College 134 Ft. Elev. +46'	Pauli Murray College Proposed Tower 134 Ft. Elev. +29'	Pierson College 136 Ft. Elev. +45'	Sheffield-Sterling-Strathcona Hall 166 Ft. (143 Ft.) Elev. +34'	Hall of Graduate Studies 189 Ft. Elev. +45'	Pauli Murray College Proposed Tower 190 Ft. Elev. +29'	Branford College Harkness Tower 216 Ft. Elev. +46'	Pauli Murray College Propsed Tower 216 Ft. Elev. +29'	Kline Biology Tower 245 Ft. Elev. +82'

4.88. Tower height comparisons, schematic design, 2010. South Tower and East Tower heights compared to other Yale towers above ground level. RAMSA.

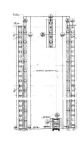
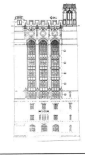

Branford College 74 Ft.	Grace Murray Hopper College 74 Ft.	Silliman College 88 Ft.	Benjamin Franklin College Proposed South Tower 90 Ft.	Pauli Murray College Proposed East Tower 90 Ft.	Silliman College 98 Ft.	Saybrook College 102 Ft.	Ezra Stiles College 105 Ft.	Bingham Tower 128 Ft. (112 Ft.)	Saybrook College 128 Ft.

4.89. **St. Michael, Cornhill (1672), London. Tower designed by Nicholas Hawksmoor (1715–22). Photograph Robert A.M. Stern, c. 1980s.** RAMSA.

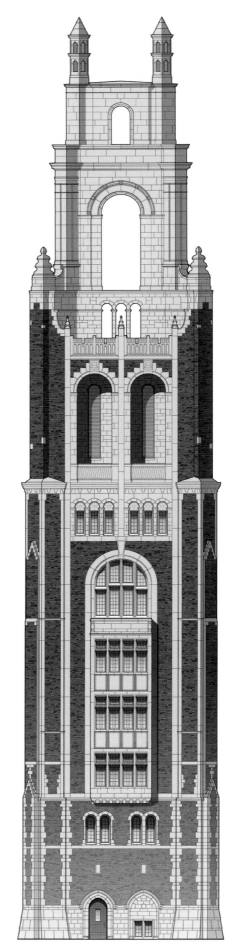

4.90. **Bass Tower elevation, design development, 2011.** RAMSA.

The other two towers, containing mostly student rooms, are positioned along Prospect Street, where the new colleges provide the long-desired connection between the central campus to the south and Science Hill to the north. The east tower of Pauli Murray College, 114 feet tall at the crenellated top of its octagonal corner turret, stands near the intersection of Prospect Street and Prospect Walk, serving as a beacon when seen from Science Hill. More visible to those traveling north on Prospect Street and punctuating its corner at Canal Street, the most acute angle of the triangular site, is the 91-foot-tall south tower of Benjamin Franklin College, with its chamfered corner, varied window types, and concentration of quoining and ornament near its crenellated crown.

The south tower's deliberately bold, light-and-dark checkerboard pattern on its upper facades recalls similar pattern work on the Hall of Graduate Studies, where it features prominently in the courtyard and on the tower. This kind of patterning can also be found in smaller increments on the Sterling Law Building and the southern end of Jonathan Edwards College, facing the Yale University Art Gallery. Rogers likely adapted such patterns from English Gothic "flushwork" masonry, in which alternating patterns of brick and stone or two kinds of stone are organized into a pattern, often a checkerboard, as realized in spectacular fashion on: the Town Hall and adjoining Trinity Guildhall in Kings Lynn, East Anglia; the Norwich Guildhall in Norwich, East Anglia; and William Butterfield's Keble College at the University of Oxford.

4.91. **Hall of Graduate Studies (James Gamble Rogers, 1930–32), Yale University. Photograph Robert A.M. Stern, May 1998.** RAMSA.

4.92. **Keble College Chapel (William Butterfield, 1873–76), University of Oxford. Photograph Graham S. Wyatt, June 1, 2009.** RAMSA.

Ribbed vaulting in both brick and stone is common in the courtyard passageways of the existing colleges, and even the relatively simple brick vaults remain harmonious with the Gothic style. In designing Benjamin Franklin and Pauli Murray Colleges' sixteen uniquely arched passageways, which connect the courtyards to each other and the surrounding streets, we faced the challenge of creating cost- and space-efficient vaults and providing integrated treatment for modern hardware such as call boxes, sprinkler heads, and electronic card readers. Each passageway, measuring about 36 feet long, has a slightly different vault design, based on a round or pointed arch profile, and is articulated into three or more repeating bays, creating moments of spatial compression between the expansive serenity of the courts. The most elaborately detailed passageways, located at the Prospect Street entrances, are also the largest at 8-1/2 feet wide and 9-1/2 feet high at the apex of the vault, spacious enough to accommodate service vehicles. The simpler and less prominently located passageways, such as those between courts or opening to the Farmington Canal Heritage Greenway, are narrower and lower by as much as a foot.

The entrance to each passage is defined by a limestone archway and one or more carved limestone plaques above. Inside, the passageway walls are lined with varying courses of brick, with Flemish garden bond interspersed in some cases with vertical, herringbone, and even circular patterns. The stone-ribbed ceilings are defined by brick-clad, precast concrete vaults, each equipped with one of a series of custom lighting fixtures. At the main entrance passageway to Pauli Murray College, the most ornate of all, stone piers seem to carry the load of the vault down to the floor, though in fact, all the vaults are suspended from the structural concrete slab above. This passageway initiates an east–west enfilade of highly detailed, axially aligned passageways leading to the main quadrangle of Pauli Murray College. By contrast, the passageways of Benjamin Franklin College do not align, instead choreographing a more casually meandering progression through space.

Before commencing design work on the nine individually designed and patterned wrought iron entryway gates needed for the two colleges, we surveyed Yale's existing exterior gates, creating a photodocumented set of references that included location plans to help us better understand the scope and breadth of ironwork on campus. Of particular interest was the work of Samuel Yellin, the Philadelphia-based artisan who forged many of Yale's exquisite metal gates and screens of the early twentieth century, and also the work of master craftsmen, such as Fritz Kuhn.

We developed a hierarchy of four tiers corresponding to the relative prominence of each gate's location, with each tier signifying an intended level of complexity and detailing. The first and second tiers included the two largest and most complex gates, which were to be completely hand forged with mechanical joints, placed at the main entrance of each college on Prospect Street. The other tiers included smaller gates to be located along Prospect Walk and the Farmington Canal Heritage Greenway, designed with simpler patterns, amenable to more expedient fabrication techniques such as welded connections, incorporating wood elements as in other gates on the Yale campus. Each college also has a designated "Sabbath entry" gate, made of a wood frame with wrought-iron ornament, that can be operated with a manual key.

The gate designs were developed through a set of hand drawings by RAMSA designers and Zoltan Kovacs, a Hungarian-trained metallurgist-artist, who, at that time, worked for Les Métalliers Champenois, a New Jersey-based

4.93. Memorial Quadrangle entryway gate at Harkness Tower on High Street, wrought iron, Samuel Yellin. *Samuel Yellin Metalwork at Yale,* catalogue of an exhibition of the same name at the Yale University School of Architecture, 1990.

4.94. Memorial Quadrangle detail of entryway gate at Harkness Tower on High Street, wrought iron, Samuel Yellin. *Samuel Yellin Metalwork at Yale,* catalogue of an exhibition of the same name at the Yale University School of Architecture, 1990.

4.95. Trumbull College entryway gate at the Head of College House on Rose Walk, monel metal, Samuel Yellin. *Samuel Yellin Metalwork at Yale,* catalogue of an exhibition of the same name at the Yale University School of Architecture, 1990.

4.96. Trumbull College detail of entryway gate at the Head of College House on Rose Walk, monel metal, Samuel Yellin. Photograph November 17, 2014. RAMSA.

4.97. Yale University Art Gallery gate in Sculpture Hall, wrought iron, Samuel Yellin. *Samuel Yellin Metalwork at Yale,* catalogue of an exhibition of the same name at the Yale University School of Architecture, 1990.

4.98. Yale University Art Gallery, detail of gate in Sculpture Hall, wrought iron, Samuel Yellin. Photograph July 20, 2017. RAMSA.

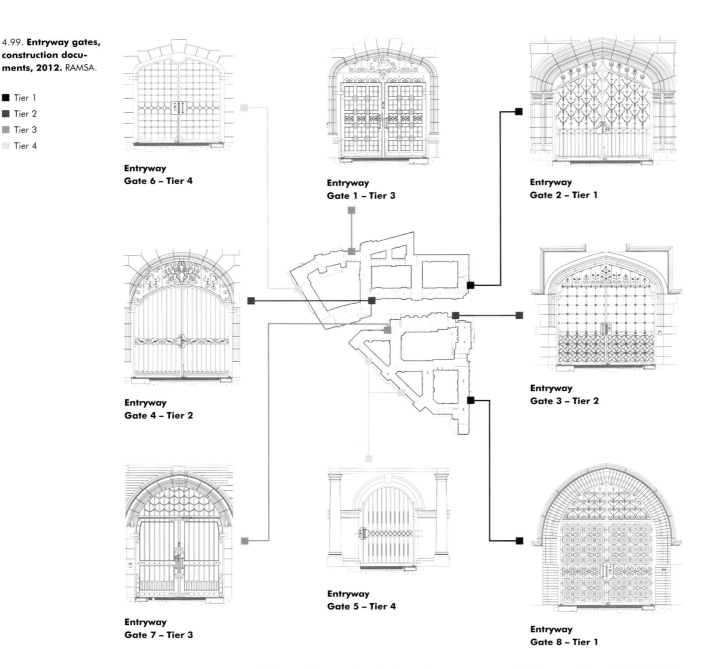

4.99. Entryway gates, construction documents, 2012. RAMSA.

■ Tier 1
■ Tier 2
■ Tier 3
■ Tier 4

**Entryway
Gate 6 – Tier 4**

**Entryway
Gate 1 – Tier 3**

**Entryway
Gate 2 – Tier 1**

**Entryway
Gate 4 – Tier 2**

**Entryway
Gate 3 – Tier 2**

**Entryway
Gate 7 – Tier 3**

**Entryway
Gate 5 – Tier 4**

**Entryway
Gate 8 – Tier 1**

architectural metalwork shop, but soon opened his own shop, COVAX. State and local flora and fauna motifs and references to Yale adorn the gates — including white-oak leaves (the Connecticut state tree), elm leaves (a reference to New Haven's nickname as the Elm City), mountain laurel blossoms (the Connecticut state flower), and the American robin (the Connecticut state bird). A sperm whale (the Connecticut state mammal) adorns the Pauli Murray College Sachem Street Gate across from Saarinen's Ingalls Rink, offering a playful reference to the rink's moniker as "the whale."

In keeping with Yale's tradition of using architecture and imagery to celebrate the life of the college and the people associated with it, Benjamin Franklin and Pauli Murray Colleges are enriched by ornament and decoration — 436 individual pieces, to be exact, from Gothic tracery to witty references to Yale, New Haven, and the site. *Ornament* denotes the stone or cast-stone pieces that articulate or embellish architectural features, such as windows and doors, while *decoration* here refers to carved stone plaques and sculptural reliefs designed for purposes of signification and commemoration.

4.100. **Pauli Murray College entryway gate on Prospect Street, construction documents, 2012.** RAMSA

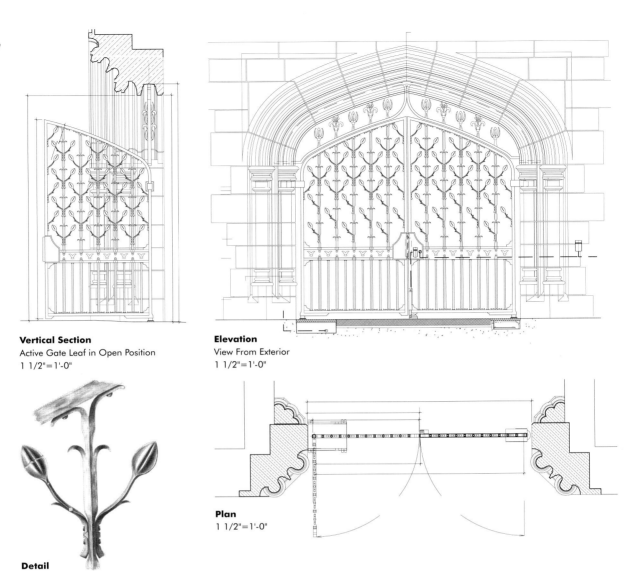

Vertical Section
Active Gate Leaf in Open Position
1 1/2"=1'-0"

Elevation
View From Exterior
1 1/2"=1'-0"

Plan
1 1/2"=1'-0"

Detail

4.101. **Entryway gate detail sketches, construction documents, 2012.** RAMSA.

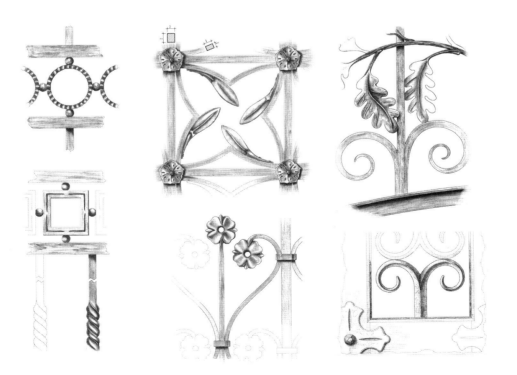

175

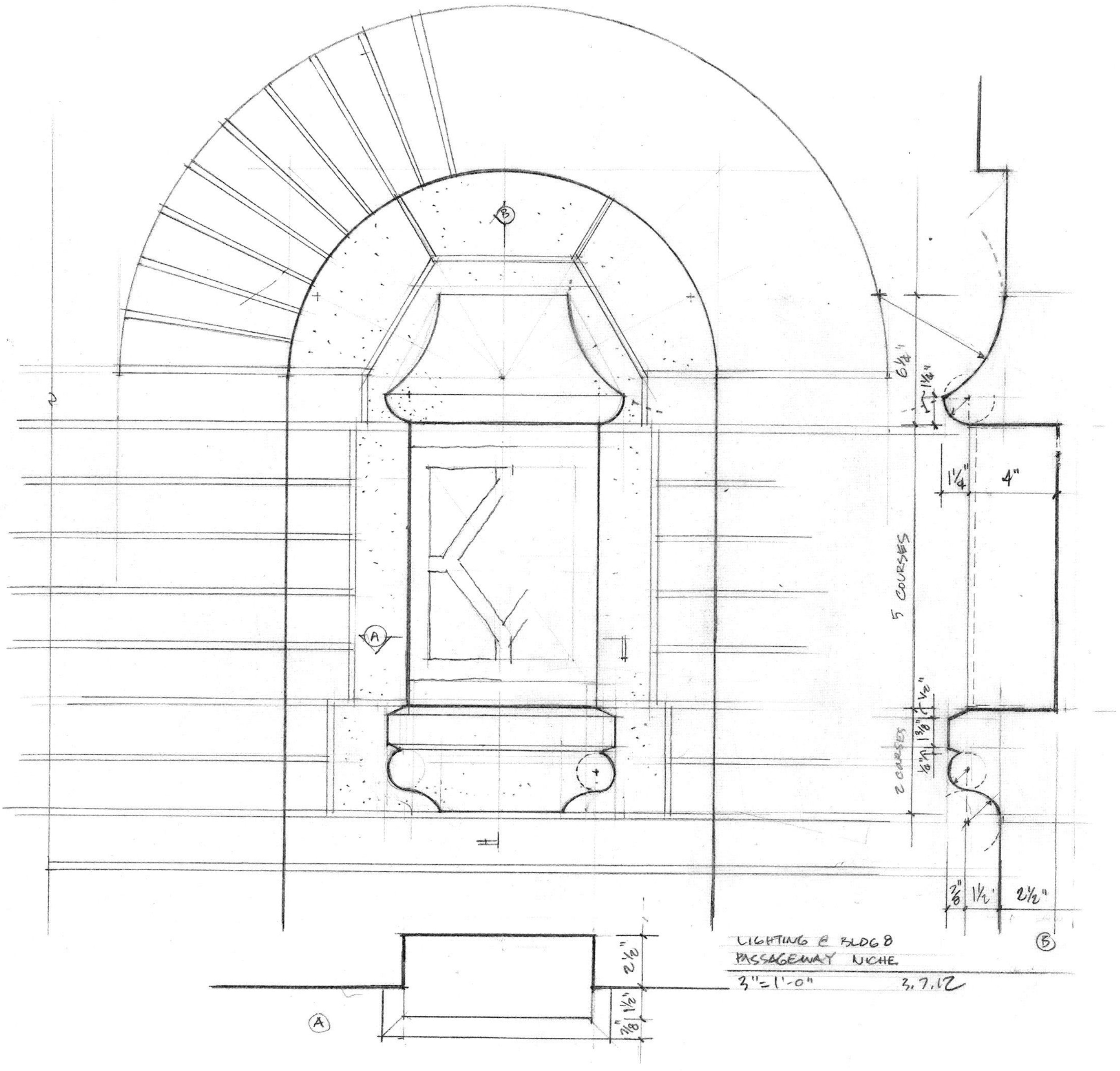
LIGHTING @ BLDG 8
PASSAGEWAY NICHE
3"=1'-0"
3.7.12
5 COURSES
2 COURSES
1¼"
4"
2½"
1½"

4.102. **Passageway niche in Pauli Murray College, elevation, plan, and section study, construction documents, 2012.** RAMSA.

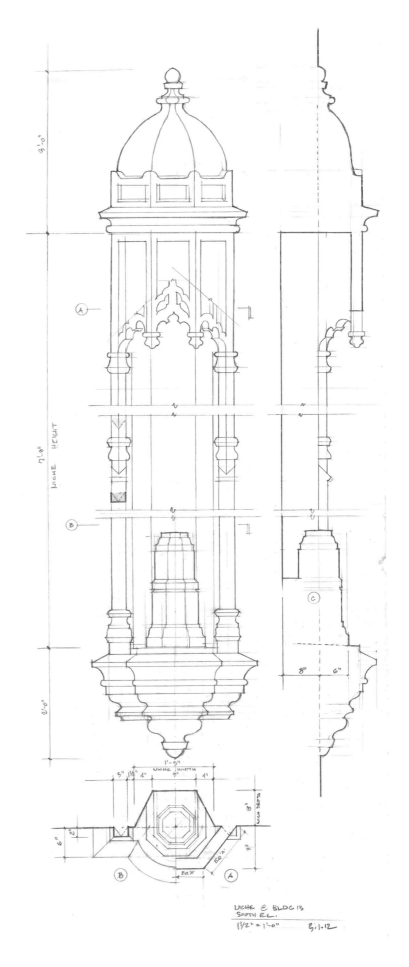

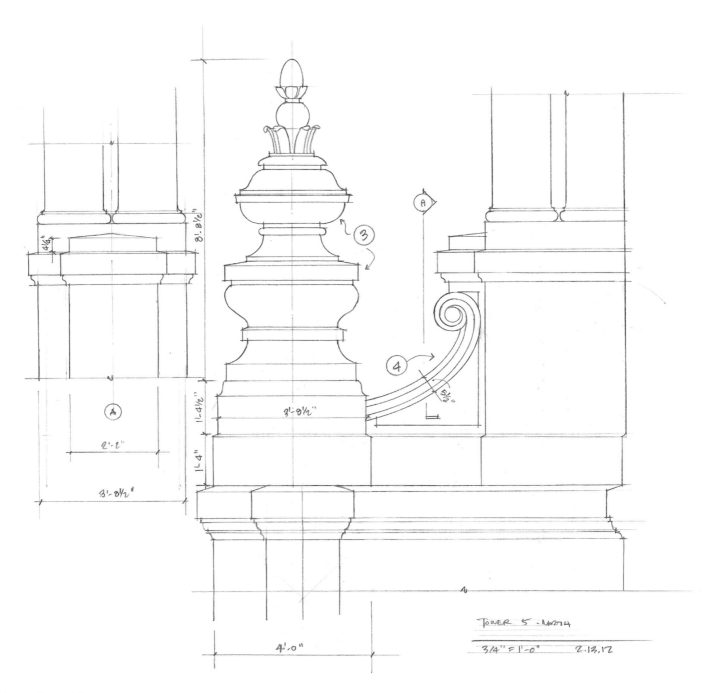

4.104. **Bass Tower finial elevation and section study, construction documents, 2012.** RAMSA.

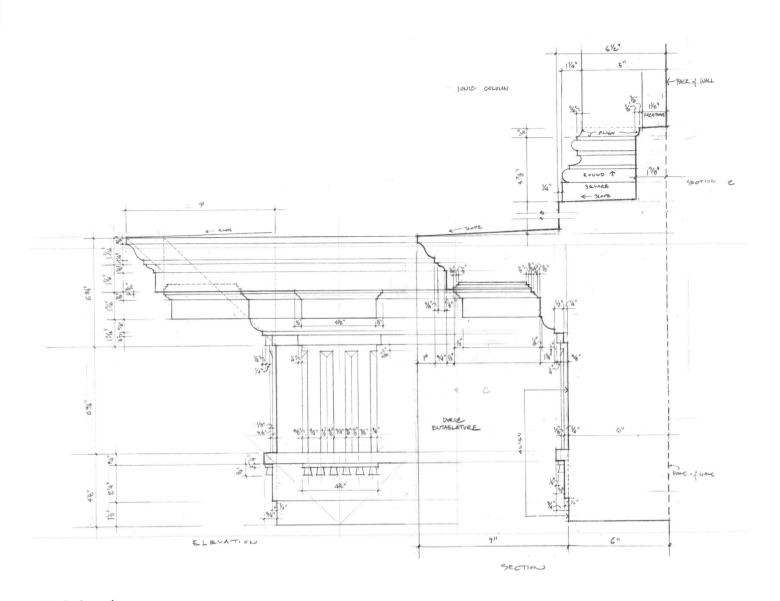

4.105. **Doric entablature elevation and section study, construction documents, 2012.** RAMSA.

4.106. **Study of typical parapet coping in Pauli Murray College, construction documents, 2012.** RAMSA.

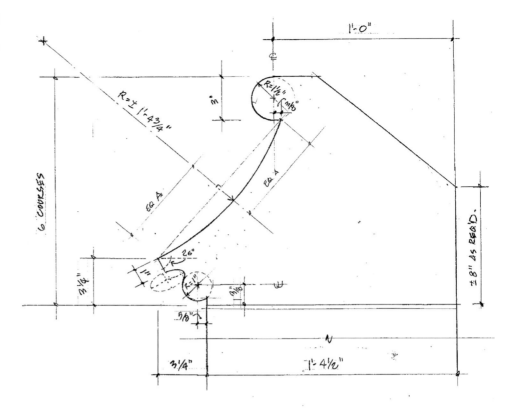

TYPICAL PARAPET COPING TYPE 1A - NORTH COLLEGE
3" = 1'-0'

4.107. **Study of typical parapet coping in Benjamin Franklin College, construction documents, 2012.** RAMSA.

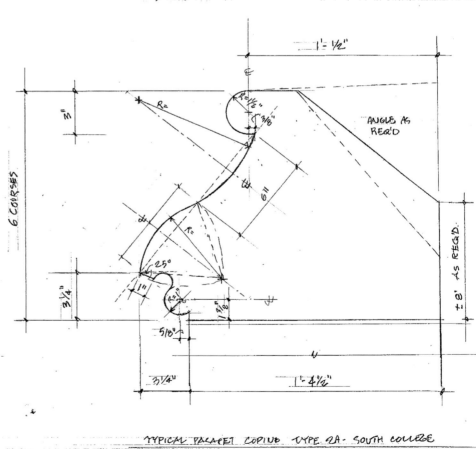

TYPICAL PARAPET COPING TYPE 2A - SOUTH COLLEGE
3" = 1'-0"

Design: From the Outside In

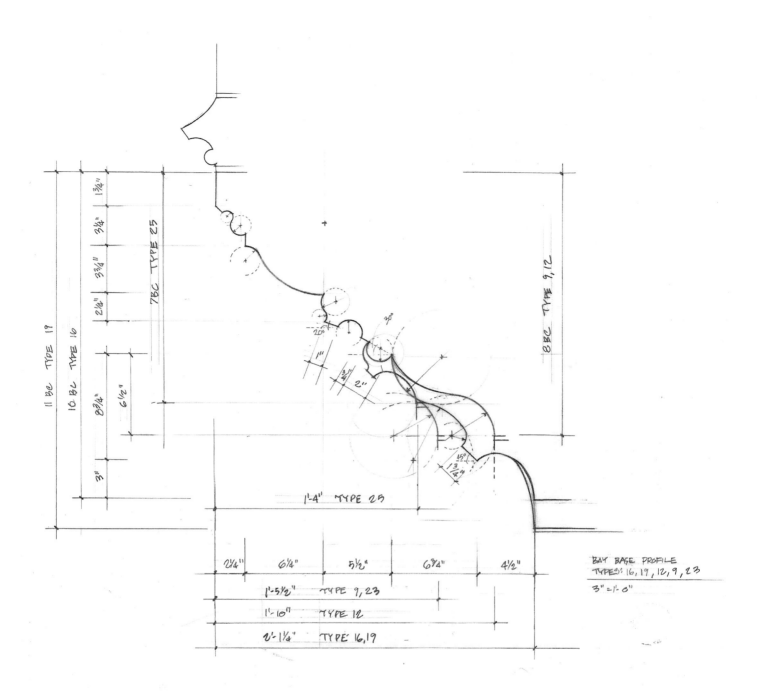

4.108. **Bay base profile study, construction documents, 2012.** RAMSA.

4.109. **Various ornament designs developed in 2013–14.** RAMSA.

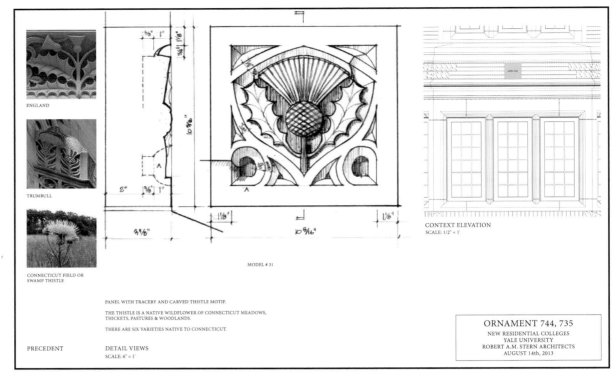

ENGLAND

TRUMBULL

CONNECTICUT FIELD OR SWAMP THISTLE

MODEL # 31

PANEL WITH TRACERY AND CARVED THISTLE MOTIF.

THE THISTLE IS A NATIVE WILDFLOWER OF CONNECTICUT MEADOWS, THICKETS, PASTURES & WOODLANDS.

THERE ARE SIX VARIETIES NATIVE TO CONNECTICUT.

PRECEDENT

DETAIL VIEWS
SCALE: 6" = 1'

CONTEXT ELEVATION
SCALE: 1/2" = 1'

ORNAMENT 744, 735
NEW RESIDENTIAL COLLEGES
YALE UNIVERSITY
ROBERT A.M. STERN ARCHITECTS
AUGUST 14th, 2013

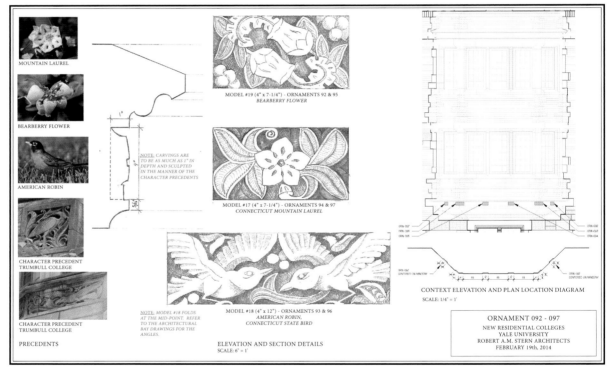

MOUNTAIN LAUREL

BEARBERRY FLOWER

AMERICAN ROBIN

CHARACTER PRECEDENT
TRUMBULL COLLEGE

CHARACTER PRECEDENT
TRUMBULL COLLEGE

PRECEDENTS

NOTE: CARVINGS ARE TO BE AS MUCH AS 1" IN DEPTH AND SCULPTED IN THE MANNER OF THE CHARACTER PRECEDENTS

MODEL #19 (4" x 7-1/4") - ORNAMENTS 92 & 95
BEARBERRY FLOWER

MODEL #17 (4" x 7-1/4") - ORNAMENTS 94 & 97
CONNECTICUT MOUNTAIN LAUREL

NOTE: MODEL #18 FOLDS AT THE MID-POINT. REFER TO THE ARCHITECTURAL BAY DRAWINGS FOR THE ANGLES.

MODEL #18 (4" x 12") - ORNAMENTS 93 & 96
AMERICAN ROBIN,
CONNECTICUT STATE BIRD

ELEVATION AND SECTION DETAILS
SCALE: 6" = 1'

CONTEXT ELEVATION AND PLAN LOCATION DIAGRAM
SCALE: 1/4" = 1'

ORNAMENT 092 - 097
NEW RESIDENTIAL COLLEGES
YALE UNIVERSITY
ROBERT A.M. STERN ARCHITECTS
FEBRUARY 19th, 2014

Design: From the Outside In

HALL OF GRADUATE STUDIES

HALL OF GRADUATE STUDIES

HALL OF GRADUATE STUDIES

PRECEDENTS

MODEL #5
ORNAMENTS 087, 161, 167, 172

NOTE: DEPTH OF CARVING
IS TO BE 1" MAXIMUM.

NOTE: ORNAMENTS 087,
090, 170, 172 ARE ROTATED
180° FROM ORIENTATION
DISPLAYED ON MODEL
DETAIL ELEVATIONS

MODEL #4
ORNAMENTS 084, 090, 163, 170

MODEL #4, #5 - ELEVATIONS
SCALE: 6" = 1'-0"

EAST FACING ELEVATION

SOUTH FACING ELEVATION

CONTEXT ELEVATIONS & LOCATION DIAGRAM
SCALE: 1/8" = 1'-0"

ORNAMENT
84, 87, 90, 161, 163, 167, 170, 172
NEW RESIDENTIAL COLLEGES
YALE UNIVERSITY
ROBERT A.M. STERN ARCHITECTS
MARCH 14th, 2014

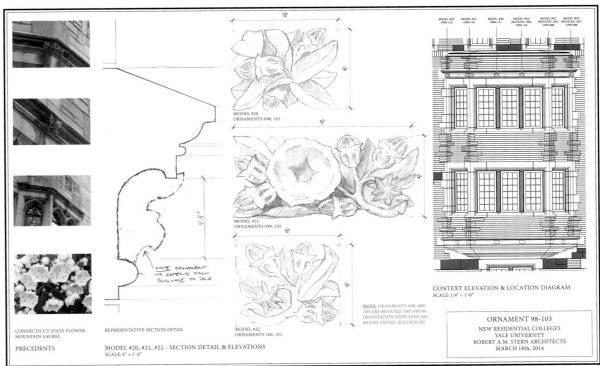

CONNECTICUT STATE FLOWER
MOUNTAIN LAUREL

PRECEDENTS

REPRESENTATIVE SECTION DETAIL

NOTE: ORNAMENT
TO EXTEND FROM
BULLNOSE TO DRIP

MODEL #20
ORNAMENTS 098, 103

MODEL #21
ORNAMENTS 099, 102

MODEL #22
ORNAMENTS 100, 101

NOTE: ORNAMENTS 098, 099,
100 ARE ROTATED 180° FROM
ORIENTATION DISPLAYED ON
MODEL DETAIL ELEVATIONS

MODEL #20, #21, #22 - SECTION DETAIL & ELEVATIONS
SCALE: 6" = 1'-0"

CONTEXT ELEVATION & LOCATION DIAGRAM
SCALE: 1/4" = 1'-0"

ORNAMENT 98-103
NEW RESIDENTIAL COLLEGES
YALE UNIVERSITY
ROBERT A.M. STERN ARCHITECTS
MARCH 18th, 2014

183

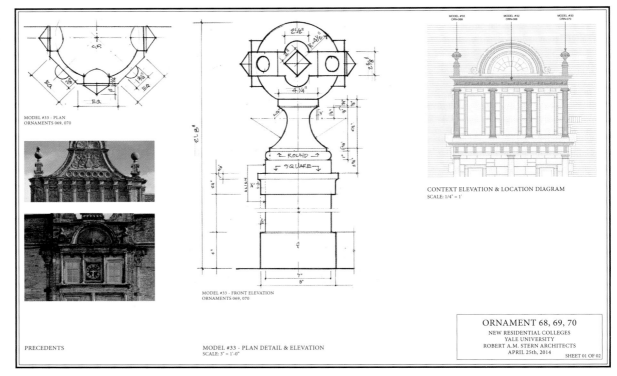

PRECEDENTS

MODEL #33 - PLAN
ORNAMENTS 069, 070

MODEL #33 - FRONT ELEVATION
ORNAMENTS 069, 070

MODEL #33 - PLAN DETAIL & ELEVATION
SCALE: 3" = 1'-0"

CONTEXT ELEVATION & LOCATION DIAGRAM
SCALE: 1/4" = 1'

ORNAMENT 68, 69, 70
NEW RESIDENTIAL COLLEGES
YALE UNIVERSITY
ROBERT A.M. STERN ARCHITECTS
APRIL 25th, 2014
SHEET 01 OF 02

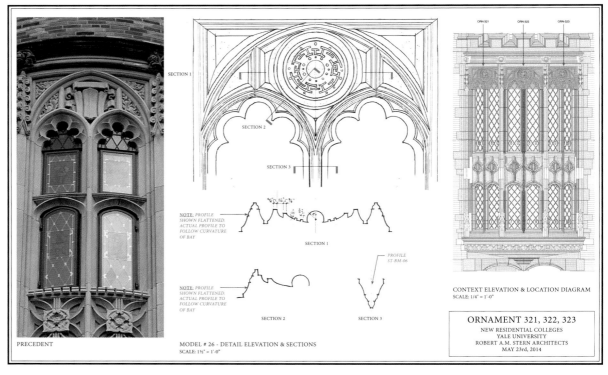

PRECEDENT

SECTION 1

SECTION 2

SECTION 3

NOTE: PROFILE SHOWN FLATTENED. ACTUAL PROFILE TO FOLLOW CURVATURE OF BAY

SECTION 1

NOTE: PROFILE SHOWN FLATTENED. ACTUAL PROFILE TO FOLLOW CURVATURE OF BAY

PROFILE ST-RM-06

SECTION 2

SECTION 3

MODEL # 26 - DETAIL ELEVATION & SECTIONS
SCALE: 1½" = 1'-0"

CONTEXT ELEVATION & LOCATION DIAGRAM
SCALE: 1/4" = 1'-0"

ORNAMENT 321, 322, 323
NEW RESIDENTIAL COLLEGES
YALE UNIVERSITY
ROBERT A.M. STERN ARCHITECTS
MAY 23rd, 2014

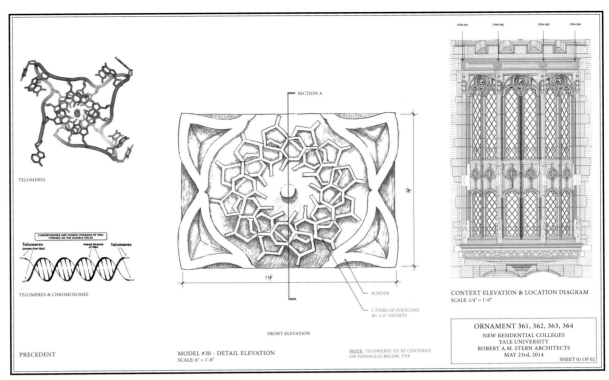

TELOMERES

CHROMOSOMES ARE PAIRED STRANDS OF DNA
FORMED AS THE DOUBLE HELIX

Telomeres
(protective tips)   Paired Strands   Telomeres
of DNA

TELOMERES & CHROMOSOMES

PRECEDENT

SECTION A

FRONT ELEVATION

MODEL #30 - DETAIL ELEVATION
SCALE: 6" = 1'-0"

BORDER

3 TIERS OF POLYGONS
W/ 1/4" OFFSETS

NOTE: TELOMERES TO BE CENTERED
ON PINNACLES BELOW, TYP.

CONTEXT ELEVATION & LOCATION DIAGRAM
SCALE: 1/4" = 1'-0"

ORNAMENT 361, 362, 363, 364
NEW RESIDENTIAL COLLEGES
YALE UNIVERSITY
ROBERT A.M. STERN ARCHITECTS
MAY 23rd, 2014
SHEET 01 OF 02

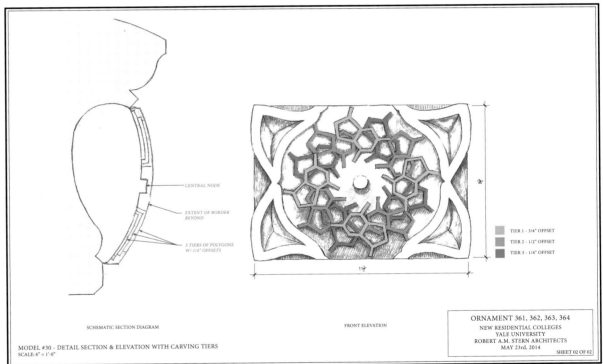

CENTRAL NODE

EXTENT OF BORDER
BEYOND

3 TIERS OF POLYGONS
W/ 1/4" OFFSETS

SCHEMATIC SECTION DIAGRAM

FRONT ELEVATION

TIER 1 - 3/4" OFFSET
TIER 2 - 1/2" OFFSET
TIER 3 - 1/4" OFFSET

MODEL #30 - DETAIL SECTION & ELEVATION WITH CARVING TIERS
SCALE: 6" = 1'-0"

ORNAMENT 361, 362, 363, 364
NEW RESIDENTIAL COLLEGES
YALE UNIVERSITY
ROBERT A.M. STERN ARCHITECTS
MAY 23rd, 2014
SHEET 02 OF 02

To guide our approach to the ornament and decoration, aiming for a sense of parity with the existing colleges, we searched the Yale archives for clues as to how the ornament program had been historically developed, thematically organized, and then realized, taking the Memorial Quadrangle as a case study. During the interwar period, Yale compiled lists of potential ornamental subjects, coordinating their distribution throughout buildings and courtyards with Rogers, and commissioning sculptors and artisans to craft them both in situ and off-site. Inspired by these findings and the 1963 publication *Yale Memorials*, we further documented and researched the significance of the ornament and commemorative iconography at Yale in an expanded examination of the Rogers-era colleges, compiling this wealth of information into a booklet to help create the framework for the design and relevant themes for the new colleges.

During the fourteen-month pause following our submission of construction documents in 2012, Yale architect and planner Alice Raucher continued to guide the development of the ornamental program, so that we were able to pick up the thread in 2013. The scope was more focused in the wake of a value engineering process, but, inspired by our earlier research findings, we once again found ways to resourcefully combine repetition with variation using hand-carved pieces in certain locations, and cast elements that could be rotated and repeated in others. Much of the architectural ornament, consisting of dozens of RAMSA-designed models or prototypes, evokes selected themes. For example, in the middle court of Pauli Murray College, the base of a two-story projecting oriel window set above the entrance to a passageway is ornamented by a horizontal band depicting double-helical strands of DNA interspersed with clusters of telomeres, a nod to nearby Science Hill.

To create a suitable body of iconographic decoration, Yale commissioned architect and historian Patrick Pinnell, author of the authoritative guidebook to the architecture of the Yale campus, to identify themes and people for commemoration and to design the stone panels. Pinnell set about matching subjects and themes to courtyards and building elevations, treating each of the two colleges as a "memory palace," inspired by the "Yale encyclopedia in stone" that is the Memorial Quadrangle, and grouping themes, he says, so that "the pieces talk back and forth with each other across the courtyards." Subjects treated through commemorative ornament include academic disciplines, student life, the history of the site, Yale architecture, famous alumni, and New Haven culture.

Pinnell's creative process, he says, was guided by the question, "How many different echoes can you make and still have them be individually coherent?" The main quadrangle of Benjamin Franklin College, for example, develops the theme of time, personified by a carved stone representation of Mnemosyne, the goddess of memory in ancient Greek mythology. "Time and Change shall not avail to break the friendships formed at Yale," a cheerful line from Yale's alma mater, appears in stone but is counterbalanced at the opposite side of the quadrangle by a representation of the cup of memory gradually disappearing beneath ocean waves — a reference to the forgetfulness caused by crossing the mythical River Lethe in Hades. The decoration along Prospect Walk has a Yale–New Haven theme: references to local food culture adorn the Pauli Murray College dining hall facade, including oyster harvesting and an homage to New Haven's two most famous pizzerias, Pepe's and Sally's. On the opposite side of Prospect Walk, a lesson in the ephemerality of monumental architecture is embedded in the walls of Benjamin Franklin College in the form of representations of

4.111. Designs for carved stone ornament, developed by Yale University and Patrick Pinnell, 2013. RAMSA/Patrick Pinnell.

Culinary Institute of America

Frisbie's Pies

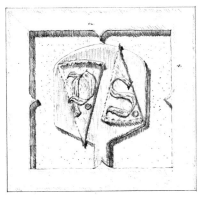

Pepe's and Sally's Pizzas

New Haven boarding houses

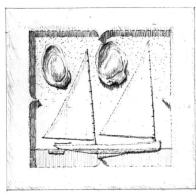

Sharpie oyster boat

Yankee Doodle Coffee Shop

4.112. Design for carved stone ornament of the Yale bulldog scupper, construction documents, 2015. RAMSA.

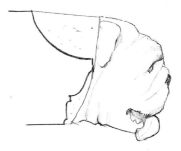

Yale bulldog

4.113. **Designs for carved stone ornament, developed by Yale University and Patrick Pinnell, 2013.** RAMSA/Patrick Pinnell.

Beatrix Jones Farrand

'Debug' and Rear Admiral Grace Hopper

Berkeley Divinity School arms

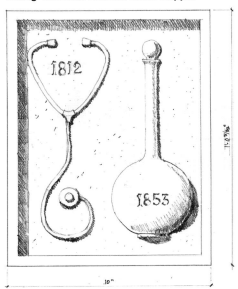

Stethoscope and chemical laboratory flask

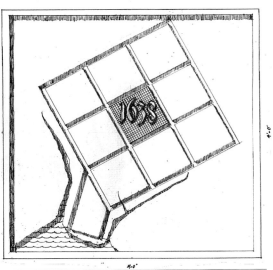

Nine Square Plan of New Haven

Arithmetic

Design: From the Outside In

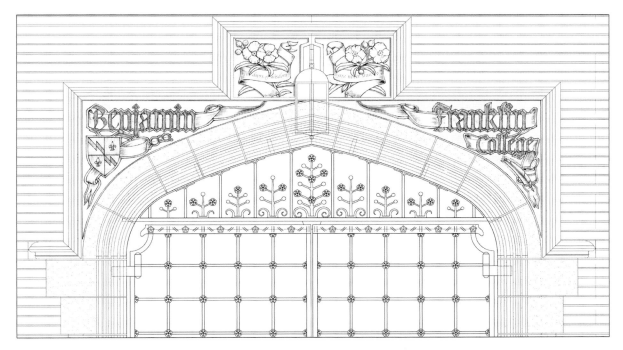

4.114. **Drawings for commemoration of the colleges' namesakes commissioned after Yale's announcement of the names on April 27, 2016.** RAMSA/The John Stevens Shop.

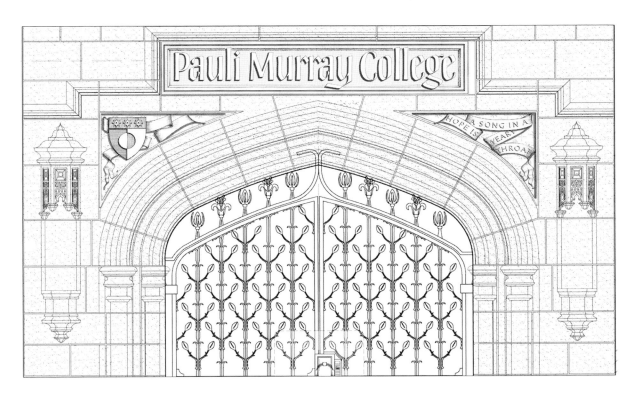

189

4.115. **Stained glass panels. Photographs December 20, 2016.** RAMSA.

TRUMBULL GALLERY
1832–1901

YALE BOAT HOUSE
1875–1910

NORTH SHEFFIELD HALL
1873–1967

BERKELEY OVAL
1894–1933

three former Connecticut State Capitol buildings erected in New Haven — including the 1827 Greek Revival statehouse designed by Ithiel Town(1784–1844) — before Hartford became the state's definitive capital in 1874 and Town's building was demolished.

Among hundreds of commemorative elements, some express a more whimsical spirit, such as lines by the composer and lyricist Cole Porter (BA 1913, 1891–1964): the words *DELIGHTFVL*, *DELICIOVS*, and *DELOVELY* are inscribed in the cornice of the Pauli Murray College dining hall, and are complemented in the Benjamin Franklin College dining hall fireplace mantle by another classic Porter line, "It was just one of those things." Both inscriptions were personally selected by Robert A.M. Stern. On an irreverent yet entirely fitting note, stone artisan Richard Carbino, cofounder of Traditional Cut Stone Ltd., the firm that fabricated the limestone ornament, took the liberty of designing a "Bobgoyle" — a gargoyle based on a Gothic treatment of the architect's likeness.

More serious themes are celebrated through stone-carved literary quotations and Pinnell-designed stone plaques engraved with pictorial references to local worthies, such as landscape gardener Beatrix Farrand, philanthropist Joseph Earl Sheffield, and the computer scientist Grace Hopper (MA 1930, PhD 1934), remembered for innovations in programming and the first known "debugging" of a computer by physically removing a moth caught in the large-scale circuitry. The 1638 Nine Square Plan of New Haven and several buildings that formerly occupied the site of the new colleges, such as Hammond Metallurgical Laboratory, are similarly commemorated in stone plaques, as are less obvious references, such as a quincunx board on the Benjamin Franklin College head of college house that refers at once to garden architecture and a traditional mathematical device.

The major donor inscriptions and archways commemorating Benjamin Franklin and Pauli Murray were designed by Nick Benson, a third-generation stone carver and MacArthur Fellow. The design of these pieces was done in consultation with Yale University Printer John Gambell, who also designed the two shields for the new colleges.

Architectural history forms the subject matter of the stained glass panels in both college dining halls. Representations of nine significant demolished Yale buildings, such as the Trumbull Gallery and North Sheffield Hall, adorn the windows of the Pauli Murray College dining hall, while the dining hall in Benjamin Franklin College shows views and plans of the Yale campus from the university's archives, including the 1793 Trumbull Plan and the 1919 Pope Plan. The tinted and leaded glass panels were fabricated by Rohlf's Stained & Leaded Glass Studio based on drawings and prints held in Yale's Manuscripts and Archives collection and the Beinecke Rare Book & Manuscript Library.

Benjamin Franklin and Pauli Murray Colleges are *Yale* through and through. Our design strategy, from basic composition to ornamental details, sought to closely integrate the new colleges with the architectural character established by James Gamble Rogers and Beatrix Farrand — the backdrop of the Yale student experience since 1917. In taking inspiration from the legacy of Gothic Yale and building upon it, we found a reservoir of meaning in the elaboration of form, image, and type.

Putting It Together: The Revenge of Girder Gothic

Modern buildings these days feel like they are assembled from a catalogue. In the olden days, buildings felt crafted.

THOMAS HEATHERWICK
Mark 36, 2015

The construction of Benjamin Franklin and Pauli Murray Colleges involved combining the most effective fabrication and building technologies of our time with still-vital artisanal techniques. The buildings recall the old paradox of "Girder Gothic," but this time with redoubled environmental performance and life safety benchmarks, new tools to coordinate design and construction, and a synthesis of handmade and factory-made elements applied in carefully planned patterns and sequences of installation.

Here, again, we found precedent in the work of James Gamble Rogers, who, though little interested in the Modernist machine aesthetic of his time, relied on industrial building technologies to realize his designs, deftly combining them with the work of skilled artisans. Having spent the early part of his career designing a range of commercial, civic, residential, and academic buildings, Rogers was familiar with the most modern building methods of his day. In building a new Yale between the two world wars, he embraced technology as a pragmatic means to an end — not as a glorification of engineering for its own sake, but as a means to realize works of architecture. Rogers sought to put technology in what he considered, and we agree, to be its rightful place: subservient to functional and cultural intentions.

To realize the quadrangles at Yale, Rogers and the builder Marc Eidlitz & Son mobilized an extended network of consultants, manufacturers, suppliers, and artisans reaching from New England to the American heartland. "All the different pieces must be made practically at one time and designed in such a way that, though made in various parts of the world, they will not only fit when brought together but form a good architectural composition and be artistically correct in their details," Rogers wrote in *The American Architect/The Architectural Review* in 1921 at the completion of Harkness Tower and Memorial Quadrangle. Rogers searched tirelessly to find high-quality building materials and skilled workers to realize his designs, but he also devised ways to save time and money by selectively using prefabricated or factory-made components, despite his stated goal to avoid a factory-made appearance.

Recounting the construction process in his book *The Memorial Quadrangle: A Book About Yale* (1929), Robert Dudley French, a professor of English and the first appointed master when the residential college system was established in 1933, remarked not only on the artisanal and artistic qualities of the buildings and courtyards but also on the elaborate marshaling of supplies and labor, revealing the spectacular contrast between the free-spirited and transcendentally contemplative end and the other almost militaristic in its minutely organized means. Building the quadrangle required the installation of 60,000 panes of glass set within 3,700 windows, 70 miles of electrical wire, 6-1/4 miles of brass plumbing pipe, and the construction of bearing walls from 7 million units of common brick, some of which was recycled from the demolished buildings on the site, according to French, and most of which was concealed behind stone cladding, surfacing only in Linonia Court and certain interior spaces. As Yale subsequently built new residential colleges and academic buildings in the 1930s, the engineering and construction techniques employed were comparable in technical ambition to New York's Rockefeller Center and other significant Depression-era building projects, reflecting the country's rapidly modernizing building industry, arguably then the most advanced in the world.

In the realization of Benjamin Franklin and Pauli Murray Colleges, we rediscovered anew the productive tension between individually detailed

5.1. **Construction of Memorial Quadrangle, East High Wing A. Mark Eidlitz & Son served as construction manager. Photograph James S. Hedden, 1920.** Yale University Library, Manuscripts and Archives. Image no. 680.

5.2. **Construction of Memorial Quadrangle, view from the corner of York and Elm Streets looking southeast [sic]. Photograph James S. Hedden, 1920.** Yale University Library, Manuscripts and Archives. Image no. 005292.

components and the rigorous coordination of the whole, with disciplined technical planning as important to the success of the project as aesthetically driven design intentions. The new colleges were constructed over a period of almost three years, compared with only two years for most of their predecessors from the 1930s and 1960s, which tended to be smaller in size and located on less logistically challenging sites. It is not just that the new colleges exceed their predecessors in sheer volume of building materials — including 33,000 cubic yards of concrete (equivalent to ten, filled Olympic-sized swimming pools), 3,200 tons of reinforcing steel, 3,155 tons of structural steel, 1-1/2 million units of face brick and decorative brick, 43,000 individually sized pieces of cut stone and cast stone, 71 miles of electrical conduit (a fraction of the total wire length), 18 miles of plumbing pipe, and 4,282 steel windows — but also that their complex ventilation systems, thermally insulated facades, roofs, and elevators required more time for coordination and installation. Additional time was also allotted to satisfy today's heightened construction safety standards.

Despite these additional requirements, Yale's analysis of historical records revealed that the new colleges cost no more per square foot than the time-adjusted costs of Eero Saarinen's Morse and Stiles Colleges constructed in 1961–63. Yale believes this to be attributable, in large measure, to the extensive use of digital documentation in the design process, which led to a high degree of coordination in the field, and strategic use of prefabrication techniques for both exterior and interior elements.

Preliminary construction services and activities began concurrently with our design commission in September 2008, as Yale engaged Turner Construction Company of New York to provide preconstruction advice on pricing, logistics, and construction methods and also to manage preliminary site work, namely upgrading the extensive underground steam, electrical, and sewer utilities serving both future colleges and nearby Science Hill.

A $250 million gift from Charles B. Johnson (BA 1954), the largest in the university's history, announced in September 2013, provided the critical impetus to resume work, starting with revised interior configurations to accommodate fifty-four more students. The few remaining buildings on the Prospect-Sachem Triangle site were removed by the end of 2013, and bid documents were issued May 1, 2014, resulting in the selection of Dimeo Construction Company of Providence, Rhode Island, as the construction manager. Remarkably, Dimeo's first step was to build their own scale model in cardboard — which they brought to their initial job interview and thereafter placed in the field office conference room for the duration of construction — as a tool for construction management, to help them understand the massing and strategize the sequence of construction operations. Foundation and preparatory site work for the new colleges began in mid-October 2014, and an official groundbreaking ceremony was held on April 16, 2015, where President Salovey looked forward to the day when the colleges would "stand in splendor" and be "teeming with life," bustling with a new community. Construction proceeded according to schedule thereafter, finishing over the summer of 2017.

Although Yale requested that we model our entire design in full detail in three dimensions using Autodesk Revit, our contract also required us to produce a set of traditional two-dimensional line drawings for construction, based upon the Revit model, to be printed and bound in the conventional way. To help organize the process, the two new colleges were divided into twenty-seven

5.3. Dimeo Construction Company cardboard model (2015) at New Haven field office. Left to right: Joe Ryan, Ken Frank, Jared Novinski. Photograph April 11, 2017. RAMSA.

5.4. Groundbreaking ceremony, April 16, 2015. Left to right: Toni Harp, Bruce D. Alexander, Joshua Bekenstein, Anita Bekenstein, Edward P. Bass, Richard C. Levin, Jane Levin, Jonathan Holloway, Marta Moret, David Swensen, Peter Salovey, Meghan R. McMahon, Charles B. Johnson, Joan E. O'Neill, G. Leonard Baker, Robert A.M. Stern, Margaret H. Marshall, Benjamin Polak. Photograph Michael Marsland. Yale University Office of Public Affairs & Communications.

5.5. Groundbreaking ceremony, April 16, 2015. President Peter Salovey at the podium. Photograph Michael Marsland. Yale University Office of Public Affairs & Communications.

5.6. Groundbreaking ceremony, April 16, 2015. Robert A.M. Stern at the podium. Photograph Michael Marsland. Yale University Office of Public Affairs & Communications.

5.7. Memorial Quadrangle, elevation of passageway entrance showing half exterior and half interior, 1919. James Gamble Rogers. Yale University Library, Manuscripts and Archives.

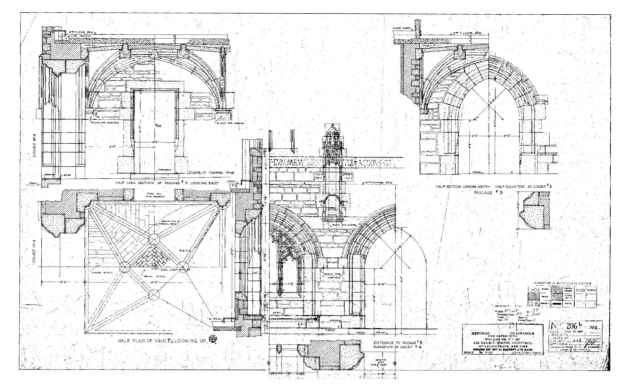

5.8. Pauli Murray College, elevation of passageway entrance showing half exterior and half interior, construction documents, 2012–14. RAMSA.

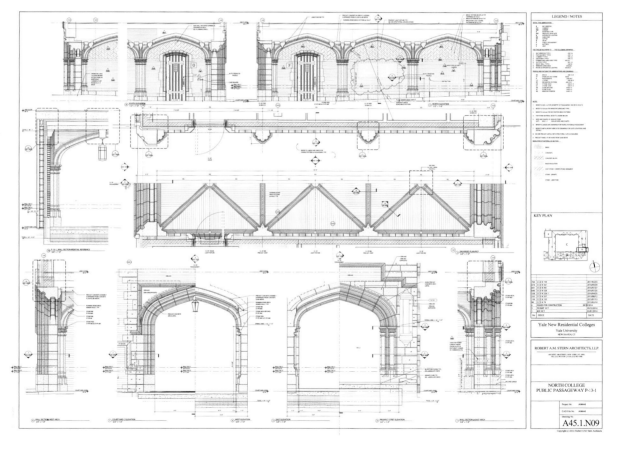

5.9. Pauli Murray College main gate passageway at Prospect Street, construction documents, 2012–14. RAMSA.

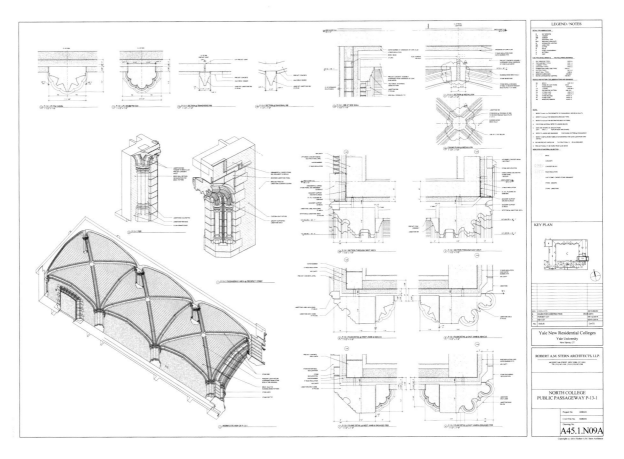

5.10. Benjamin Franklin College buttress details, construction documents, 2012–14. RAMSA.

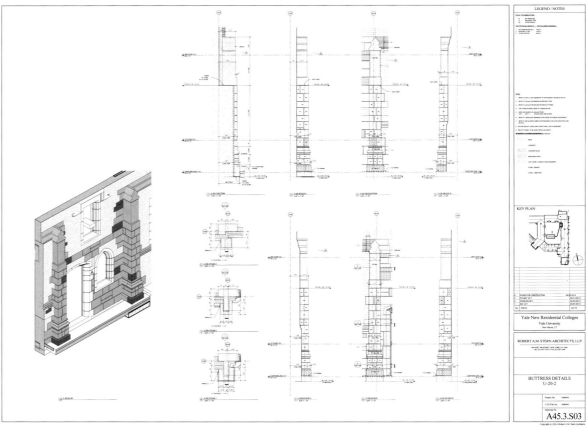

5.11. Pauli Murray College bay window, construction documents, 2012–14. RAMSA.

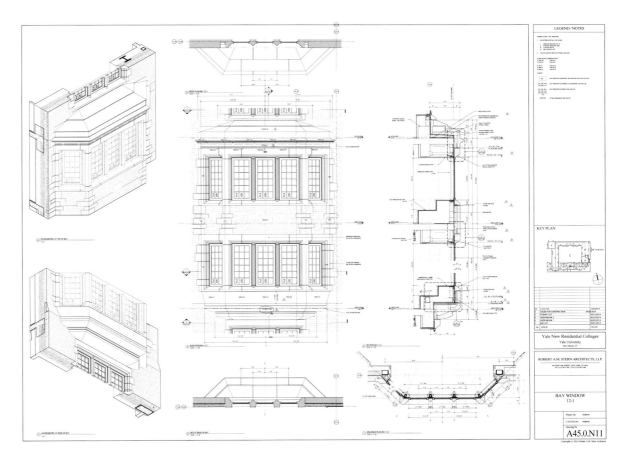

5.12. Pauli Murray College entryway details, construction documents, 2012–14. RAMSA.

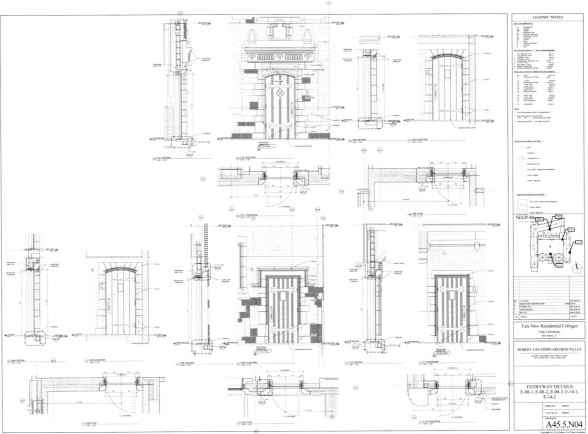

contiguous buildings, each with its own set of plans, sections, and elevations, similar to those in Rogers's archived drawing sets. We also borrowed some of his efficient graphic strategies for representing Gothic features, such as bisecting the elevation of passageway entrances to show half of the exterior and half of the interior, thereby saving space on the page, and assigning a number to each individual architectural component. Our sheets representing bay windows show section, plan, and elevation in a similar configuration to what Rogers used, and we also incorporated his system for numbering each individual bay window, passageway, and other components. Revit enabled us to place three-dimensional isometric views of these components on the same sheet with two-dimensional plans, sections, and elevations.

The construction document set for Benjamin Franklin and Pauli Murray Colleges came to include a total of 2,311 printed sheets, compared with an estimated 691 sheets prepared for the construction of the Memorial Quadrangle almost a century earlier. The greater number of drawings can be attributed not only to the comparatively larger size and programmatic complexity of the new colleges but also to the need for a greater number of technical drawings, including many produced by engineering consultants. Other factors contributing to the increased size of this and other modern drawing sets include the need to limit liability by reducing the risk of misunderstanding in the field and the long-term historic shift toward more explicit instructions to builders and artisans.

Despite the fact that the two-dimensional drawings came from the three-dimensional model, Revit does not produce a clear set of drawings without substantial additional work. Modeling techniques appropriate for developing the three-dimensional model, whether to create legible visualizations or produce accurate and useful component data, are often incongruous with the approach required to create legible two-dimensional line drawings. In short, construction documents may differ in both ends and means from a three-dimensional virtual model. Our team therefore had to adjust or "clean up" the line work of the Revit drawings not because they lacked accuracy but because they needed an added level of abstraction, long established in architecture and the building trades, in order to be clear and communicative to the builders who must interpret them. We encountered this need to improve clarity through abstraction—culling extraneous data and selectively emphasizing the most relevant aspects—whenever we cut a wall section or a plan through the digital model, for example, or depicted a corner detail. Certain architectural elements, such as dormers, consistently fared poorly in the automated translation from digital model to drawing, even though our modelling of them was geometrically correct.

Still, this extra effort was to some extent compensated by the significant gains derived from Revit's visualization and data management capabilities, which enabled us to match the intimate scale of Rogers-era construction while coordinating far more intricate modern building systems within. As expected, the use of a three-dimensional BIM model enabled us to streamline the review process with consultants and builders, reducing the likelihood of unforeseen conflicts in the field between structural or mechanical elements and complex facade components involving multiple building trades. Landscape and engineering systems, such as irrigation, geothermal wells, tree roots, and drainage, also required—and benefitted from—extensive coordination via the shared three-dimensional BIM model.

5.13. **Full-scale mockup. James Gamble Rogers. Photograph 1917.**
Richard Benson, *A Yale Album: The Third Century* (New Haven: Yale University Press, 2000), image no. 27.

5.14. **Full-scale mockup. Photograph February 21, 2012.** RAMSA.

We had also anticipated taking advantage of the direct-to-fabrication capability of Gehry Technologies's Digital Project, which we used to model geometrically complex stone profiles. One of the known virtues of Digital Project is its ability to provide fabricators with a data-rich, technically accurate model, circumventing the need to translate the design into hand-drawn shop drawings, which can introduce opportunities for error. However, the preconstruction manager's preference for a more traditional workflow using manual shop drawings, which were executed while the project was on hold in 2012, resulted in a missed opportunity and in some complications that could have been avoided. Despite this setback, Digital Project was used and was invaluable for managing and realizing major components such as prefabricated passageways and the panelized tower cladding.

Prior to the start of construction, our research into building techniques and component assemblies culminated in the ultimate in physical study models, a full-scale mockup that helped solidify decisions about the composition and construction of the 1-1/2 miles of facade that would wrap Benjamin Franklin and Pauli Murray Colleges. Erected a few blocks from the site on Winchester Avenue, the 30-foot-tall mockup effectively demonstrated technical and aesthetic qualities of the facade for both the builders and the client, tested assumptions about constructibility and cost, and set quality standards for subcontractors later asked to submit bids. It featured a fragment of a typical elevation of face brick, limestone and granite trim, cast-stone coping and window surrounds, a slate roof, a limestone-capped buttress, zinc gutters and downspouts, and a solid wood door. Its various types of windows, including a bay window, were supplied by five different manufacturers being considered for the job. The mockup also included invisible but equally important technical elements, such as flashing, waterproofing, insulation, and an air cavity.

Rogers had similarly relied upon demonstration walls, erected first in New York City and then in New Haven, "to get satisfactorily the stone jointing, texture, color, and mortar," as reported in *Architectural Record* in February 1918, and he subsequently used mockups to facilitate the detailing and construction of the

201

5.15. Limestone fabrication at Bybee Stone Company. Photograph May 21, 2015. RAMSA.

5.16. Weymouth granite mockup. Photograph January 6, 2015. RAMSA.

5.17. Mold and resulting cast-stone ornament. Photographs June 3, 2015. RAMSA.

residential colleges after 1930. Robert Dudley French, writing about Rogers's use of mockups for the Memorial Quadrangle, observed, "It is always easier to show a man what you want done than it is to tell him."

We explored potential sources for building materials throughout the design process, though decisions were not necessarily finalized until after bidding and construction began in 2014. Our search for the best sources of cut limestone, granite, slate, and bluestone was aided by stone consultant Malcolm Swenson. To avoid bottlenecks in supply and fabrication, the contract for 17,433 pieces of rustic buff limestone ashlar, quoins, and trim was split in two: the limestone for Benjamin Franklin College was supplied by Reed Quarries, Inc. and fabricated by Indiana Limestone Fabricators, both of south-central Indiana; the limestone for Pauli Murray College, virtually indistinguishable from its counterpart in color and quality, was sourced from the quarries of the Indiana Limestone Company and fabricated by the Bybee Stone Company, located in the same region.

For the 8,000 pieces of Weymouth granite trim, including some split-face and some seamface, we turned to Plymouth Quarries Inc. of Hingham, Massachusetts, which had previously supplied the granite for the Memorial Quadrangle and other historic Yale buildings. We initially encountered some competition from Boston College, which had ordered a significant amount of granite for several building projects of its own. Thanks to Dimeo's just-in-time delivery approach, the quarry was able to meet the demands of both projects, providing the stone to Yale in multiple phases, rather than all at once as some construction managers would require.

As important as sourcing limestone accents for the facades was the sourcing of an approximately equivalent number of cast-stone units that resembled the limestone in tone and texture. The smooth, fine texture of cast stone, a specialized type of concrete, results from the use of stone dust as an aggregate, allowing it to take on precisely molded shapes, often for purposes of creating decorative or detailed elements more economically than if carved from quarried blocks. Dyes are added to adjust the color as desired. Technical expertise and attention to detail were paramount, so the choice of the Québec firm BPDL (Béton Préfabriqué du Lac) as the fabricator of 17,110 pieces of cast stone cladding was taken only after a series of factory visits and discussions.

The most significant cladding material by surface area is brick, which we carefully selected for color and texture based upon our analysis of Linonia Court in Branford College. A custom three-color blend of hand-molded face brick, imparting subtle tonal variety, was developed in consultation with the Mack Brick Company and the manufacturer, Old Virginia Brick Co., to be placed by masons on-site in the Flemish garden wall bond; however, after Old Virginia unexpectedly suspended operations in April 2015, the same month our brick order was to be placed, we scrambled to identify a suitable replacement blend from other manufacturers based upon brick varieties already in production, expediting mockups for review within a week and comparing each one with the other cladding materials.

Fortunately, neither the construction schedule nor the design concept were compromised as the contract for 1.4 million individual units of molded face brick was awarded to Glen-Gery, a firm founded in 1890, which manufactured the bricks at its Shoemakersville, Pennsylvania–based plant, in a color blend similar to that seen in the courtyards of Grace Hopper (formerly Calhoun) College.

Glen-Gery also provided 105,000 specially shaped bricks that were installed in decorative patterns.

The natural-cleft slate roofing, considered integral with the facade design, matches the quality of that used in other Yale buildings and is expected to last for many generations. The sloping roofs of varying heights are topped with 165,000 square feet, or approximately fifty truckloads, of multi-hued slate sourced from the Vermont Structural Slate Co., founded in 1859. After splitting the metamorphic stone into the varying thicknesses and lengths specified for the graduated roof panels, the fabricator loaded a mix of colors into each pallet so that the contractors could easily achieve the desired heterogeneous appearance across all the roof surfaces.

All of these carefully sourced cladding materials, essential to the character of the new colleges, are nothing without the reinforced concrete and steel structure, designed and engineered by Weidlinger Associates (now Thornton Tomasetti), as discussed in Chapter 4. To build the reinforced concrete slabs, columns, and beams, over 3,300 truckloads of high-quality concrete from a New Haven mixing facility were pumped and poured in place under the supervision of general contractors J. L. Marshall & Sons, Inc. and Manafort Brothers, Inc. The ingredients of the concrete mix were sourced relatively locally, including basalt aggregate quarried in Meriden, Connecticut, cement manufactured in Ravena, New York, and sand from Cape Cod, Massachusetts, all mixed with New Haven municipal water. The 3,200 tons of steel reinforcing bars embedded within the concrete were manufactured in Connecticut, using over 99 percent recycled steel; 3,155 tons of structural steel were manufactured in Roanoke, Virginia, and southern Québec.

As the building complex visibly took shape from 2015 to 2017, the construction site was buzzing with hundreds of workers from different trades (at the peak reaching 608 construction workers and an average of 432 workers on a daily basis during the most labor-intensive phases). Approximately 25-1/2 percent of the workforce was composed of minorities or women under Equal Employment

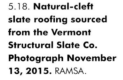

5.18. **Natural-cleft slate roofing sourced from the Vermont Structural Slate Co. Photograph November 13, 2015.** RAMSA.

5.19. **Foundations. Photographs April 29, 2015.** RAMSA.

5.20. **Steel erection. Photograph September 2, 2015.** RAMSA.

5.21. **Steel framing. Photograph October 14, 2015.** RAMSA.

5.22. **Construction sequence, 2015–17.** Yale University Office of Development.

March 13, 2015

April 8, 2015

June 5, 2015

July 21, 2015

October 8, 2015

October 27, 2015

April 26, 2016

May 31, 2016

August 26, 2016

September 29, 2016

March 13, 2017

March 30, 2017

Putting It Together: The Revenge of Girder Gothic

April 23, 2015

May 8, 2015

May 21, 2015

August 3, 2015

September 8, 2015

September 23, 2015

November 22, 2015

February 9, 2016

February 28, 2016

June 14, 2016

July 7, 2016

July 29, 2016

November 4, 2016

February 2, 2017

February 15, 2017

May 11, 2017

June 25, 2017

August 4, 2017

5.23. **Aerial view of site with four tower cranes looking northeast. Photograph Don and Roy Couture, November 21, 2015.**
Aerial Photography of Don Couture.

Opportunity guidelines, and New Haven residents worked over 13 percent of the total hours logged in the project's construction. Four tower cranes and up to eleven smaller cranes worked in concert while a tireless corps of mixing, pumping, lifting, and delivery vehicles performed their choreography on the ground.

Dimeo developed a series of strategies to deal with the limits of the triangular site, constrained as it was by the Greenway and the busy urban thoroughfare of Prospect Street, with little room to maneuver and store materials and heavy equipment. They planned the sequence of work across the site from east to west, from Prospect Street toward the Greenway, to enable subcontractors to follow each other in an orderly manner. The schedule of operations was precisely orchestrated down to individual building components, since both space and time were seen as limited resources. Courtyard facades were completed prior to the north- and west-street facades, since the installation of passageway vaulting would at some point necessarily limit access for the construction vehicles. Toward the end of construction, as Dimeo finished the interiors, they proceeded according to the spatial logic of vertical entryways, rather than by floor level, mirroring the social and physical organization of the buildings.

To accommodate the lack of an expansive on-site staging area, Dimeo devised a just-in-time delivery system, establishing an intricately organized staging area at a warehouse ten miles away in Northford, Connecticut, where all building supplies were delivered, sorted, and repackaged according to their designated location and sequence of installation. This system — effectively pre-assembling the entire job off-site, piece by piece and pallet by pallet — allowed

5.24. **Dimeo ornament storage warehouse. Photograph 2015.** RAMSA.

the builders on-site to install components much more efficiently. Each of the thousands of individually distinct pieces of cut and cast stone, for instance, were available for inspection prior to delivery to the site, thanks in part to the use of unique, scannable identification tags for each component.

To also reduce time and labor cost expenditures at the construction site, many building components were manufactured off-site, including the 72 stairways serving the residential suites, consisting of 325 precast concrete stair runs of varying dimensions. A more complex and self-concealing version of precast technology is found in the 45 chimneys, clad in the same brick and stone veneer used in the facade but cast into a concrete backing in the controlled shop environment of BPDL. The resulting chimney towers are thinner and lighter than traditional masonry construction and were efficiently transported and installed as fully formed units.

The trade-off for faster installation on-site by means of precast elements was a series of logistical challenges related to staging, loading, and rigging the massive units at carefully specified points and times, usually at night, when the delicate, two-hour job of placing each precast stair or chimney would not hamper other construction activities or unduly monopolize one of the tower cranes. These operations drew attention in late 2015, when the freestanding chimneys suddenly began appearing atop the buildings' exposed structural framing, causing no end of comment from sidewalk superintendents.

Jon Olsen, Yale's project manager for the construction of the colleges, praised the time-saving use of precast technology for the 36-foot-long vaulted Gothic passageways, similarly fabricated by BPDL as a series of concrete shells cast with face brick and stone on their inner surface: "You just slap it on a truck, you drive it down, you rig it into place and, 'boom' it's on." The sixteen passageway vaults may look structural, but they are suspended from the structural concrete slab above by threaded rods—recalling Rogers's controversial use of nonstructural rib vaulting inside Sterling Memorial Library, his infamous "Girder Gothic" masterpiece. Additional prefabricated elements on Benjamin Franklin and Pauli Murray Colleges include the many dormers, which were framed and sheathed in a factory before being placed along the roof.

5.25. **Precast chimney, type F, at BPDL's plant in Alma, Quebec, Canada. Face brick matches the facades. Photograph June 28, 2016.** RAMSA.

5.26. **Precast chimney, type B, hoisted in place on roof of Pauli Murray College. Photograph March 8, 2016.** RAMSA.

5.27. **Precast chimney, type A3, on unfinished roof of Benjamin Franklin College. Photograph December 8, 2015.** RAMSA.

Putting It Together: The Revenge of Girder Gothic

5.28. Construction of passage to Calliope Court in Memorial Quadrangle. Photographs 1920. James Gamble Rogers, "The Memorial Quadrangle of Yale University and the Harkness Memorial Tower," *Architecture* v.44, n.4 (October 1921): 299.

5.29. Precast passageway vault to be installed in Pauli Murray College Bekenstein Court. Photograph March 8, 2017. RAMSA.

5.31. Passageway vault in Benjamin Franklin College, viewed from Prospect Walk. Photograph March 23, 2017. Fly on the Wall Productions.

5.30. Precast passageway vault suspended from structural slab, viewed from common room in Pauli Murray College. Photograph June 8, 2016. RAMSA.

5.32. **Prefabricated dormer. Photograph February 11, 2016.** RAMSA.

5.33. **Prefabricated dormer hoisted in place on roof of Pauli Murray College. Photograph April 21, 2016.** RAMSA.

Following today's best practices for durable and energy-efficient cavity wall construction, the typical assembly for Benjamin Franklin and Pauli Murray Colleges is designed to minimize thermal transfer. Its typical cross-section, starting from the exterior, consists of the face brick, a 1-3/8–inch airspace, three inches of rigid insulation, a vapor barrier, and structural concrete affixed with steel angles to support the cladding. A 6-inch nonbearing wall of concrete masonry units (CMUs) is set with mortar and fills the nonwindow gaps between structural elements. On the interior side of the concrete lies a layer of nonrigid insulation, metal stud framing, and gypsum wallboard.

A similarly multilayered, approximately 1-foot-thick roof assembly, far exceeds the energy and environmental performance of Rogers-era precedents while closely matching their outward appearance. Specifically, the slates of Benjamin Franklin and Pauli Murray Colleges were installed over a vapor barrier, multiple layers of rigid insulation panels, a waterproofing membrane, sheathing board, and corrugated decking over the steel structure.

The 4,282 windows—visually similar to Rogers's steel-frame casements but providing vastly superior thermal performance—were manufactured by Crittall in England and assembled in Connecticut by Berlin Steel. Each window has three layers of glass: a modern insulated unit comprising two sealed panes,

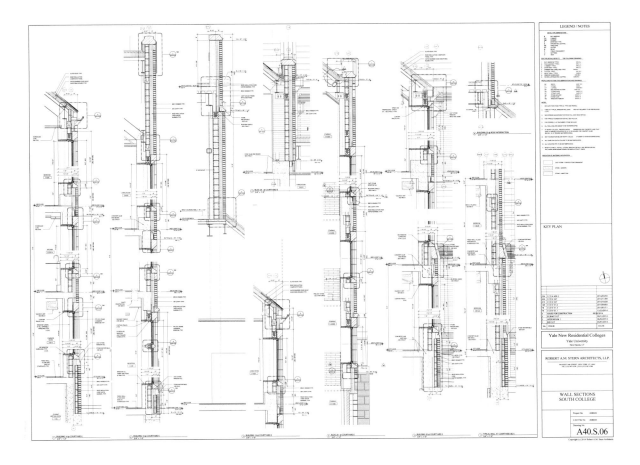

plus an external vented layer of ornamental leaded glass fabricated by Rohlf's Stained & Leaded Glass Studio in Mount Vernon, New York. The leaded glass panels are made by handcutting the desired sizes from imported mouth-blown glass, then adding subtle color tints, lead came, cross members, waterproofing, and in some cases steel reinforcing bars. Rohlf's, a firm that dates to 1920, has restored or replicated thousands of leaded glass window panels throughout Yale's Collegiate Gothic buildings, taking inspiration from the legacy of G. Owen Bonawit of New York, the artisan who designed much of Yale's leaded glass in the interwar period, and continuing the decorative practice of "grapevining" to simulate a long history of breakage and repairs.

Dimeo devised an efficient way to build the rough openings for the windows, once again relying on off-site fabrication to increase reliability as well as speed. Forgoing the time-consuming process of preparing each window opening with a sequence of components added one at a time—waterproofing, wood framing, vertical steel tubes between adjacent windows, wood blocking, and a vapor barrier—they elected to have unitized blocking assemblies for each window or row of windows built in wood in a controlled factory setting, precisely measured to match the specified opening. During construction, the installation of a plastic barrier behind this unitized window blocking served at once as a weather shield and as a safety barrier, saving the time and expense of installing temporary railings. Later, cast-stone profiles surrounding the window openings were fastened to the concrete structure. The steel-framed windows were then clipped into place and sealed from inside and outside, and oak trim was installed to form the deep jambs.

Skilled masons and their assistants placed the roughly 43,000 pieces of limestone, cast stone, and brick, subcontracted through a joint venture of

Grande Masonry and Joe Capasso Mason Enterprises Inc. Members of the construction management team believe that more masons were at work on the facades of Benjamin Franklin and Pauli Murray Colleges in 2016 than on any other project in the country. As Yale's Jon Olsen observed, "You can't necessarily just snap your fingers and get eighty masons," but in this case they came from four different states, taking pride in their work and welcoming the opportunity to pass their skills on to younger employees. At least one senior mason is said to have postponed his retirement and pension in exchange for the opportunity to practice his craft one last time on a memorably detailed and complex project.

The majority of the stone on the project was set with hoists, beams, trolleys, and chains, the same tools masons have used for centuries—but using electricity or vehicle motors to power the hoists. During the winter, as is standard to ensure proper curing of mortar and masonry, pieces of stone scheduled to be installed were first brought into a heated area and acclimated for several days, then installed within a heated tent erected around the building facade.

The numerous carved stone profiles used on the project were produced by means of planers—machines introduced in the late nineteenth century that

5.36. **Masons at work at the site. Photograph March 8, 2017.** RAMSA.

5.37. **Masons at work at the site. Photograph April 12, 2017.** Dimeo Construction, Seth Jacobson Photography.

5.38. **Masons at work at the site. Photographs April 12, 2017.** Dimeo Construction, Seth Jacobson Photography (left); RAMSA (right).

5.39. **Formwork for cast-stone ornament. Photograph June 3, 2015.** RAMSA.

5.40. **Window surrounds, cast-stone ornament. Photograph October 8, 2015.** RAMSA.

5.41. **Cast-stone ornament. RAMSA team member Asdren Matoshi. Photograph November 19, 2015.** RAMSA.

5.42. **Cast-stone ornament. Photographs January 3, 2017.** RAMSA.

Putting It Together: The Revenge of Girder Gothic

5.43. **Carved-stone ornament, Mnemosyne or Memory designed by Patrick Pinnell. Photograph September 11, 2015.** RAMSA.

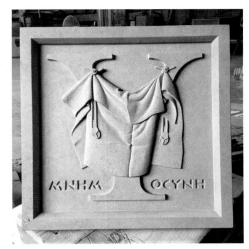

5.44. **Carved-stone ornament, Janus designed by Patrick Pinnell. Photograph September 23, 2015.** RAMSA.

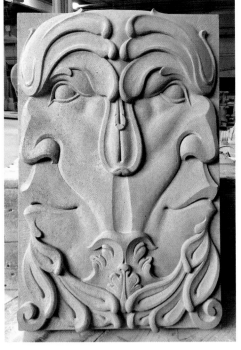

5.45. **Carved-stone ornament, Gothic triglyph using Yale College initials designed by Patrick Pinnell. Photograph October 8, 2015.** RAMSA.

5.46. **Carved-stone ornament. Photograph October 8, 2015.** RAMSA.

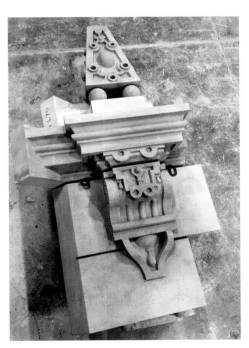

5.47. **Carved-stone ornament designed by Patrick Pinnell. Photograph October 8, 2015.** RAMSA.

217

cut evenly along the edge of a stone slab — and also by computer-numerical-controlled (CNC) cutters. Corners and angles were finished by hand with the aid of air-powered chisels. Ornamental carved limestone elements were fabricated and delivered in stages by Traditional Cut Stone Ltd., based in Mississauga, Ontario, selected by Yale from among four firms that we visited and interviewed. Ornamental cast-stone elements, requiring more steps but ultimately saving labor time due to their repeating use, were formed within CNC-cut molds in foam, wood, or resin, depending on the number and type of casts to be made, by BPDL. Some of these molds, such as those used to cast the finials, were created based on hand-carved masonry models provided by Traditional Cut Stone Ltd. according to our designs.

To realize the commemorative plaques designed by Patrick Pinnell, Traditional Cut Stone Ltd. modeled his drawings at full scale in clay, making adjustments based on feedback from Pinnell, our team, and the client. Each approved plasticine model was laser scanned to create a high-fidelity digital model, which in turn was used to carve the final relief in stone using a combination of computer-numerical-controlled tools and hand-carving techniques. We were assisted by sculptor David Simon in mapping out the process for developing, pricing, and fabricating all 436 pieces of ornament and decoration, including both carved and cast units.

Fabrication of the nine different wrought-iron gates, embellished with figural and abstract ornament, was overseen by Zoltan Kovacs, who had collaborated with our team during the design process (see Chapter 4), drawing upon his technical expertise to bring to light both the challenges and opportunities involved in the process of shaping chunks of malleable, low-carbon "mild" steel into delicately detailed patterns. The results can be seen in the chamfered corners of straight bars, the twisted metal strands of a one-of-a-kind door pull, and a chiseled back plate with an undulating edge detail, among many other aspects of the gates. Each piece of metal was mechanically fastened into place; the visible fastener heads impart an ornamental as well as functional quality. Electronic components for the key card readers are concealed within the gates' mid-sections and door pull assemblies.

The four largest and most ornate gates were forged by Kovacs's own firm, COVAX, and the five smaller gates were fabricated by Connecticut-based Engineered Building Products in consultation with Kovacs. Taking pride in the integrity of his craft, Kovacs wanted to put aside the tiered hierarchy according to which the gates were designed, insisting that "there are no second-tier gates." He thus echoed the conviction of his predecessor Samuel Yellin, the fabricator of numerous Rogers-era gates at Yale, who once refused a request to provide an estimate for ornamental ironwork in "rustless iron," an early variant of stainless steel that he found unworthy of the metalworker's art. Preferring to work in wrought iron or Monel metal, Yellin wrote to Rogers in 1935:

> It is absolutely impossible to carry out these designs in that material, unless the work is done in the most artificial and commercial manner, such as sticking the various members together (or shall I say "glueing" them together?) by means of machine welding etc. I feel certain that you especially would not approve of such unnecessarily poor work.

5.48. **Benjamin Franklin College, Class of 1964 Gate detail. Photograph January 25, 2017.** RAMSA.

5.49. **COVAX metalwork shop with hand-forged entryway gates in background. Left to right: Benjamin Franklin College Main Gate, Pauli Murray College Main Gate. Photograph January 25, 2017.** RAMSA.

5.50. **Benjamin Franklin College Main Gate at COVAX shop. Left to right: Zoltan Kovacs, Kurt Glauber. Photograph January 25, 2017.** RAMSA.

5.51. **Benjamin Franklin College Main Gate detail. Photograph January 25, 2017.** RAMSA.

5.52. **Pauli Murray College Main Gate at COVAX shop. Photograph January 25, 2017.** RAMSA.

5.53. **Pauli Murray College Main Gate detail. Photograph January 25, 2017.** RAMSA.

5.54. **Pauli Murray College Main Gate installation. Photograph May 18, 2017.** RAMSA.

Other ironwork was touched by hand in order to appear handmade, even though it was made in a factory. The standardized welded steel railings along the entryway staircases were brought to the forge to be lightly hammered in a manner evocative of traditional wrought iron and embellished with rosettes at the joints. Such subtly refined architectural components exemplify a consistent level of commitment to detail, even in less important areas, relying on more economical means and, in the spirit of Rogers, a kind of sleight-of-hand to make standard-issue parts feel handcrafted.

The construction of Bass Tower presented some particular challenges. Cast-in-place concrete buttresses support the tower's first six floor plates to a height of roughly 68 feet, and the reinforced concrete framing continues up to 103 feet, just past the eighth-floor plate. From there all the way to the top of the crown, the structure consists of a bolted steel frame with diagonal bracing, clad with precast units in various forms—rounded arches, finials, and a dome inside the crown, to name a few. These 275 precast ornamental and cladding components were modeled in Digital Project, which allowed for precise analysis of the size, weight, and jointing of each piece for ease of shipping and installation. The cladding elements rest upon concealed support clips or angles, the locations of which were determined by the structural engineer, with the hardware itself designed by the precast manufacturer in coordination with the structural steel subcontractor. The large dimensions of some precast cladding units dictated that the builder install several of these units prior to completing the structural frame, since diagonal bracing would obstruct the placement of large precast panels and shells. As a result, a portion of the tower's masonry cladding first appeared high

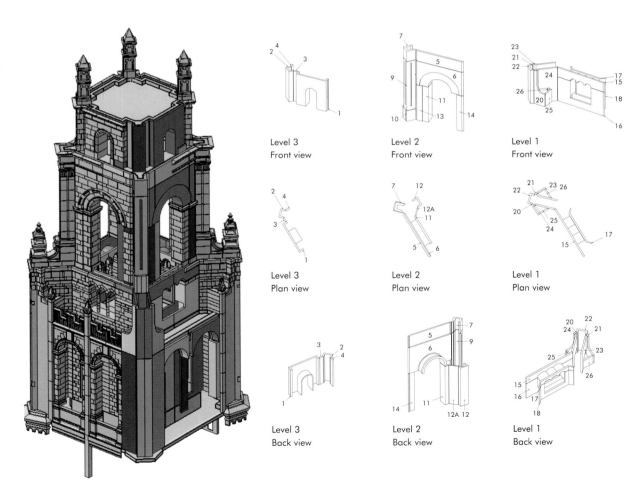

5.55. **Pauli Murray College Bass Tower relational parametric modeling, design development, 2010.** RAMSA.

Level 3
Front view

Level 2
Front view

Level 1
Front view

Level 3
Plan view

Level 2
Plan view

Level 1
Plan view

Level 3
Back view

Level 2
Back view

Level 1
Back view

5.61. Bass Tower elevation and plan details, construction documents, 2012–14. RAMSA.

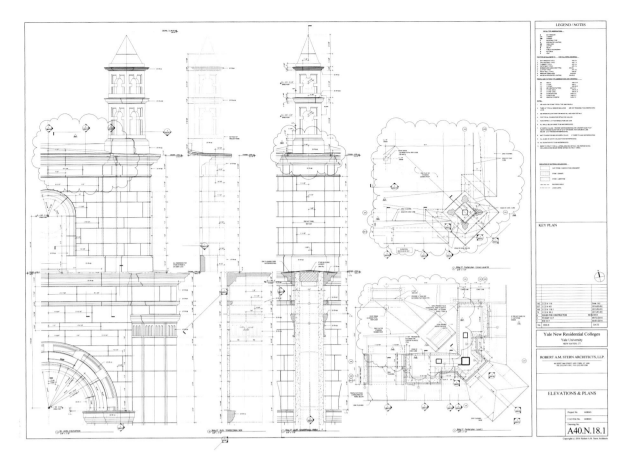

5.62. Bass Tower elevation details, construction documents, 2012–14. RAMSA.

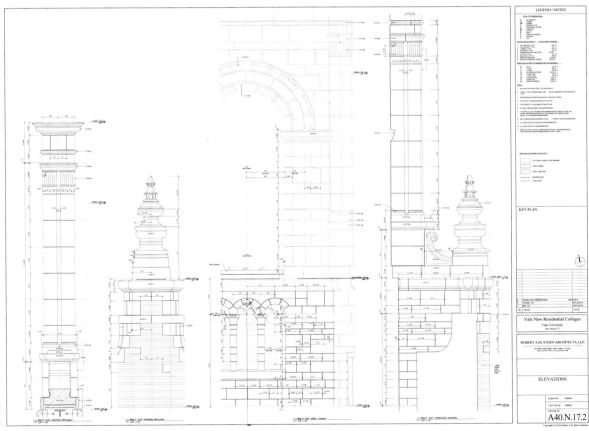

5.63. Millwork, prefabricated components. Photograph October 12, 2016. RAMSA.

5.64. Millwork, window casing. Photograph January 28, 2016. RAMSA.

5.65. Millwork, window casing. Photograph January 28, 2016. RAMSA.

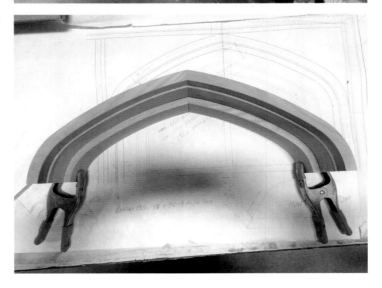

5.66. **Millwork, prefabricated components in the Pauli Murray College dining hall. Photographs May 18, 2017.** RAMSA.

5.67. **Red oak harvested from the Yale Myers Forest in northern Connecticut. Photograph May 18, 2016.** RAMSA.

5.68. **Benjamin Franklin College dining hall construction compared to 2010 rendering. Robert A.M. Stern and Ken Frank. Photograph April 16, 2017.** RAMSA.

225

5.69. Pauli Murray College, tree lowered onto raised courtyard. Photograph April 26, 2017. RAMSA.

5.70. Pauli Murray College, trees planted in small courtyard. Photograph April 11, 2017. RAMSA.

5.71. Benjamin Franklin College Nyburg Baker Court (large courtyard), bluestone pavers installation. View looking west. Photograph March 23, 2017. Fly on the Wall Productions.

5.72. RAMSA team construction site visit. Photographs March 21, 2017. RAMSA.

Top left **Left to right: Graham S. Wyatt, Melissa DelVecchio, Kurt Glauber, Robert A.M. Stern.**

Bottom left **Left to right: Melissa DelVecchio, Robert A.M. Stern.**

Right **Left to right: Ken Frank, Melissa DelVecchio, Kurt Glauber, Robert A.M. Stern, Jennifer Stone, Graham S. Wyatt, Tiffany Barber.**

on its shaft while the crown awaited its final beams and braces and the lower section remained a bare skeletal frame.

By fall 2016, the structural framing, roofing, and most of the facade work were substantially complete, allowing the contractors to shift their attention to the equally labor-intensive work of roughing out and finishing the interiors as well as planting the courtyards. The most significant challenges with respect to interior construction and fit-out were posed by wood millwork and carpentry. The overall quantities of wood required were so large — 27 miles of window trim, 13 miles of baseboards, 14 miles of casing around doors and windows, 2-1/2 miles of chair rail, 1,900 interior doors, and 42,500 square feet of veneer plywood — that each production decision had an outsize effect on time and cost.

The wood millwork subcontractor, Millwork One of Cranston, Rhode Island, reduced on-site labor while maintaining a high level of detail and quality, taking the unusual step of preparing dimension-cut bases and casings, mitered corners, and other details off-site in their shop. The time savings achieved by this method nonetheless required additional logistical organization to ensure that each component reached its assigned position intact and on schedule, as facilitated by the use of individual bar codes to track each individual millwork piece. In keeping with LEED sustainable construction guidelines, the wood was sourced predominantly from manufacturers in the region, and in particular the red-oak flooring for the dining halls and common rooms was sustainably harvested from the Yale Myers Forest in northern Connecticut.

Landscape contractor Central Nurseries oversaw the planting and paving of the quadrangles and courtyards. The OLIN team selected each individual tree included in the project, looking not only for healthy specimens but also forms and proportions befitting their specific place in the courtyard in relation to the buildings. When a 30-foot-tall bur oak was being planted in the medium-sized courtyard of Pauli Murray College, OLIN partner Richard Newton recalls the contractor slowly swiveling the tree until he and his colleague identified "exactly the right orientation for all the critical views." Bluestone pavers, sourced from American Bluestone, LLC in Sidney, New York, were bush-hammered to create an irregular surface texture, thereby increasing the material's solar reflectance index (SRI), or ability to reflect (rather than absorb) the heat of the sun, to meet LEED criteria, while also staying true to the paving material used in the historic colleges. The variously-sized bluestone slabs and the gridded 4-by-4-inch granite setts (blocks) were laid carefully to align their joints.

The ambition behind the construction of Benjamin Franklin and Pauli Murray Colleges was to equal the aesthetic standard set by James Gamble Rogers using contemporary modeling and manufacturing techniques to economize fabrication, coordinate construction, navigate more complex requirements, and achieve more ambitious performance goals. The intricately combined use of industrial and craft building techniques, adapted to the given limits of time and cost, allows artisanal work to shine in the most important locations. In using high-quality materials to realize a historically contextual facade over technically sophisticated underpinnings, the construction effort reaffirms that craft traditions are not dead — but they do require significant resources and a dedicated creative effort to flourish in tandem with modern construction techniques.

Benjamin Franklin College and Pauli Murray College: A Portfolio

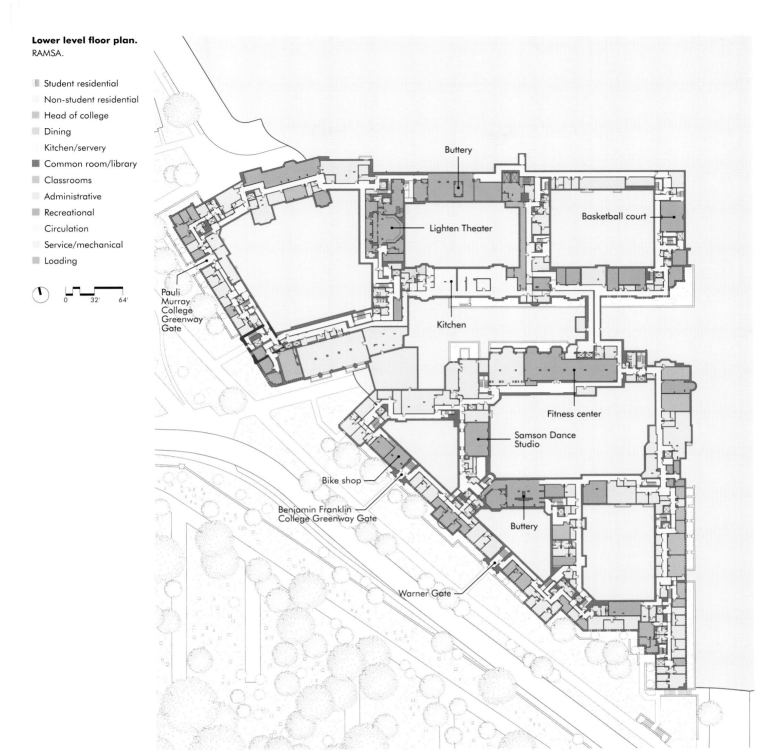

Lower level floor plan.
RAMSA.

- Student residential
- Non-student residential
- Head of college
- Dining
- Kitchen/servery
- Common room/library
- Classrooms
- Administrative
- Recreational
- Circulation
- Service/mechanical
- Loading

0   32'   64'

Buttery

Basketball court

Lighten Theater

Pauli
Murray
College
Greenway
Gate

Kitchen

Fitness center

Samson Dance
Studio

Bike shop

Benjamin Franklin
College Greenway Gate

Buttery

Warner Gate

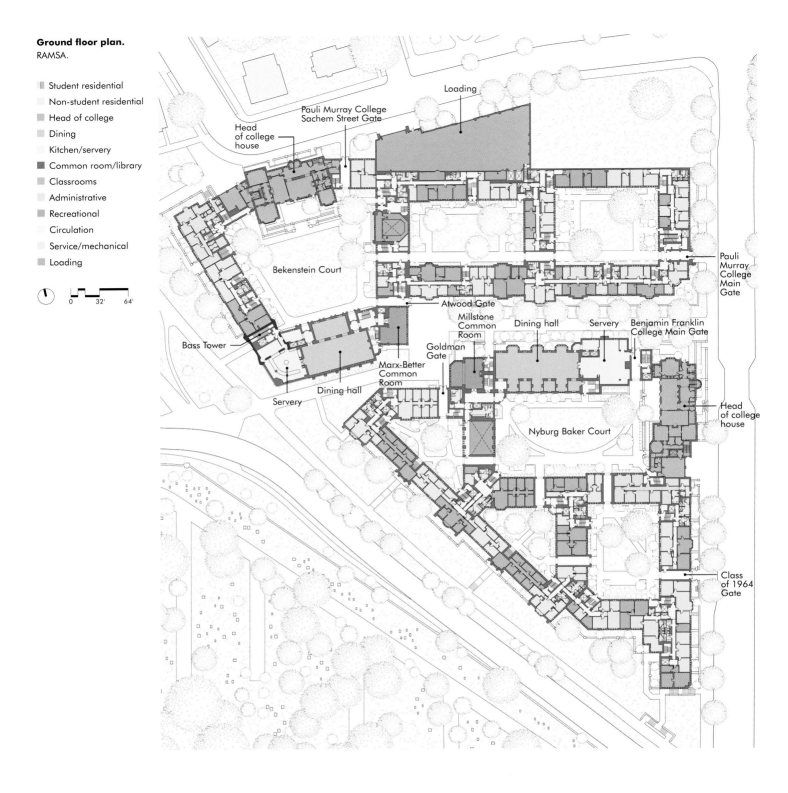

Ground floor plan.
RAMSA.

Student residential
Non-student residential
Head of college
Dining
Kitchen/servery
Common room/library
Classrooms
Administrative
Recreational
Circulation
Service/mechanical
Loading

0   32'   64'

Loading

Pauli Murray College
Sachem Street Gate

Head
of college
house

Bekenstein Court

Pauli
Murray
College
Main
Gate

Atwood Gate

Bass Tower

Millstone
Common
Room

Dining hall   Servery   Benjamin Franklin
College Main Gate

Goldman
Gate

Marx-Better
Common
Room

Dining hall

Servery

Nyburg Baker Court

Head
of college
house

Class
of 1964
Gate

Benjamin Franklin College and Pauli Murray College: A Portfolio

- Student residential
- Non-student residential
- Head of college
- Dining
- Kitchen/servery
- Common room/library
- Classrooms
- Administrative
- Recreational
- Circulation
- Service/mechanical
- Loading

0   32'   64'

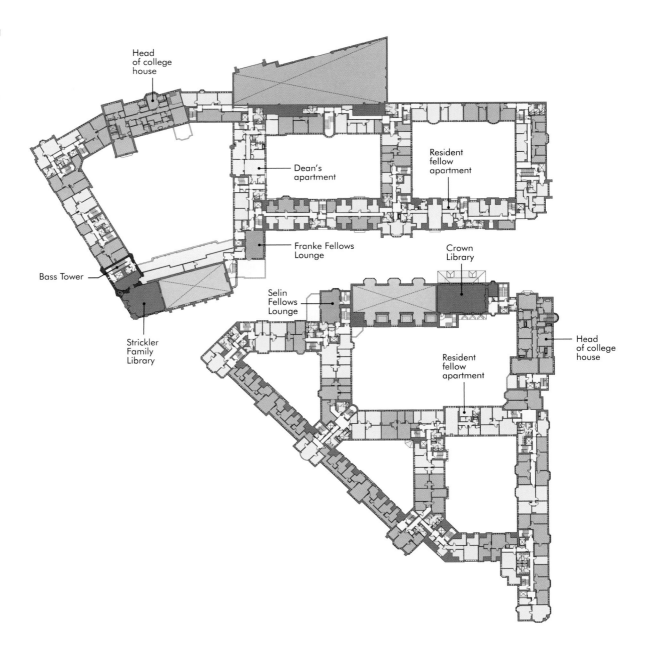

Head of college house

Dean's apartment

Resident fellow apartment

Franke Fellows Lounge

Crown Library

Bass Tower

Selin Fellows Lounge

Head of college house

Resident fellow apartment

Strickler Family Library

Third floor plan.
RAMSA.

Student residential
Non-student residential
Head of college
Dining
Kitchen/servery
Common room/library
Classrooms
Administrative
Recreational
Circulation
Service/mechanical
Loading

0   32'   64'

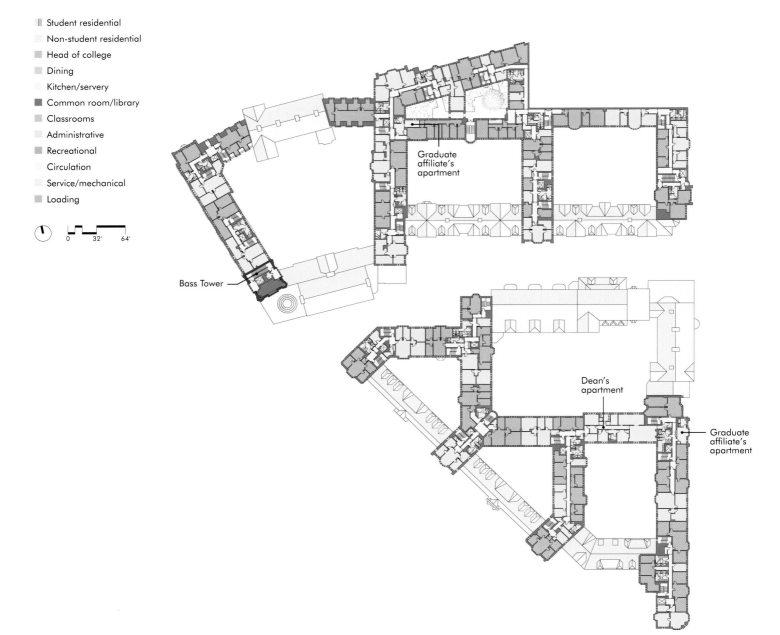

Graduate
affiliate's
apartment

Bass Tower

Dean's
apartment

Graduate
affiliate's
apartment

Fourth floor plan.
RAMSA.

- Student residential
- Non-student residential
- Head of college
- Dining
- Kitchen/servery
- Common room/library
- Classrooms
- Administrative
- Recreational
- Circulation
- Service/mechanical
- Loading

0   32'   64'

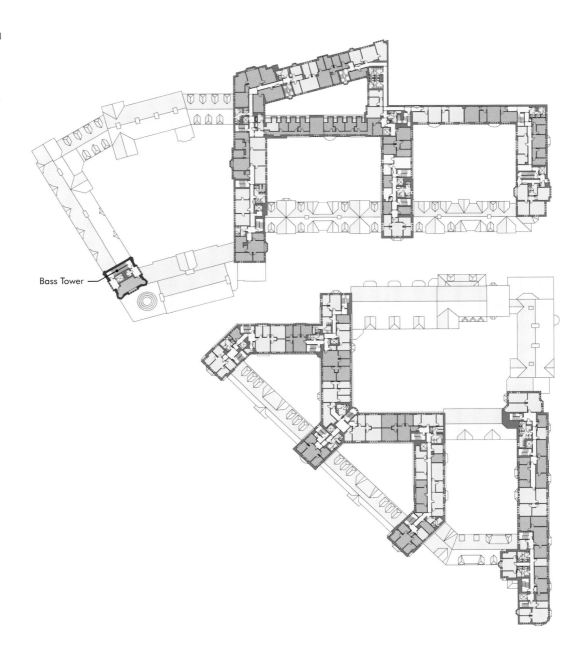

Bass Tower

Fifth floor plan.
RAMSA.

- ▐ Student residential
- ▢ Non-student residential
- ▨ Head of college
- ▨ Dining
- ▢ Kitchen/servery
- ■ Common room/library
- ▨ Classrooms
- ▨ Administrative
- ▨ Recreational
- ▢ Circulation
- ▢ Service/mechanical
- ▨ Loading

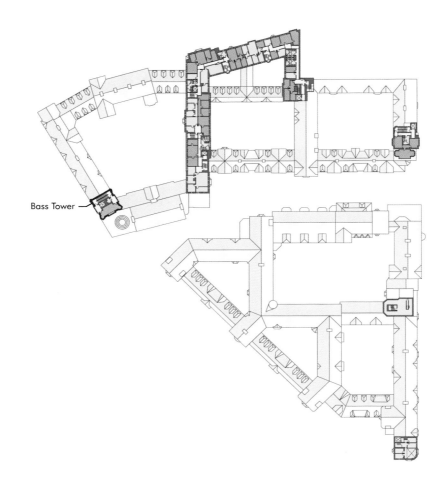

Bass Tower

0 32' 64'

Sixth floor plan.
RAMSA.

- ▐ Student residential
- ▢ Non-student residential
- ▨ Head of college
- ▨ Dining
- ▢ Kitchen/servery
- ■ Common room/library
- ▨ Classrooms
- ▨ Administrative
- ▨ Recreational
- ▢ Circulation
- ▢ Service/mechanical
- ▨ Loading

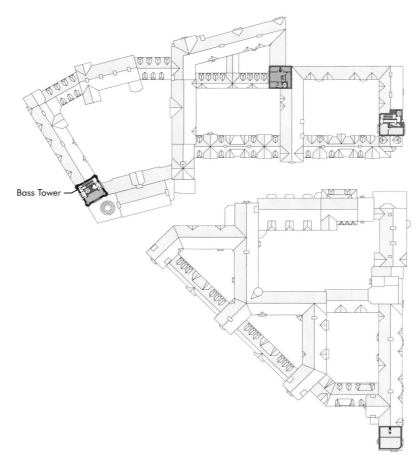

Bass Tower

0 32' 64'

Seventh floor plan.
RAMSA.

- Student residential
- Non-student residential
- Head of college
- Dining
- Kitchen/servery
- Common room/library
- Classrooms
- Administrative
- Recreational
- Circulation
- Service/mechanical
- Loading

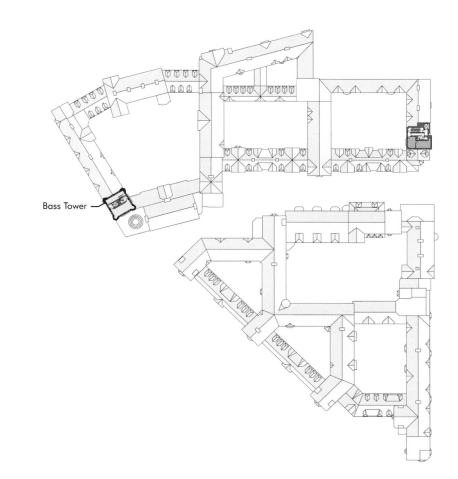

Bass Tower

0   32'   64'

Eighth floor plan.
RAMSA.

- Student residential
- Non-student residential
- Head of college
- Dining
- Kitchen/servery
- Common room/library
- Classrooms
- Administrative
- Recreational
- Circulation
- Service/mechanical
- Loading

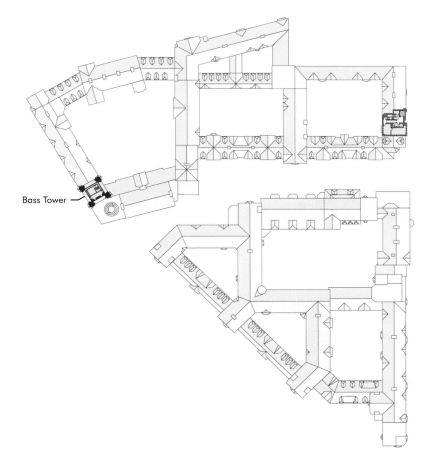

Bass Tower

0   32'   64'

View north with Grove Street Cemetery in the foreground and Kline Biology Tower (Philip Johnson Associates, 1965) in the background, right.

Benjamin Franklin College and Pauli Murray College: A Portfolio

241

Benjamin Franklin
College, view south-
west along Prospect
Street.

245

Pauli Murray College, view southwest from Sachem Street. Loading dock on the left and head of college house on the right.

Benjamin Franklin College and Pauli Murray College: A Portfolio

Prospect Walk, view west. Benjamin Franklin College on the left and Pauli Murray College on the right.

Below: **Prospect Walk, view southeast toward Benjamin Franklin College dining hall, the Millstone Common Room, and Goldman Gate.**

Bottom: **Prospect Walk, view northeast with Pauli Murray College dining hall on the left.**

Below: **Prospect Walk, view north toward Pauli Murray College.**

Bottom: **Prospect Walk, view northwest toward Bass Tower, Pauli Murray College dining hall, and the Marx-Better Common Room.**

255

Benjamin Franklin College and Pauli Murray College: A Portfolio

257

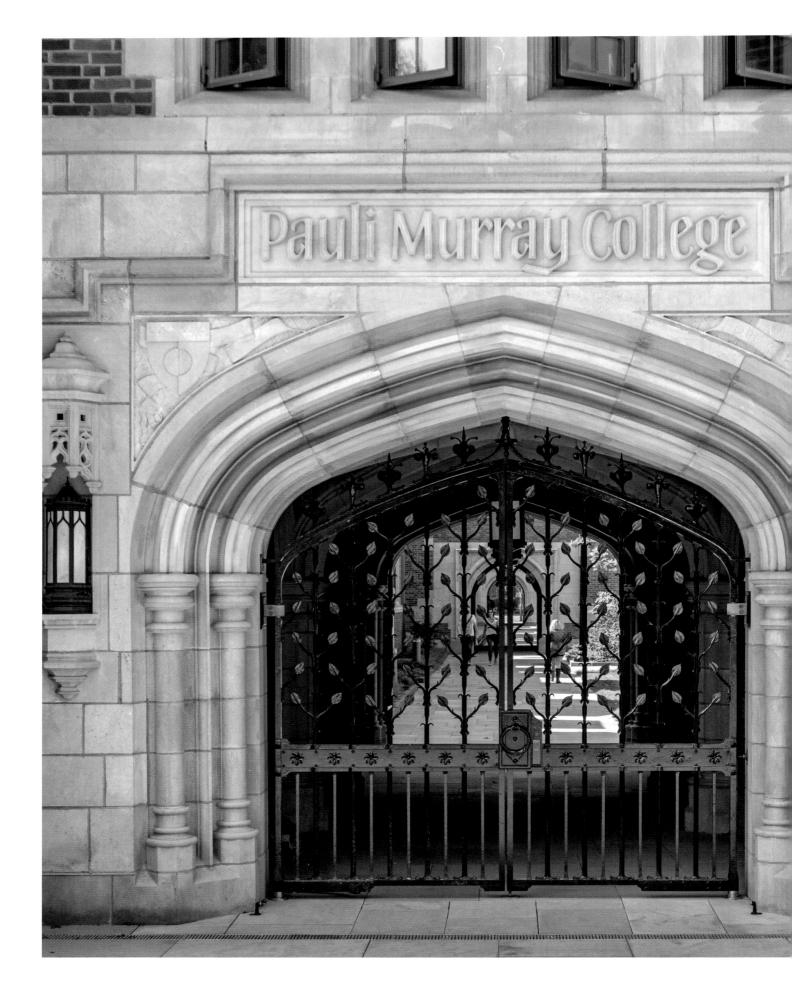

Benjamin Franklin College and Pauli Murray College: A Portfolio

Opposite: **Pauli Murray College Main Gate, view from Prospect Street.**

Left: **Pauli Murray College Sachem Street Gate and passageway, view from Bekenstein Court.**

Below: **Pauli Murray College Sachem Street Gate referencing the Ingalls Rink across the street, commonly referred to as "The Yale Whale."**

Benjamin Franklin College Nyburg Baker Court, view west toward Samson Dance Studio with the dining hall on the right.

263

Below: **Benjamin Franklin College south triangular courtyard, view southeast.**

Bottom: **Benjamin Franklin College north triangular courtyard, view northwest.**

267

Benjamin Franklin College and Pauli Murray College: A Portfolio

269

Benjamin Franklin College and Pauli Murray College: A Portfolio

Opposite: **Pauli Murray College**, view east from Bekenstein Court through enfilade.

Left top: **Pauli Murray College**, view east from center courtyard through enfilade.

Left center: **Pauli Murray College**, view west from center courtyard through passageway to Bekenstein Court.

Left bottom: **Pauli Murray College** Greenway passageway, view northeast toward Bekenstein Court.

Right top: **Benjamin Franklin College** Greenway Gate, view northeast from Farmington Canal Heritage Greenway.

Right center: **Pauli Murray College**, view west from east courtyard through enfilade to Bekenstein Court.

Right bottom: **Pauli Murray College** Atwood Gate, view east from Bekenstein Court.

273

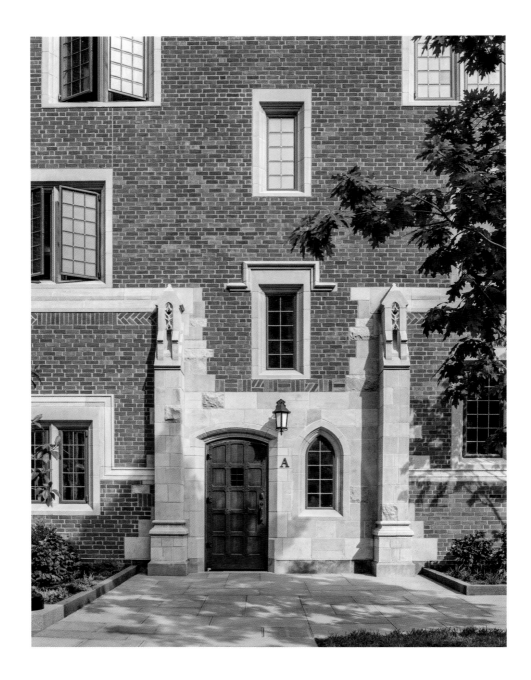

277

285

Below: **Benjamin
Franklin College
Millstone Common
Room, view toward
Prospect Walk.**

Bottom: **Pauli Murray
College Marx-Better
Common Room, view
toward Prospect Walk.**

Below: **Pauli Murray
College Marx-Better
Common Room.**

Overleaf: **Benjamin
Franklin College
dining hall.**

Below: **Benjamin Franklin College Crown Library, view of window to dining hall.**

Bottom: **Benjamin Franklin College dining hall fireplace with Cole Porter (BA 1913) lyric.**

Overleaf: **Pauli Murray College dining hall, with Cole Porter lyric above the arches.**

Below: **Pauli Murray College dining hall alcove, view toward Bekenstein Court.**

Bottom: **Pauli Murray College servery.**

Opposite: **Pauli Murray College dining hall, view of Strickler Family Library above the servery.**

Below and opposite:
**Benjamin Franklin
College and Pauli
Murray College
stained glass details
in dining halls.**

301

Below: **Benjamin Franklin College brickwork detail above Class of 1964 Gate, view west from Prospect Street.**

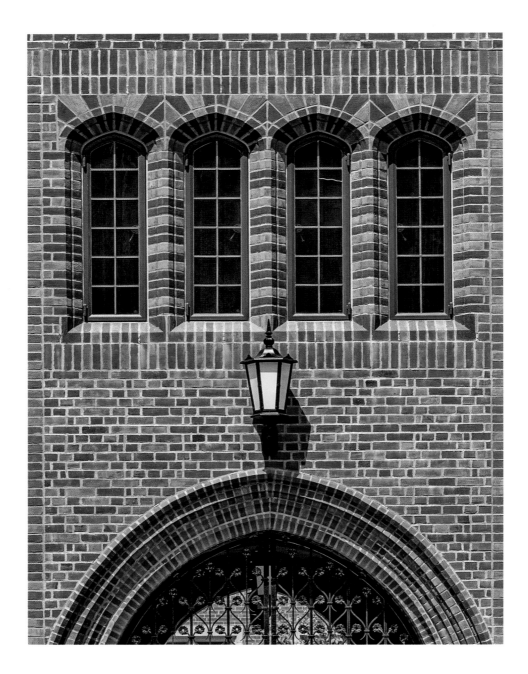

303

Benjamin Franklin College and Pauli Murray College: A Portfolio

Opposite: **Pauli Murray College ornament.** "Know the Difference" is drawn from the famous Serenity Prayer attributed to Reinhold Niebuhr (BA 1914, MA 1915). The hedgehogs flanking the arch refer to both Sir Isaiah Berlin's *The Hedgehog and the Fox: An Essay on Tolstoy's View of History* and Edward Tenniel's illustration of the croquet game in Lewis Carroll's *Alice's Adventures in Wonderland.*

Left top: **Pauli Murray College "Ghost Ship"** pedimental sculpture above an arrangement of golden rectangles.

Left center: **Benjamin Franklin College** quincunx board.

Left below: **Pauli Murray College ornament** referencing nerve cells.

Below: **Pauli Murray College oriel window ornament with double spiral DNA and nerve cells commemorating Yale's strong history of contributions to neuroscience.**

307

Below, top to bottom:
Benjamin Franklin College bulldog scupper (left) and Class of 1954 commemorative ornament (right);
Pauli Murray College "Bobgoyle" (left) and ornament referencing Janus (right).

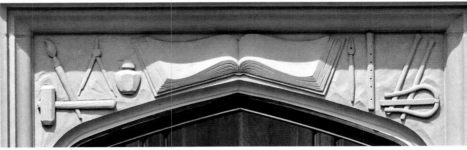

REGINA VIRTUS

libra excellentia

Below, top to bottom:
Benjamin Franklin College ornament commemorating the Canal Railway; Benjamin Franklin College ornament commemorating the arts. Flanking an open book are a sculptor's hammer, painter's brush, architect's compass, ink bottle, pen, flute, drumsticks, and jaw harp; Pauli Murray College ornament of illusionist and film director George Méliès's *Voyage dans la Lune* (left) and ornament of composer and songwriter Cole Porter (BA 1913) (right); Pauli Murray College ornament referencing architectural treatises by Andrea Palladio (left) and A. W. N. Pugin (right).

Benjamin Franklin College and Pauli Murray College: A Portfolio

Opposite: **Benjamin Franklin College Nyburg Baker Court turret, view southwest.**

Left: **Gutter and leader head details.**

Pauli Murray College head of college house, view northwest from Bekenstein Court.

Below: **Pauli Murray College head of college house, entrance hall and living room.**

Bottom: **Pauli Murray College head of college house, family kitchen.**

Benjamin Franklin College head of college house, view west from Prospect Street.

Prospect Walk, view east toward Prospect Street and garden facade of 46 Hillhouse Avenue (Aaron N. Skinner House, A. J. Davis, 1832.)

Overleaf: **Benjamin Franklin College passageway ornament, view north from Nyburg Baker Court.**

to break the Friend-
ships formed
at Yale

Project Credits

Managing the team for the design and construction administration of Benjamin Franklin and Pauli Murray Colleges was like managing a sizeable office within an office. The team grew quickly — starting with about twelve people at the beginning of concept design, swelling up to twenty by the end of that phase, and hovering between twenty and thirty until the final push to complete construction documents, when extra help was required and the number jumped to forty. Over the nine years we worked on this project, between 2008 and 2017, more than 140 people from our office were involved, logging a combined total of 237,708 hours, the equivalent of one person working forty hours per week for 114 years.

Owing to the project's complexities and long duration from conception to construction, team organization was important and needed reevaluation at several points. We found ourselves cycling between an arrangement that related to the vertical organization of the entryways — assigning people to one or more of the twenty-seven "buildings" or seven main courtyards — which helped to create both spatial coherence and variety and had certain benefits for coordination. At other times, team organization tracked one of numerous "assemblage systems" such as windows, chimneys, or mechanical systems to bring clarity to our detailing strategy, which was key to creating an efficient set of construction drawings and managing cost.

In addition to leadership for the entire team — Robert A.M. Stern, Melissa DelVecchio, Graham S. Wyatt, Jennifer Stone, and Kurt Glauber — we also had several sub-teams focused on areas of the building during different design phases. These teams were led by Lara Apelian, Rebecca Atkin, George de Brigard, and Ken Frank. In addition to those who led teams, others had substantial contributions, over multiple phases, focused on specific aspects of the design. William West led our BIM implementation and strategy, Sungchan Park led structural coordination and development of technical details, and Jennifer Bailey led mechanical coordination. Anya Grant and Jonathan Kelly developed many of the distinctive features of the exterior, including its detailing, Michael Mesko developed stone profiles and ornament, and Christopher McIntire led the development of the head of college houses, exterior gates, and stone ornament. When we walk through the site, currently in the final stages of construction as we write in 2017, we are struck by the collaborative teamwork it represents, but at the same time we associate various elements with the individuals who were so instrumental in creating them.

We worked hard, keeping a sense of humor to balance the intensity. We occasionally held competitions for prizes — for example, who could find a digital Yale bulldog hidden in the BIM model? Or who could predict the total number of sheets in our final Design Development drawing set? We exchanged April Fool's jokes with our counterparts at Yale and celebrated key milestones with team dinners. A high point was a party held October 17, 2012, to destroy the room-sized 1/4"=1'-0" design development model, which had served us and our clients so well through a meticulous process of assembly and review, but eventually had to be cleared — ruthlessly but with a hint of ceremony — to make way for new projects.

The following directory identifies RAMSA team members involved in each phase of the project, listed as part of the core team, or as contributors who worked at least 100 hours in a given phase, illustrated by the candid photographs in this section. Consultants and members of the Yale administration who were our clients are also listed. We extend our thanks to all who contributed their talent and expertise to the project and were so dedicated to its success for such a sustained period.

Robert A.M. Stern Architects, Architect

Concept Design (September 2008– April 2009)
CORE TEAM
Lara Apelian
Rebecca Atkin, *Associate*
Jennifer Bailey
George de Brigard
Mia Gorretti Layco
Clay Hayles
Jonathan Kelly
Kathryn Lenehan
Christopher McIntire, *Associate*
William West
Young Jin Yoon
CONTRIBUTORS
David Abecassis
Alex Boardman
Kathleen Casanta
Yolanda Cheung
Milton Hernandez
Bruce Lindsay
George Punnoose, *Associate*
Tin Yiu Lo

Schematic Design (May 2009–April 2010)
CORE TEAM
Lara Apelian
Rebecca Atkin, *Associate*
Jennifer Bailey
George de Brigard
Anya Grant
Jonathan Kelly
Jennifer Lee
Kathryn Lenehan
Katherine Lobalbo
Asdren Matoshi
Christopher McIntire, *Associate*
Cristian Oncescu
Sungchan Park
Leo Stevens
William West
CONTRIBUTORS
David Abecassis
Alex Boardman
Seth Burney
Kenneth Fyfe
Mia Gorretti Layco
Kevin Hasselwander
Christopher Heim
Carlos Hurtado

Ann N. Johnson
Victor Marcelino
Tehniyet Masood
Michael Ryan
Benjamin Salling, *Associate*
Charles Yoo
Young Jin Yoon
INTERIOR DESIGN
Philip Chan
Shannon Ratcliff, *Associate*

Design Development (May 2010–April 2011)
CORE TEAM
Lara Apelian, *Associate*
Rebecca Atkin, *Associate*
Jennifer Bailey
George de Brigard, *Associate*
Delia Conache
Ken Frank
Anya Grant
Jonathan Kelly
Jennifer Lee
Tanya Lee
Katherine Lobalbo
Asdren Matoshi
Christopher McIntire, *Associate*
Cristian Oncescu
Sungchan Park
Janice Rivera-Hall
Leo Stevens
Michael Weber, *Senior Associate*
William West
Young Jin Yoon
CONTRIBUTORS
David Abecassis
Alex Boardman
Richard Box
Seth Burney
Thomas Fryer
Kenneth Fyfe
Kevin Hasselwander
Christopher Heim
Daniel Hogan
Kathryn Lenehan
Tehniyet Masood
Anthony McConnell
Nalina Moses
Thomas Politi
Temitayo Shajuyigbe
Mike Soriano, *Associate*
INTERIOR DESIGN
Lawrence Chabra
Megan Dohmlo
Shannon Ratcliff, *Associate*

Construction Documents (May 2011– March 2012)
CORE TEAM
Lara Apelian, *Associate*
Jennifer Bailey, *Associate*
Elizabeth Baldwin
Richard Box
George de Brigard, *Senior Associate*
Ken Frank, *Associate*
Anya Grant, *Associate*
Preston Gumberich, *Partner*
Alan Infante
Jonathan Kelly, *Associate*
Jennifer Lee, *Associate*
Tanya Lee, *Associate*
Katherine Lobalbo
Marissa Looby
Sonal Mathur
Asdren Matoshi
Christopher McIntire, *Associate*
Sungchan Park, *Associate*
Janice Rivera-Hall
Therese Roche
Christopher Rountos
Sara Rubenstein, *Senior Associate*
Mike Soriano, *Associate*
Leo Stevens, *Associate*
Michael Weber, *Senior Associate*
William West, *Associate*
Young Jin Yoon
CONTRIBUTORS
Everald Colas
Delia Conache
Enid DeGracia, *Associate*
Lindsey DuBosar
Ji Hye Ham
Kevin Hasselwander, *Associate*
Tehniyet Masood
Matthew Masters
Anthony McConnell
Michael Mesko
Paul Naprstek
David Rinehart, *Associate*
Alex Rothe
Colin Slaten, *Associate*
Susan Son
Alexandra Thompson
Marek Turzynski, *Senior Associate*

INTERIOR DESIGN
Lawrence Chabra, *Associate*
Crystal Palleschi

Construction Administration (October 2014– July 2017)
CORE TEAM
Tiffany Barber
C. Gavet Douangvichit
Ken Frank, *Associate*
Monica Gaura
Asdren Matoshi
Christopher McIntire, *Senior Associate*
Michael Mesko
Sungchan Park, *Senior Associate*
Janice Rivera-Hall, *Associate*
Therese Roche, *Associate*
CONTRIBUTORS
Jennifer Bailey, *Associate*
Jose Cruz
Aaron Dresben
Thomas Friddle
Carlos Gamez
Jules Gianakos
Caroline Grieco
Zhenyuan Han
Avnee Jetley
Kwangtaek Kim
Rachel Kim
Jennifer Lee, *Associate*
Andrew McIntyre, *Associate*
Raphael Ogoe
Kasey Puls, *Associate*
Sangeeta Ramakrishnan
Patrick Riordon
Susan Son, *Associate*
Huaxia Song
Douglas West
Kim Yap, *Senior Associate*
INTERIOR DESIGN
Ross Alexander, *Associate*
John Boyland, *Associate*
Manrique Cartin
Lawrence Chabra, *Associate*
Lauren Kruegel, *Associate*
May Liu
Youngjin Park
Carly Silver

Tighe & Bond, Civil Engineer
John W. Block, PE, LS, *Senior Vice President*
Charles J. Croce, PE, *Senior Project Manager*
Andrew P. White, PE, *Project Manager*
Christopher O. Granatini, PE, *Senior Project Manager*

OLIN, Landscape Architect
Richard Newton, *Partner in Charge*
Laurie Olin, *Consulting Partner*
Jean Weston, *Associate (Schematic Design)*
Josh Leaskey, *Associate (Concept - Construction Documentation)*
Eve Kootchick, *Associate (Construction Documentation - Construction Administration)*
Takashi Sato, *Associate (Design Development - Construction Administration)*
Allison Harvey, *Senior Landscape Architect (Construction Administration)*
Judy Venonsky, *Landscape Architect (Schematic Design)*
Ed Confair, *Landscape Architect (Construction Documentation)*
Eric Schuchardt, *Landscape Architect (Concept Design)*

Thornton Tomasetti, Structural Engineer
Stephen Lew, *Senior Principal*
Shawn Leary, *Associate Principal/Project Manager*
Vladimir Gluzov, *Project Engineer*
Tim Foy, *Project Engineer*
Han Xu, *Project Engineer*
Joshua Crawford, *Project Engineer*
Richard Miller, *Project Modeler*
Sandy Jiminian, *Project Modeler*

Philip R. Sherman, Building Code Consultant
Philip R. Sherman, PE

Cini-Little International, Food Service Consultant
Richard H. Eisenbarth, *President & COO*
Garin Wong, *Associate Project Manager*
Marleen St. Marie, *Associate*
Theodore E. Farrand, *Director of Management Advisory Services*

Jaffe Holden, Acoustical/Audio Visual Consultant
Russ Cooper, *Principal Acoustician*
Ben Bausher, *Senior AV Designer*

BuroHappold Consulting Engineers, PC, MEP/ FP/Sustainability Consultant IT & Telecom/Security/ Lighting Consultant
Denzil Gallagher, *Project Principal*
James Hanley, *Project Manager*
Patrick Regan, *Technical Director, MEP Engineering*
Sal Rachiele, *Associate Principal, MEP Engineering*
Rachel Modica, *Engineer, MEP Engineering*
Samantha Bernstein, *Graduate Engineer, MEP Engineering*
Nathan Gubser, *Graduate Engineer, MEP Engineering*
Bob Kearns, *Associate Principal, MEP Engineering*
Michael Huang, *Associate, MEP Engineering*
Dennis Burton, *Associate, MEP Engineering*
John Pulley, *Technical Director, MEP Engineering*
Robin Mosley, *Associate, MEP Engineering*
Gabe Guilliams, *Associate Principal, Lighting Design*
Nick Mykulak, *Lighting Designer*
Sarah Sachs, *Associate Principal, Sustainability*

Ana Serra, *Associate, Sustainability*
Signal Shemesh, *Graduate Engineer, Sustainability*
Paul McGilly, *BIM Manager*

Haley & Aldrich, Geotechnical & Environmental/ Geothermal
Chris Harriman, LEP, *Environmental Professional/Team Leader*
Tim Danaher, *Chief Field Technician*
Jeremy Haugh, PE, *Project Manager*
Paul Ormond, *Geothermal System Designer*
John Dugan, PE, *Principal Geotechnical Engineer (Retired)*
John Difini, PE, *Principal Geotechnical Engineer*
Andrew Chan, *Geothermal and Geotechnical Engineer*
Jen Buchanon, PE, *Project Engineer*
Rich Genovesi, *Project Engineer*
Jeffery Miller, *Environmental Engineer*
Lindsay Strole, *Field Engineer*
Craig Toscano, *Field Technician*
Katrina Perez, *Field Engineer*

Curtain Wall Design & Consulting Inc, Facade, Roof & Waterproofing Consultant
Stephen Rodier, *Project Executive*
Mark Allego, *Site Operations*

Van Deusen & Associates, Inc., Vertical Transportation
Michael Munoz, *Senior Associate*
Eugene Marchetto, *Associate*
Christopher Marino, *Senior Associate*

Spagnola & Associates, Graphics & Wayfinding
Tony Spagnola, *Principal*
Nico Curtis, *Designer*
Kyle Green, *Designer*
Dustin Tong, *Designer*
Elliot Langejans, *Designer*

Moberg Fireplaces, Fireplace Consultant
Walter Moberg, *President*
Debbie Webb, *Senior Administrative Manager*
Charles MacEachen, *Design Director*
Emile Lemoine, *Fabrication Manager*
Christopher Agnew, *Production Manager*
Matt Garner, *Project Manager*
Vonda Moberg, *Communications Director*

Lynch & Associates, Irrigation Consultant
Brendan Lynch, *Principal*
Daniel Lynch, *Project Manager*
Chwan Lee, *Designer*

The John Stevens Shop, Stone Carver
Nicholas Benson, *Owner and Creative Director*

Whitechapel Bell Foundry, Consultant
Alan Hughes

Theatre Projects, Theater Consultant

Integrated Design Consulting and BIM Training
Autodesk
CASE Inc.
Gehry Technologies
Microdesk

Dimeo, Construction Manager
Stephen Rutledge, *Senior VP of Operations*
Paul Aballo, *VP of Construction/Project Executive*
Mike Fuchs, *VP of Preconstruction*
Andy Schiff, *Senior Project Manager*
Blair Oliver, *Construction Manager*
Craig Bolton, *Senior Project Manager Exterior Envelope*
Jeff Sturtevant, *Project Manager Exterior Envelope*
Pablo Garcia, *Project Manager Envelope*
Tim Cohen, *Project Manager Interiors/ Gates/Carvings/Millwork*
Kerri Zavistowski, *Project Manager Structures & Residential Areas*
Vin Pilla, *Project Manager Financial Management*
Joe Ryan, *Project Manager Food Service*
Jared Novinski, *Project Manager Schedule/ Common Area*
Steve Depaola, *Lead MEP Project Manager*
Jonathan Mcnulty, *MEP Project Manager*
Mike Manzolillo, *Superintendent MEP*
Ryne Wallace, *MEP Engineer*
Clair Percival, *Cost Manager*
James Kohnke, *Engineer Cost/Change Management*
Krista LaScola, *Cost Accounting/Requisition*
John Vaslet, *Superintendent Building Structures*
Joe Tomasino, *Lead Superintendent Pauli Murray*
Bruce Hoff, *Lead Superintendent Benjamin Franklin*
Ed Giesbrandt, *Superintendent Pauli Murray*
Mike Marocco, *Superintendent Site & Structures*
Brent Derrick, *Superintendent Sitework Landscaping/Logistics*
Jeff Mansfield, *Superintendent Structures*
Mark Toper, *Superintendent Envelope*

Eric Majewski, *Superintendent Structures*
Nick Bitsis, *Assistant Superintendent Benjamin Franklin*
Maricel Valcarcel, *Assistant Superintendent*
Matt Leone, *Assistant Superintendent*
Bob Kunz, *Corporate Safety Director*
Jody DeCarolis, *Senior Site Safety Manager*
Brett Dootson, *Site Safety Manager*
Adam Daigle, *Assistant Superintendent Envelope/ Stairs/Elevators*
Pat Percichino, *Virtual Building Engineer*
Emily Brenner, *Project Engineer*
Andrew Piquette, *Project Engineer*
Peter Botelho, *VDC Manager*
Libby Cote, *Project Scheduler*

Project Credits

325

Project Credits

7.10

7.11

7.12

7.13

7.14

7.15

7.16

7.17

7.18

7.19

Project Credits

7.50

7.51

7.52

7.1. Front row, left to right: Melissa DelVecchio, Robert A.M. Stern, Graham S. Wyatt; Back row, left to right: Tina Hu, Shannon Rataitt, Brandan Lee, Kate Lenehan. Photograph October 1, 2008.

7.2. Left to right: Robert A.M. Stern, Melissa DelVecchio, Milton Hernandez, Alex Boardman, Lara Apelian. Photograph October 14, 2008.

7.3. Clockwise from left: Ken Frank, George de Brigard, Christopher Heim, Tanya Lee, Sungchan Park, Robert A.M. Stern. Photograph September 28, 2009.

7.4. Left to right: Melissa DelVecchio, Robert A.M. Stern, Jennifer Stone, Kurt Glauber, Lara Apelian, Leo Stevens. Photograph November 4, 2009.

7.5. Clockwise from left: George de Brigard, Kurt Glauber, Leo Stevens, Melissa DelVecchio, Robert A.M. Stern. Photograph November 4, 2009.

7.6. Left to right: Jonathan Kelly, Robert A.M. Stern, Melissa DelVecchio. Photograph November 11, 2009.

7.7. Front row, left to right: Robert A.M. Stern, Melissa DelVecchio, Jennifer Stone; Back row: Benjamin Salling. Photograph December 2, 2009.

7.8. Clockwise from left: Benjamin Salling, Melissa DelVecchio, Michael Ryan, Jennifer Stone, Robert A.M. Stern. Photograph December 2, 2009.

7.9. Team bowling event. Front row, left to right: Lara Apelian, Jennifer Lee, Kate Lenehan, Beverly Johnson-Godette, Rebecca Atkin, Jennifer Bailey; Back row, left to right: George de Brigard, Charles Prettyman, Sungchan Park, William West, Michael Ryan, RAMSA guest, Leo Stevens, Kurt Glauber, Jonathan Kelly, Cristian Oncescu, Jennifer Stone, David Abecassis, Melissa DelVecchio, Alex Boardman, Christopher McIntire. Photograph December 14, 2009.

7.10. Left to right: Christopher McIntire, Melissa DelVecchio, Robert A.M. Stern. Photograph January 5, 2010.

7.11. Jonathan Kelly. Photograph January 26, 2010.

7.12. Clockwise from left: Christopher McIntire, Rebecca Atkin, Cristian Oncescu, Jennifer Lee, Melissa DelVecchio, Robert A.M. Stern. Photograph June 15, 2010.

7.13. Front row, left to right: Kate Lenehan, Robert A.M. Stern, Melissa DelVecchio; Back row, left to right: William West, Jonathan Kelly, Jennifer Bailey, George de Brigard, Anya Grant, Rebecca Atkin. Photograph March 10, 2010.

7.14. Clockwise from left: George de Brigard, Leo Stevens, Jennifer Lee, Kate Lenehan, Jennifer Stone, Melissa DelVecchio, Robert A.M. Stern. Photograph June 16, 2010.

7.15. Clockwise from left: Kurt Glauber, Robert A.M. Stern, Graham S. Wyatt, Jennifer Stone, Melissa DelVecchio. Photograph June 17, 2010.

7.16. Clockwise from left: Robert A.M. Stern, Melissa DelVecchio, Graham S. Wyatt, Jennifer Stone, Jonathan Kelly, Christopher McIntire, David Abecassis. Photograph July 14, 2010.

7.17. Robert A.M. Stern. Photograph July 20, 2010.

7.18. Left to right: Thomas Fryer, Asdren Matoshi, Andreea Cojocaru, Robert A.M. Stern, Melissa DelVecchio, Jennifer Stone. Photograph July 20, 2010.

7.19. Clockwise from left: Melissa DelVecchio, Jonathan Kelly, Rebecca Atkin, Jennifer Stone, Robert A.M. Stern. Photograph July 20, 2010.

7.20. Left to right: Robert A.M. Stern, Leo Stevens, Delia Conache. Photograph July 20, 2010.

7.21. Clockwise from left: Kurt Glauber, Tanya Lee, Jennifer Stone, Christopher McIntire, Rebecca Atkin, Ken Frank, Melissa DelVecchio, Jonathan Kelly, Robert A.M. Stern. Photograph July 20, 2010.

7.22. Left to right: Melissa DelVecchio, Robert A.M. Stern, Sungchan Park, Jennifer Stone, Christopher McIntire. Photograph July 21, 2010.

7.23. Front row: Rebecca Atkin; Back row, left to right: Delia Conache, Andreea Cojocaru, Christopher McIntire, Ken Frank. Photograph July 20, 2010.

7.24. Rebecca Atkin. Photograph July 20, 2010.

7.25. Left to right: Lara Apelian, Jennifer Stone, Robert A.M. Stern, Melissa DelVecchio, Sungchan Park, Rebecca Atkin, Jonathan Kelly. Photograph July 21, 2010.

7.26. Jonathan Kelly. Photograph August 10, 2010.

7.27. Clockwise from left: Melissa DelVecchio, Tehniyet Masood, Leo Stevens, Jonathan Kelly, Robert A.M. Stern. Photograph August 24, 2010.

7.28. Robert A.M. Stern. Photograph August 24, 2010.

7.29. Front row: Robert A.M. Stern; Back row, left to right: Jonathan Kelly, Jennifer Bailey, Kurt Glauber, Leo Stevens, Melissa DelVecchio, Cristian Oncescu. Photograph September 14, 2010.

7.30. Left to right: Robert A.M. Stern, Lawrence Chabra. Photograph August 9, 2011.

7.31. Design development model demolition party. Front row, left to right: Jennifer Stone, Melissa DelVecchio, Robert A.M. Stern, Jennifer Lee, Graham S. Wyatt; Middle row, left to right: William West, Preston Gumberich, Kurt Glauber, Christopher McIntire, Sara Rubenstein, Katherine Lobalbo, Therese Roche; Back row, left to right: Colin Slaten, Kevin Hasselwander, Ken Frank, Jonathan Kelly, Paul Naprstek, Lawrence Chabra, George de Brigard, Victor Marcelino, Asdren Matoshi, Youngjin Yoon, Jennifer Bailey, Anya Grant, Sungchan Park, Tehniyet Masood. Photograph October 17, 2012.

7.32. Design development model demolition party. Robert A.M. Stern. Photograph October 17, 2012.

7.33. Design development model demolition party. Robert A.M. Stern. Photograph October 17, 2012.

7.34. Design development model demolition party. Front row: Robert A.M. Stern; Middle row, left to right: Katherine Lobalbo, Kurt Glauber, Graham S. Wyatt; Back row: George de Brigard, Jennifer Stone, Jonathan Kelly, Christopher McIntire. Photograph October 17, 2012.

7.35. Design development model demolition party. Front row: Robert A.M. Stern; Middle row, left to right: Katherine Lobalbo, Kurt Glauber, Graham S. Wyatt; Back row: Melissa DelVecchio, Ken Frank, George de Brigard, Jennifer Stone, Jonathan Kelly, Christopher McIntire, Asdren Matoshi. Photograph October 17, 2012.

7.36. Design development model demolition party. Front row, left to right: Preston Gumberich, Kurt Glauber, Robert A.M. Stern; Middle row, left to right: Jennifer Lee, Asdren Matoshi, Graham S. Wyatt; Back row, left to right: Tehniyet Masood, Sara Rubenstein, Colin Slaten, William West, George de Brigard, Ken Frank, Jonathan Kelly, Jennifer Stone. Photograph October 17, 2012.

7.37. Design development model demolition party. Clockwise from left: Asdren Matoshi, Jonathan Kelly, Ken Frank, Jennifer Stone, Graham S. Wyatt, Therese Roche. Photograph October 17, 2012.

7.38. Design development model demolition party. Kurt Glauber, Robert A.M. Stern. Photograph October 17, 2012.

7.39. Design development model demolition party. Left to right: Robert A.M. Stern, Melissa DelVecchio, Graham S. Wyatt. Photograph October 17, 2012.

7.40. Design development model demolition party. Front row, left to right: Lawrence Chabra, Preston Gumberich, Paul Naprstek, Therese Roche, Robert A.M. Stern, Youngjin Yoon, Tehniyet Masood, Anya Grant, Jennifer Bailey; Middle row, left to right: Kevin Hasselwander, Tanya Lee, Melissa DelVecchio, Katherine Lobalbo, Jennifer Lee, Kurt Glauber, Asdren Matoshi, Graham S. Wyatt. Back row, left to right: Sara Rubenstein, Colin Slaten, William West, George de Brigard, Jonathan Kelly, Ken Frank, Jennifer Stone, Christopher McIntire. Photograph October 17, 2012.

7.41. Left to right: Robert A.M. Stern, Lawrence Chabra, May Liu. Photograph June 23, 2015.

7.42. Left to right: Robert A.M. Stern, Lawrence Chabra. Photograph June 23, 2015.

7.43. Left to right: Kurt Glauber, Christopher McIntire, Robert A.M. Stern. Photograph September 9, 2015.

7.44. Left to right: Joe Tomasino, Kurt Glauber, Graham S. Wyatt, Jennifer Stone, Robert A.M. Stern. Photograph April 13, 2017.

7.45. Left to right: Robert A.M. Stern, Jennifer Stone, Graham S. Wyatt, Kurt Glauber, Monica Gaura, Tiffany Barber, Joe Tomasino. Photograph April 13, 2017.

7.46. Front row, left to right: Ken Frank, Jennifer Stone; Back row, left to right: C. Gavet Douangvichit, Therese Roche, Tiffany Barber, Kurt Glauber, Jules Gianakos. Photograph August 19, 2016.

7.47. Left to right: Kurt Glauber, Jennifer Stone, Melissa DelVecchio, Graham S. Wyatt, Ken Frank, Tiffany Barber. Photograph April 13, 2017.

7.48. Left to right: Jennifer Stone, Kurt Glauber, Robert A.M. Stern. Photograph April 13, 2017.

7.49. Melissa DelVecchio. Photograph July 19, 2017.

7.50. Left to right: Leonard DelVecchio, Melissa DelVecchio, Jennifer Stone, Tiffany Barber, Mike Soriano, Jules Gianakos, Tanya Lee, Michael Weber, Kurt Glauber, Tehniyet Masood, Lawrence Chabra, David Abecassis, Paul Naprstek, Ken Frank, Colin Slaten, C. Gavet Douangvichit, Caroline Grieco, Jennifer Bailey, George de Brigard. Photograph July 28, 2016.

7.51. Clockwise from left: Tiffany Barber, Caroline Grieco, Jules Gianakos, Eric Majewski, Ron Foster. Photograph June 29, 2016.

7.52. Left to right: Tehniyet Masood, David Abecassis, Colin Slaten, George de Brigard, Mike Soriano, Paul Naprstek, Jennifer Stone, Lawrence Chabra, Michael Weber, Melissa DelVecchio, Tanya Lee, Kurt Glauber, Graham S. Wyatt, Jennifer Bailey, Ken Frank, Jules Gianakos, C. Gavet Douangvichit, Tiffany Barber, Caroline Grieco, Sungchan Park. Photograph July 28, 2016.

Project Credits

Bibliography

Adkisson, Kevin. "How Science Was Built: 1701–1900." *Yale Scientific Magazine*, October 2010.

——. "Science Goes up Prospect Street." *Yale Scientific Magazine*, December 2010.

Bedford, Steven McLeod. *John Russell Pope: Architect of Empire*. New York: Rizzoli, 1998.

Bergin, T. G. *Yale's Residential Colleges: the First Fifty Years*. New Haven, CT: Yale University Press, 1983.

Betsky, Aaron. *James Gamble Rogers and the Architecture of Pragmatism*. Cambridge, Mass.: The MIT Press, 1994.

——. "James Gamble Rogers and the pragmatics of architectural representation," 64–87. In W. Lillyman, M. F. Moriarty, and D. Neuman, eds., *Critical Architecture and Contemporary Culture*. New York: Oxford University Press, 1994.

Brody, Alison E., and Kenneth J. Brody, eds. *Yale: A Celebration*. Portland, Ore: Old Ivy Press, 2001.

Brown, Elizabeth Mills. *New Haven: A Guide to Architecture and Urban Design*. New Haven: Yale University Press, 1976.

"Buildings of Yale University," edited by Lottie G. Bishop. *Bulletin of Yale University*, series 61, no. 3 (February 1, 1965).

Bunting, Bainbridge. *Harvard: An Architectural History*. Completed and edited by Margaret Henderson Floyd. Cambridge, Mass.: The Belknap Press of Harvard University Press, 1985.

Carley, Rachel D. "Tomorrow is Here: New Haven and the Modern Movement." New Haven: The New Haven Preservation Trust, 2008.

Carter, Angela. "Yale eyes vacant Lock Street dump site for townhouses." *New Haven Register*, March 19, 2001.

Chittenden, Russell Henry. *History of the Sheffield Scientific School of Yale University, 1846–1922*. New Haven: Yale University Press, 1928.

Chua, Yen Pin. "Dim Sum Tower." *Mark 36* (June/July 2015).

Conniff, Richard. "Kroon Hall Rises." *Journal of the Yale School of Forestry and Environmental Studies* vol. 8, no. 1 (Spring 2009).

Cooper, Robertson & Partners. *Yale University: A Framework for Campus Planning*. New Haven: Yale University, 2000.

——. *Yale University: A Framework for Campus Planning–Supplement*. New Haven: Yale University, 2009.

Coulson, Jonathan, Paul Roberts, and Isabelle Taylor. *University Planning and Architecture: The Search for Perfection*. New York: Routledge, 2010.

"Design by Postcard: James Gamble Rogers's Postcard Collection." *Perspecta 41* (2008): 180–82.

Dickens, Charles. *American Notes for General Circulation*. London: Chapman and Hall, 1842.

Duke, Alex. *Importing Oxbridge*. New Haven: Yale University Press, 1997.

Dwight, Timothy. "Yale College; Some Thoughts Respecting Its Future," *New Englander*, vol. 29–30 (July 1870–October 1871).

Foster, Jodie. "Class Day Remarks, May 23rd, 1993," *Yale Banner* vol. 152 (1993). New Haven: Yale University, 1993.

French, Robert Dudley. *The Memorial Quadrangle*.

New Haven: Yale University Press, 1929.

Goldberger, Paul. "Romantic Pragmatism: The Work of James Gamble Rogers at Yale University." Unpublished senior thesis, Yale University, 1972.

——. "James Gamble Rogers and the Shaping of Yale in the Twentieth Century," in *Yale in New Haven: Architecture & Urbanism*, edited by Lesley K. Baier, 264–91. New Haven: Yale University Press, 2004.

Goodyear, William H. "The Memorial Quadrangle and the Harkness Memorial Tower at Yale." *The American Architect–The Architectural Review* vol. 70, no. 2379 (October 26, 1921): 300–21.

Gordon, Joseph, William Sledge, Penelope Laurans, et al. "Report of the Study Group to Consider the New Residential Colleges." New Haven: Yale University, 2008.

Haight, Charles Coolidge. Architectural drawings and papers. Avery Architectural and Fine Arts Library, Columbia University.

Hale, William Harlan. "Art vs. Yale University," *The Harkness Hoot* vol. 1 (November 15, 1930): 17–32.

——. "Yale's Cathedral Orgy," *The Nation* (April 29, 1931): 471–72.

——. "Out of the Gargoyles and into the Future." *Horizon 1*, no. 5 (1959). Quoted in Robert A.M. Stern, "Library Architecture at Yale" in *Yale Library Studies Volume 1: Library Architecture at Yale*, edited by Geoffrey Little, 12–65. New Haven: Yale University Press, 2010.

Havemeyer, Loomis. *Sheff Days and Ways:*

Undergraduate Activities in the Sheffield Scientific School, Yale University, 1847–1945. New Haven: s.n., 1958.

Hill, Everett Gleason. *A Modern History of New Haven and Eastern New Haven County* vol. II. New York: The S. J. Clarke Publishing Company, 1918.

Holden, Reuben A. *Yale: A Pictorial History*. New Haven: Yale University Press, 1967.

Hopkins, Jonathan. "Developing Dixwell to Connect and Buffer the Yale Campus." *Urbanismo* www.newhavenurbanism. org. Accessed October 1, 2016.

Kelley, Brooks Mather. *Yale: A History* (Revised). New Haven: Yale University Press, 1999.

Klauder, Charles Z., and Herbert C. Wise. *College Architecture in America*. New York: Scribner & Sons, 1929.

Levin, Richard C. *The Work of a University*. New Haven: Yale University Press, 2003.

Lynn, Catherine. "Building Yale and Razing It from the Civil War to the Great Depression." In *Yale in New Haven: Architecture & Urbanism*, edited by Lesley K. Baier, 101–232. New Haven: Yale University Press, 2004.

Maynard, W. Barksdale. *Princeton: America's Campus*. University Park, Pa.: Pennsylvania State University Press, 2012.

Miller, Mary, Ben Polak, et al. "Report of the Ad Hoc Committee on Yale College Expansion." New Haven: Yale University, 2014.

Morand, Michael. "Construction of new residential colleges an 'optimistic affirmation of Yale's future,' say leaders." *YaleNews* April 17, 2015.

Morison, Samuel Eliot. *The Founding of Harvard College*. Cambridge, Mass.: Harvard University Press, 1935 (1963).

——. *Three Centuries of Harvard, 1636–1936*. Cambridge, Mass.: Harvard University Press, 1936 (2001).

Nichols, George. "The Memorial Quadrangle of Yale University and the Harkness Memorial Tower." *Architecture* vol. 44, no. 4 (October 1921): 293–96; 299–307.

Pearson, Marjorie A. "The Writings of Russell Sturgis and Peter B. Wight: The Victorian Architect as Critic and Historian." PhD diss., City University of New York, 1999.

Pennoyer, Peter, and Anne Walker. *The Architecture of Delano & Aldrich*. New York: Norton, 2003.

Pierson, George Wilson. *A Yale Book of Numbers: Historical Statistics of the College and University, 1701–1796*. New Haven: Yale University Press, 1983.

——. *Yale: The University College: 1921–1937*. New Haven: Yale University Press, 1955 (1966).

Pinnell, Patrick. *Yale University: An Architectural Tour*. 2nd ed. New York: Princeton Architectural Press, 2013.

Pope, John Russell. Illustrations by O.R. Eggers. *Yale University: A Plan for Its Future Building*. New York: Cheltenham Press, 1919.

Porphyrios, Demetri. *Porphyrios Associates: The Allure of the Classical*. New York: Rizzoli, 2016.

Porter, Noah. *The American Colleges and the American Public*. New Haven: Charles C. Chatfield & Co./The College Courant, 1870.

Rees, William. H. "How We Stopped the Ring Road." *New Haven Independent*. February 4, 2014.

Robbins, Ruth. *Oscar Wilde*. London: Bloomsbury, 2011.

Roberts, Russell B. "The Changing Architecture of Yale." *The Harvard Crimson*, May 14, 1962.

Robinson, Deborah, and Edmund P. Meade. "Traditional Becomes Modern: The Rise of Collegiate Gothic Architecture at American Universities." In *Proceedings of the Second International Congress on Construction History* vol. 3, 2673–93. Cambridge, UK: Queens' College, Cambridge University, 2006.

Rogers, James Gamble. "The Harkness Memorial Quadrangle, Yale University. The Architectural Plan." *Architecture* vol. 44, no. 4 (October 1921): 287–92.

——. "The Memorial Quadrangle, Yale University, New Haven, Conn. A Communication from James Gamble Rogers, Architect." *The American Architect/The Architectural Review* vol. 120 no. 2380 (November 9, 1921): 333–40.

——. "Notes of Impressions After Visiting Oxford, Cambridge, St. Andrews University, Scotland, Bristol University, Harrow and Eton." Unpublished typescript, June 9, 1927. Commonwealth Fund Archives, Rockefeller Archives Center.

——. "Oxford-Cambridge" Unpublished typescript, undated. Commonwealth Fund Archives, Rockefeller Archives Center.

——. James Gamble Rogers Papers (MS 396). Yale University Library, Manuscripts and Archives.

Saarinen, Eero. *Eero Saarinen on His Work*, edited by Aline B. Saarinen. New Haven: Yale University Press, 1962.

Schiff, Judith. "How the colleges were born." *Yale Alumni Magazine*. May/June 2008.

——. "A mover and shaker of the Gilded Age." *Yale Alumni Magazine*. September/October 2011.

Schuyler, Montgomery. *A Review of the Work of Chas. C. Haight*. New York: Architectural Record Company, 1899.

——. "The Works of Cram, Goodhue & Ferguson," *Architectural Record* vol. 29 no. 1 (January 1911): 4–112.

Scully, Vincent. *American Architecture and Urbanism*. New York: Praeger, 1969.

——. "Modern Architecture at Yale: A Memoir." In *Yale in New Haven: Architecture & Urbanism*, edited by Lesley K. Baier, 293–353. New Haven: Yale University Press, 2004.

Scully, Vincent, Thomas H. Beeby, Kent Bloomer, et al. *Samuel Yellin Metalwork at Yale*. New Haven: Yale University School of Architecture, 1990.

Seasonwein, Johanna G. *Princeton and the Gothic Revival: 1870–1930*. Princeton, N.J.: Princeton University Press, 2012.

Shaw, Paul. "An Interview with Matthew Carter." *Print*. March 2, 2011.

Snow, Charles Percy. "The Two Cultures." *New Statesman*. (October 6, 1956), 413.

——. *The Two Cultures and the Scientific Revolution*. Cambridge, UK: Cambridge University Press, 1959.

Stern, Robert A.M. *On Campus: Architecture, Identity, and Community*. New York: The Monacelli Press, 2010.

Stern, Robert A.M., and Jimmy Stamp. *Pedagogy and Place: 100 Years of Architecture Education at Yale*. New Haven: Yale University Press, 2016.

Stone, Melissa. "Another Time, Another SSS: A Brief History of the Sheffield Scientific School." *Yale Scientific Magazine*. November 2008.

Turner, Paul Venable. *Campus: An American Planning Tradition*. Cambridge, Mass: The MIT Press, 1990.

"The Harkness Memorial Quadrangle and Memorial Tower, Yale University." Editorial. *Architecture* vol. 44, no. 4 (October 1921): 297–98.

"Two Branford Memorials." *Bulletin of Branford College* vol. 1, no. 10 (May 10, 1938).

Vogt, Erik. "Cultivating Types: The Rise and Fall of Brick Row." In *Yale in New Haven: Architecture & Urbanism*, edited by Lesley K. Baier, 53–100. New Haven: Yale University Press, 2004.

Walker, Gay. "Brilliance All Around: The Stained Glass of Sterling and Its Maker," Presented January 27, 2006, at the Sterling Memorial Library, Yale University. www.library.yale.edu/75th/walker_brilliance.pdf

Wilcox, Marrion. "The Memorial Quadrangle of Yale College." *The Architectural Record* vol. 43, no. 2 (February 1918): 148–59.

Wilde, Oscar. *The Importance of Being Earnest*. London: Leonard Smithers and Co.: 1898.

Wood, John Seymour. *Yale Yarns: Sketches of Life at Yale University*. New York: G.P. Putnam's Sons, 1903.

Yale University. *Yale Memorials*. New Haven: Yale University Office of the Secretary, 1963.

Yale University. *The residential colleges at Yale University*, edited by Richard C. Carroll. 3rd edition. New Haven: Office of the Secretary, Yale University, 1977.

"Yale's Property Line Expands Again, to Neighbors' Ire." *New York Times* (NY/Region). April 26, 1999.

Yale Daily News

Armstrong, Steven V. "New Interstate 91 Brings Plans for Tunnel Link Under Campus." Jan. 7, 1966.

Williams, Tarryn. "Yale Police will move to Dixwell." Oct. 12, 2001.

Sullivan, Will. "University paves way for new Rose Center." Apr. 23, 2004.

Needham, Paul. "'New campus' proponent Pope's legacy lives on." Jan. 28, 2008.

Kaplan, Theodore. "Levin urges Corporation to approve expansion plans." Feb. 18, 2008.

"Corporation Should Endorse Expansion." Editorial. Feb. 22, 2008.

Kaplan, Thomas. "Corporation directs administrators to plan for two new residential colleges." Feb. 23, 2008.

Needham, Paul. "To Grove Street Cemetery: Tear down that wall." Apr. 4, 2008.

Harden, Steven. "Stern offers elegance over absurdity." Sept. 8, 2008.

Caro, Ryan. "Stern should trade luxury for novelty." Sept. 15, 2008.

Randall, Eric. "Students to have input on colleges." Nov. 10, 2008.

Lasley, Taylor, and Baobao Zhang. "Cemetery wall alteration plan withdrawn." Oct. 14, 2009.

Holmes, Tao Tao. "The New Party Suites." Nov. 8, 2011.

Bashin-Sullivan, Brendan. "The Giant Hole on Sachem Street." Apr. 7, 2013.

Taft, Isabelle. "New colleges redefine a neighborhood." Sept. 25, 2015.

Hamid, Zainab. "New colleges transfer process completes." Feb. 23, 2017.

Gittler, Ryan, and David Yaffe-Bellany. "New colleges near completion." Mar. 8, 2017.

Hamid, Zainab. "New colleges attract established groups." Mar. 31, 2017.

Odermann, Myles. "For New Haven, new colleges bring opportunity for growth." Apr. 7, 2017.

Interviews

Bruce D. Alexander
Vice President for New Haven and State Affairs and Campus Development, 2006–present; Vice President and Director of New Haven and State Affairs, 1998–2006; BA 1965.

Edward P. Bass
Trustee, 2001–13; Senior Fellow of the Yale Corporation, 2011–13; Chair of the Buildings and Grounds Committee, 2011–12; Buildings and Grounds Committee, 2008–12; BS 1967, BS 1968, Arch 1972, Hon. MA 2001.

Phillip G. Bernstein
Vice President of Strategic Relations at Autodesk, 2000–16; Lecturer at the Yale School of Architecture, 1989–present; BA 1979, MArch 1983.

Roland Betts
Trustee, 1999–2011; Senior Fellow of the Yale Corporation, 2004–11; Chair of the Buildings and Grounds Committee, 2008–10; BA 1968.

Laura A. Cruickshank
University Planner, 2005–13.

Denzil Gallagher
Principal, BuroHappold Engineering, New York.

Eve Kootchick
Associate, OLIN, Philadelphia.

Penelope Laurans
Special Assistant to the President, 1993–2016; Associate Professor in English; Senior Adviser; Head of Jonathan Edwards College, 2009–16.

Shawn Leary
Associate Principal, Thornton Tomasetti, Boston.

Richard C. Levin
22nd President of Yale University, 1993–2013; Frederick William Beinecke Professor of Economics; Chair of the Economics Department; Dean of Yale's Graduate School of Arts and Sciences; PhD 1974.

Richard Newton
Partner, OLIN, Philadelphia.

Jon Olsen
Associate Director, Facilities Planning and Project Management, 2007–present.

Patrick Pinnell
Author of *The Campus Guide: Yale University, an Architectural Tour* and founder of Architecture & Town Planning LLC; BA 1971, MArch 1974.

Alice J. Raucher
Senior Architect, Major Projects Planner, and Chair of the Design Steering Team, 2007–15.

Peter Salovey
23rd President of Yale University, 2013–present; Provost of Yale University, 2008–13; Chris Argyris Professor of Psychology; MS 1983, MPhil 1984, PhD 1986.

Index